ETHNIC HUMOR IN MULTIETHNIC AMERICA

ETHNIC HUMOR IN MULTIETHNIC AMERICA

DAVID GILLOTA

RUTGERS UNIVERSITY PRESS
New Brunswick, New Jersey, and London

Library of Congress Cataloging-in-Publication Data
Gillota, David, 1977–
Ethnic humor in multiethnic America / David Gillota.
pages cm
Includes bibliographical references and index.
ISBN 978–0–8135–6149–3 (hardcover : alk. paper) — ISBN 978–0–8135–6148–6 (pbk. : alk. paper) — ISBN 978–0–8135–6150–9 (ebook)
1. Ethnic wit and humor—United States—History and criticism. 2. American wit and humor—History and criticism. 3. Wit and humor—Social aspects—United States. I. Title.
PN6149.E83G55 2013
818'.60208—dc23 2012040294

A British Cataloging-in-Publication record for this book is available from the British Library.

Visit our website: http://rutgerspress.rutgers.edu

Manufactured in the United States of America

CONTENTS

ACKNOWLEDGMENTS

Contemporary popular culture can be a slippery subject to write about. As soon as I feel I have a particular idea nailed down, a new sequel will come out, a new episode will air, or a new stand-up comedian will emerge, seemingly from nowhere, to make me reconsider everything. There is no way I could have even pretended to keep up with all of this if it weren't for the numerous friends, colleagues, and students who were aware of my interest in contemporary ethnic humor and would tell me about a show they had seen, or e-mail me a stand-up clip from YouTube, or pass along a book or DVD that seemed useful. It may be impossible to thank everybody who helped while I was working on this, but I am going to give it a shot.

I would like to first thank the many friends who read portions of this work in its earliest form: Amy Parsons, Laura Beadling, Janet Neary, Russ Brickey, Justin Ponder, and Doug Anderson. Their comments have been invaluable, their continued encouragement has kept me motivated, and their friendship has kept me sane. I presented an early draft of chapter 2 at the Klutznick-Harris symposium on "Jews and Humor" in 2009. I would like to thank the organizer, Leonard Greenspoon, and all of the presenters at the symposium for providing insight into my own work and for presenting a series of fascinating papers that encouraged me to think about my research in new ways. I would also like to thank the English Department at the University of Miami, especially Joe Alkana, Lindsey Tucker, and the late Zack Bowen. While I didn't realize it at the time, my work on this book really started while I was finishing my graduate work under their tutelage. I would like to thank both the Office of Sponsored Programs and the Humanities Department at the University of Wisconsin–Platteville for providing funding for this project. The entire staff at Rutgers University Press has been very supportive, and the manuscript reviewers provided incredibly helpful comments. My copy editor, Beth Gianfagna, has also provided invaluable support. I would especially like to thank my editor at Rutgers, Katie Keeran, for her insights and for helping me to navigate the maze of publishing my first book.

Many of the ideas in this work were fleshed out while I was teaching courses in American humor, film, and ethnic studies at the University of Miami and the University of Wisconsin–Platteville. I would like to thank all of my students at both universities for serving as sounding boards while my ideas were still in their earliest form. Also, many of the works of humor discussed in this book I only became aware of after reading about them in a student's paper. I would also like to thank my students, then, for keeping me current.

I am forever indebted to my mom, Ferne Gillota. She was my earliest film and television teacher, and I learned more from her than I did through all my years of formal education. My son Isaac, who is almost two and a half as I write this, is funnier than any comedian I have ever seen. He has also reminded me every day that there are more important things than writing books. Finally, I don't even know how to begin to thank my wife, Amanda Tucker. She has read and commented on every word of this book, and we have had countless conversations about ethnic humor. When I read over the pages here, I am astonished at how many of the best ideas *and* sentences are actually hers. It should go without saying—but I will say it anyway—that without her love, friendship, and encouragement this book would have never been written.

Portions of this work were previously published and are reprinted here with permission:

"Negotiating Jewishness: *Curb Your Enthusiasm* and the Schlemiel Tradition," *Journal of Popular Film and Television* 38, no. 4 (Winter 2010): 152–161.

"The New Jewish Blackface: African American Tropes in Contemporary Jewish Humor," in *Jews and Humor: Studies in Jewish Civilization*, vol. 22, ed. Leonard J. Greenspoon (West Lafayette, IN: Purdue University Press, 2011), 225–236.

"'People of Colors': Multiethnic Humor in *Harold and Kumar Go to White Castle* and *Weeds*," *Journal of Popular Culture* 45, no. 5 (October 2012): 960–978.

ETHNIC HUMOR IN MULTIETHNIC AMERICA

INTRODUCTION

The Boundaries of American Ethnic Humor

IN ONE OF his many oft-quoted routines, Lenny Bruce provides some unexpected distinctions between Jewish and *goyish* cultures:[1]

> Now I neologize Jewish and *goyish.* Dig: I'm Jewish. Count Basie's Jewish. Ray Charles is Jewish. Eddie Cantor's *goyish.* B'nai Brith is *goyish;* Hadassah, Jewish. Marine Corps—heavy goyim, dangerous. Kool-Aid is *goyish.* All Drake's cakes are *goyish.* Pumpernickel is Jewish, and, as you know, white bread is very *goyish.* Instant potatoes—*goyish.* Black cherry soda's very Jewish. Macaroons are very Jewish—very Jewish cake. Fruit salad is Jewish. Lime Jello is *goyish.* Lime soda is very *goyish.* Trailer parks are so *goyish* that Jews won't go near them. *Jack Paar Show* is very *goyish.* Underwear is definitely *goyish.* Balls are *goyish.* Titties are Jewish. Mouths are Jewish. All Italians are Jewish. Greeks are *goyish*—bad sauce. Eugene O'Neill—Jewish; Dylan Thomas—Jewish.[2]

The objects of Bruce's humor are multiple. On one level, he is clearly making fun of *goyish* culture—presented here as bland and tasteless—and privileging Jewish culture, which he presents as much richer. The humor of this bit, though, lies not in the specific commentary that Bruce provides about Jewish or *goyish* tastes but rather in the unexpected manner in which Bruce redefines, or "neologizes," his terms. In the mid-1960s, when this bit was initially performed, audience members, particularly Jewish ones, would have been very familiar with Jewish/*goyish* distinctions between items like white bread and pumpernickel. The African American musicians Ray Charles and Count Basie, however, are not Jewish at all. Eugene O'Neill is Irish American, and while some Sephardic Jews are indeed Italian, all Italians, by any recognized definition, are not Jewish. For that matter, the entertainer Eddie Cantor, born

Edward Israel Iskowitz, was very Jewish and was in fact a prominent supporter of the Zionist movement. The Jewish fraternal organization B'nai Brith is also, by definition, Jewish.

We can often see, though, what Bruce is getting at. While Eddie Cantor may have been technically Jewish, his popularity as the star of bland Hollywood musicals such as *Whoopee!* (1930) firmly establishes him as an entertainer for *goyish* America. And Bruce's designation of Ray Charles and Count Basie as Jewish points to both an ongoing and long-standing identification between African and Jewish Americans, which I will discuss more fully in chapter 2. So while there is an odd sort of logic to many of Bruce's designations, it also seems as if Bruce is simply listing the things he likes as Jewish and those he does not as *goyish*. Aside from being funny and surprising, Bruce is challenging his audiences to rethink the ways in which ethnic and/or religious affiliation are defined. Rather than viewing essential categories as determined by blood, ethnic identifications, for Bruce, are performative, cultural, and open to personal interpretation. Despite this seemingly progressive view of ethnicity, Bruce's distinctions between Jewish and *goyish* are also extremely reductive. The items on his list include a wide spectrum of ethnic affiliations: white, Jewish, African American, Italian, Irish American, and Greek. But rather than allow each affiliation a particularity, Bruce forces each of them onto one side or the other of a simple Jewish/*goyish* dichotomy. Part of the joke, of course, is the ridiculousness of doing this, but the routine is nevertheless driven by a dualistic view of ethnicity, with *goyish* representing the tasteless, mainstream cultural center and Jewish representing the livelier and more transgressive margins.

This sort of insider/outsider or center/margins binary drives most ethnic humor throughout the twentieth century, and—even more important—it underlies the ways in which we often talk about race and ethnicity. Bruce's broad distinctions between *goyish* and Jewish may today be rewritten, respectively, as majority/minority or white/persons of color, all of which are terms that obscure, rather than explore, specific ethnic affiliations. In many arenas, though, the ways in which we talk about race and ethnicity are changing. This is particularly true in contemporary ethnic humor. Indian Canadian (but U.S.-based) comic Russell Peters discusses ethnic particularity in a manner that stands in sharp contrast to Bruce's reductive binary. In his stand-up special *Russell Peters: Outsourced* (2006), for example, Peters gives his audience a lesson on the difference between various Asian groups because he claims that Americans seem to think that all Asians are Chinese. After asserting that Indians like himself are also Asian, he explains that in America one can tell the difference between other Asian groups "by the way that they speak English." He follows this up with a series of impersonations of Korean, Chinese, and Vietnamese speakers. Peters exaggerates his voices for comic effect, and he embodies humorous characters, but the accents are clearly distinct from each other, and Peters has obviously spent time listening to speakers from each group and studying their speech patterns. The most striking thing here is the emphasis on diversity; the point of the routine is to demonstrate the multiplicity of Asian groups so that Westerners will not lump them all together. Peters even goes so far as to explain that in China there are two principal languages, Mandarin and Cantonese, and numerous local dialects. In discussions with audience members, he also displays a passing knowledge about which regions of China speak which language. Some may argue that Peters's knowledge in this routine is fairly superficial, but what is important is the way in which he embraces the *idea* of ethnic specificity and works against the tendency, found in the Lenny Bruce routine above, to paint different groups in as broad strokes as possible.

The contrast between these two routines is about much more than the particular difference of two individual comedians. The work of both comics reflects—even if it also challenges—the ethnic ideology of their day. Bruce was performing in an America in which Jews were a visible ethnic group and white Christians were an overwhelming majority. Peters is performing in a time in which Jews are largely considered white and after which waves of immigration from Mexico, South America, Asia, and the Middle East have drastically altered the country's ethnic demographic and threatened the dominance of the white majority. Bruce performed before the institutionalization of multiculturalism, whereas Peters is performing in a cultural climate in which nearly every university offers ethnic studies courses and in which cultural "diversity" is something that every corporate entity strives for, at least officially. Peters's routine thus serves as a signal that in at least some areas of popular culture, the ways in which ethnicity is discussed is drastically different from how it was fifty years ago.

In the years roughly from 2000 to 2010, in particular, there have been significant developments in the manner in which ethnicity is performed and defined in popular humor. These developments are characterized by the increased tendency of comic artists and performers to place multiple ethnic groups in sustained conversation with each other. While these developments are by no means apparent in *all* ethnic humor, they do constitute an important trend. I suggest that this trend of interethnic dialogue in American ethnic humor is a result in part of the increased influence of multiculturalism on how we speak and think about cultural difference. *Multiculturalism,* of course, is a notoriously slippery term. I use it here and throughout to refer to an ideology that promotes the active celebration and embracing of ethnic, racial, religious, or cultural difference. While it is not necessarily a dominant ideology, the tenets of multiculturalism, since the late 1960s, have permeated nearly every aspect of the culture, through university ethnic studies programs, corporate diversity seminars, media watchdog organizations that monitor representations of nonwhite groups, and an array of affirmative action programs.

The other primary catalyst for the new trend in popular ethnic humor is the diversification of the national demographic, marked particularly by a significant increase in Latino and Asian American populations. While multiculturalism refers specifically to a set of ideas, the diversity of the American population refers to the *fact* that there are many different ethnic groups coexisting in the nation. This has always been true to some extent, but the growth patterns in the past ten to fifteen years are forcing many Americans of all ethnic backgrounds to rethink their position in the population and their relationship to other ethnic groups. For example, in the 2000 census, the African American and Hispanic/Latino populations were approximately the same size, with each group accounting for slightly more than 12 percent of the population. In the 2010 census, however, Latinos shot ahead to constitute more than 16 percent of the population, thus unseating African Americans as the largest nonwhite group. During the same period, Asian Americans replaced Latinos as the fastest-growing nonwhite group, with a growth rate of more than 43 percent. These growth rates, of course, continue to chip away at the white majority, and it is projected that by 2050, white people will make up less than 50 percent of the total U.S. population. All of this suggests the need for a reconceptualization of what it means to be black, Latino, Asian American, or white in the contemporary United States.[3]

This book does not offer such a reconceptualization. Rather, I argue that a close analysis of contemporary ethnic humor can provide insight into the manner in which different ethnic groups view themselves in relation to each other. Most media scholars have followed the traditional lines of ethnic formation, created in response to each ethnic group's particular history of trauma, oppression, and segregation; these traditional ethnic divisions require that each group is viewed either in isolation or only in relation to the dominant (i.e., white) culture. However, this approach cannot account for the full complexity and nuance of contemporary ethnic relations or contemporary ethnic humor. Contemporary ethnic humorists often emphasize community building and intercultural dialogue. This sort of dialogue spans a wide range of genres, including stand-up, sketch comedy, film, television, and new media. Very often, these formats blur into each other, as stand-up comedians tend to also appear frequently in film and television comedy. In all cases, I focus on examples that participate, either knowingly or not, in conversation across cultural lines. At times, the comic works under discussion reflect and critique the actual struggles of living in a multiethnic society, and in other moments, they project a fantasy of how we would like to see ourselves. Their work, then, can reveal startling insights into the nature of multiethnic America.

ETHNIC HUMOR IN THEORY

It is typical for academic books about humor to provide a survey of the most prominent philosophies of humor.[4] This overview of humor theory usually includes discussions of serious thinkers like Freud, Hobbes, Bergson, and Kant and in some ways serves as a defense of the subject matter itself, for humor is often overlooked in academic discussion. Theories of humor, however, do not drive this book. I am not ultimately concerned with humor in the abstract, nor do I believe that a theory of humor can ever wholly explain why we laugh at certain things and not at others. Humor is largely context specific, but I have enough experience teaching humor in the classroom to know that not everybody, even those who share a cultural background, finds the same material funny. There are very few things, for example, that make me happier than watching Larry David embarrass himself in episode after episode of *Curb Your Enthusiasm* (2000–), but my wife, who otherwise often shares my tastes, usually has to leave the room after the first five minutes. What I find funny, she finds agonizingly uncomfortable.

Nevertheless, there are three broad ideas about humor that may prove relevant in understanding the workings of contemporary American ethnic humor. The first is Thomas Hobbes's "superiority theory." Hobbes argues that "laughter is nothing else but *sudden glory* arising from some sudden conception of some *eminency* in ourselves, by *comparison* with the *infirmity* of others."[5] It is easy to see how this theory could be transferred to a specifically ethnic humor. Whites make jokes about African Americans because they feel superior; Jews make fun of Christians for the same reason, and so forth. The next relevant theory belongs to Sigmund Freud, and it is sometimes referred to as "aggression theory." Freud asserts that jokes "make possible the satisfaction of an instinct (whether lustful or hostile) in the face of an obstacle that stands in its way."[6] We joke about race and ethnicity because it is often socially unacceptable to talk about these issues openly. Humor provides a socially sanctioned release valve.

Finally, ethnic humor is often defined as "self-deprecating," meaning that humorists often make jokes about their own ethno-racial group. Self-deprecation is most often associated with Jewish humor, but as Christie Davies points out, "the telling of self-mocking jokes is very widespread among all manner of minorities."[7] In the broadest sense, self-deprecating humor is fundamental to most contemporary ethnic humor, but because self-deprecation can be explained in multiple ways, it does not tell us very much about how ethnic humor works. For example, self-deprecating humor may suggest that the humorist really does dislike his or her own ethnic group, in part or in whole, or has internalized stereotypes perpetuated by the majority group. Very often, though, self-deprecating humor actually celebrates a particular stereotype and turns it into a positive; in this sense, the humor is, like the Lenny Bruce routine above, directed most forcefully at the dominant group. Self-deprecating humor can also be seen as a sort of psychological defense mechanism, as marginalized groups will joke about themselves in order to intercept or redirect aggression from the dominant group.[8] These contradictory explanations suggest that self-deprecating humor needs to be considered in a context-specific, situational basis. The concepts of superiority, aggression, and self-deprecation should certainly be kept in mind when considering contemporary ethnic humor, but as I argue below, the work of scholars in ethnic studies ultimately provides a more productive framework for my subject matter.

Indeed, in his classic study of American ethnic cultures, *Beyond Ethnicity*, Werner Sollors provides what may be our most useful definition of ethnic humor. "Laughing at others," Sollors explains, "is a form of boundary construction." He goes on to note that "the community of laughter itself is an ethnicizing phenomenon, as we develop a sense of we-ness in laughing with others."[9] Sollors's comments are insightful on numerous levels. His initial emphasis on laughing *at* others resonates with Hobbes's superiority theory; while his later shift to laughing *with* others recalls Freud's assertion that humor requires at least three people: a teller, an object, and a receiver. The joke-teller and the receiver produce a community that excludes the object of the joke itself. Hence, a boundary is formed. Ethnic humor, then, is about including and excluding. This is true of ethnic humor created by and for the dominant culture and at the expense of marginalized groups, but it is equally true of ethnic humor that is created by the marginalized groups themselves. In the latter case, the ethnic humor has the potential to build group solidarity and to critique the dominant cultural framework.

Sollors's definition is at the heart of this book, for I explore the ways in which contemporary ethnic humorists are using their humor to defend, redraw, or challenge the traditional boundaries that have been used, for decades or even centuries, to separate and define various ethnic groups. Humor may not initially seem like an obvious site for a serious discussion of contemporary race relations, but as Bambi Haggins asserts in her important study of African American humor, *Laughing Mad*, "comedy is a powerful discursive tool; the notion . . . that if one gets an audience laughing, then while their mouths are open, you can shove the truth in, seems quite applicable here."[10] Humorists, as we know, go for the laugh. But, as Haggins suggests, they also make arguments. This is especially true for ethnic humorists, for they use their humor to continually negotiate their ethnic positions. These arguments embedded within ethnic humor can provide a window into the complex web of ethnic relations in contemporary American culture.

AN OVERVIEW OF AMERICAN ETHNIC HUMOR

In order to fully understand the current state of American ethnic humor, it is necessary to know something about the traditions upon which contemporary ethnic humorists are building and the preconceptions that they are often working against. Of course, a true history of American ethnic humor could fill several volumes, and a discussion of the implications of that history could fill several more. Therefore, I will necessarily limit myself to a broad discussion of what I see as the most important trends that have occurred in American ethnic humor throughout the years. While all ethnic groups have a rich heritage of wit, this section—like the early chapters of this book—will primarily focus on African Americans and Jewish Americans. As John Lowe points out, African and Jewish Americans "have given us many of our ethnic jokes, and arguably, between the two of them, have provided the main foundation for contemporary American humor."[11] Furthermore, both groups have been the object of comic ridicule at the hands of the Christian white majority and have used their humor as a method of defense and/or retaliation. Perhaps most important, the humor of both groups has inspired a wealth of scholarly investigations, for nearly all work focusing on American ethnic humor discusses either African American or Jewish American humor.[12]

American ethnic humor is usually divided into two main periods.[13] The first period occurs from the beginnings of the nation until the middle of the twentieth century and entails humor directed at marginalized groups for the entertainment of the mainstream, white culture. Prominent examples include ethnic caricatures in newspaper cartoons, which would depict hook-nosed Jews, simian blacks, or drunken Irishmen. Ethnic stereotypes also manifested themselves on the stage, most famously in minstrel shows but also in a series of plays that featured comic Jewish villains who were inevitably devious and miserly.[14] And as Donald Bogle and others have pointed out, black stereotypes such as the complacent "Tom" or the nurturing "Mammy" continued to survive throughout much of the twentieth century in film and television productions.[15] Throughout this history, ethnic performers themselves were often complicit in these representations. African American performers would black-up for a minstrel show, and Jewish actors would don a hook-nose to play villains such as Shakespeare's Shylock or Dickens's Fagin. There was no other recourse for ethnic performers who wished to make a living in show business.

The second phase of American ethnic humor emerged during and became prominent after the civil rights movement and saw, as a result of various "ethnic pride" movements, the control over mainstream ethnic humor shift somewhat into the hands of minority groups themselves. Black humorists such as Dick Gregory and Richard Pryor and Jewish humorists such as Lenny Bruce, Woody Allen, and Mel Brooks were empowered to speak frankly not only about their own ethnic positions but also about mainstream culture. These humorists would rework familiar ethnic stereotypes, often collapsing or subverting them. More important, as we saw in the Bruce routine discussed above, they turned the tables and provided pointed critiques of whites and/or Christians. If the most prominent example of racist humor directed at minority groups is minstrelsy, in which whites would don blackface and perform blackness in comic and reductive ways, then the most striking example of later ethnic humorists critiquing whiteness lies in the inverse of minstrelsy: black comics impersonating nervous or uptight whites (for a fuller discussion of this sort of humor, see chapter 1).

This overview of American ethnic humor is a useful starting place and provides a broad outline of American ethnic humor, but it only tells part of the story. While humor opened up in this time period for ethnicity, the same does not necessarily hold true for gender. Even though the post–civil rights era saw a marked increase in the number of successful ethnic humorists, the overwhelming majority of these "crossover" comics were men. In fact, mainstream mass media has a long-standing history of discrimination against female humorists, for comedy is often thought of as a purely masculine realm.[16] And this discrimination is even worse in terms of female humorists from marginalized groups. Successful white female humorists have been increasing slowly since the 1960s, and things look even better in the wake of Tina Fey's tenure as head writer for *Saturday Night Live*, in which she secured more creative control for a number of other female comics, including Amy Poehler and Kristen Wiig. However, the number of nonwhite female humorists who have achieved any measure of mainstream success remains startlingly small even today.[17] These facts necessarily affect the readings of ethnicity that can be gleaned from American ethnic humor, for the comic representations of both men and women have been largely controlled by men. Even in this project, unfortunately, the number of male humorists discussed greatly outnumbers the female humorists. And as we will see, many male ethnic humorists are often brilliant when it comes to discussing race but fairly conservative and two-dimensional in discussions of gender.

We must also remember that even during the first phase of American ethnic humor, when whites were using ethnic humor to reinforce stereotypes, marginalized groups themselves maintained a private, subversive humor of their own. In his massive history of African American humor, *On the Real Side*, Mel Watkins maintains that while whites were lampooning black culture on the stage and screen, blacks maintained their own folk humor within their communities. Professional black humorists, such as Redd Foxx and Moms Mabley, made a living performing in black clubs on the "chitlin' circuit" and also recorded a number of comedy albums that circulated underground in black communities. These humorists influenced later generations of crossover comedians led by Dick Gregory, Flip Wilson, Bill Cosby, and Richard Pryor.[18] Jewish American humor has a similarly complex history. In the early twentieth century, Jewish entertainers would downplay their ethnicity for mainstream audiences but would perform a more distinctive "Jewish" humor for audiences in the Catskills and other Jewish community venues. More important, Jewish humorists drew from a long history of Jewish humor that can be traced back to the *shtetls,* or small villages, of eastern Europe. Jewish Americans adapted (and are still adapting) this *shtetl* humor for an American context.[19]

It is also important to note that the two periods of American ethnic humor that we have established are not as fixed as they initially seem. As Eric Lott has argued, minstrel shows themselves were more complex than a simple manifestation of racism. Rather, they represented a white fascination with, and fear of, black culture—what Lott calls a "dialectical flickering of racial insult and envy."[20] And although later works like the 1950s sitcoms *Amos 'n' Andy* (1951–1953) and *Beulah* (1950–1952) are now considered a repository for racist stereotypes, in their day, these shows, especially *Amos 'n' Andy,* proved popular with black audiences, who felt that the actors were able to bring to their roles a semblance of genuine African American folk humor. Moreover, even though ethnic humorists began to have greater control of their material in the late 1960s, they were not always applauded for their efforts by their own ethnic community. Jewish humorists have long been accused of being "self-hating Jews" or of ultimately aiding the cause of anti-Semitism. And as late as 2005, African American comic Dave Chappelle abandoned his successful television series because he feared that his humor was ultimately reinforcing stereotypes rather than challenging them. In ethnic humor, though, there is always a fine line between reinforcing and collapsing a stereotype.

We must also remember that just because ethnic humorists have managed to wrest some control over the ways in which their identities are performed does not mean that the old patterns of whites controlling ethnic images have disappeared. Ethnic humorists, no matter how innovative they may be, still must convince mostly white studio executives and sponsors to allow them to perform in mainstream venues. Very often, corporate interest exerts its power over ethnic humor and presents ethnicity in the simplest, least threatening manner possible. As I argue in chapter 4, for example, reductive and damaging stereotypes still survive in mainstream pop cultural genres such as the children's film and the thirty-minute sitcom. Simple racist humor has not gone away either. While the most malicious forms of racist humor have become unacceptable in mainstream media like film and television, racist humorists have been able to find a home for their "work" on the Internet. Michael Billig, for example, provides a frightening study of "nigger joke" websites that are loosely affiliated with the Ku Klux Klan and that use their humor to disseminate and reinforce racial hatred.[21]

Finally, any discussion of ethnic representations must also take into account the ways in which gender affects our understanding of ethnic identification. Although our culture assigns broad ethnic stereotypes to various groups—stereotypes that are in turn the building blocks of most ethnic humor—these stereotypes usually manifest themselves in different ways, depending on whether they are directed at men or women. For example, African Americans are frequently stereotyped as simple, childlike, and mentally inferior, but these traits may manifest themselves differently in relation to each gender. For example, the stereotype of the criminal and sexually aggressive black male—what Donald Bogle refers to as a "Black Buck"—was created in response to fears of African American men seducing or raping white women. Other black male stereotypes (the Tom or the Coon) served to diffuse the threat of black masculinity by painting blacks as either emasculated saints or objects of comic ridicule. For black females, the stereotype of the "Mammy" or the "Aunt Jemima" served to desexualize black women, transforming them into little more than asexual, and occasionally comic, domestic servants.[22] Similar points could be made about the stereotypes for other ethnic groups, for example, the Jewish American Princess or the neurotic Jewish man. Gender and ethnic identification are thus intertwined.

Regardless of whether ethnic humor is wielded by men or women, racist whites or ethnic humorists themselves, there *is* one constant that can be found in most iterations of nineteenth- and twentieth-century ethnic humor. Until very recently, ethnic humor in America tended to focus on only one nonwhite ethnic group at a time. While ethnic humor often focuses on intra-ethnic issues, most ethnic humor is comparative and based on juxtapositions between a marginalized group and the dominant (i.e., white) majority. Very often, the dominant group remains unseen or simply implied. When a cartoonist draws an exaggerated hook nose on a stereotypical Jewish moneylender, for example, that nose is comic only in relation to a smaller, "normal," WASP nose. Likewise, when an African American humorist impersonates an uptight white person who dances poorly, this impersonation is funny in comparison with the looser, more relaxed persona of the African American comic herself. So-called self-deprecating humor focuses on only one group, turning itself inward and relying on smaller distinctions within a single ethnic community. More often than not, self-deprecating humor is equally dependent on the unseen dominant group. Jewish humorists, for example, are well known for making self-deprecating jokes about cheap Jews; the stereotype of the cheap Jew, though, comes from the dominant group itself.

Traditional ethnic American humor, then, does not only construct rigid group boundaries, but until very recently, it does so almost always between white and a single Other. There are occasional exceptions. Mel Brooks's western spoof *Blazing Saddles* (1974)—which was cowritten by Richard Pryor and is driven by both black and Jewish sensibilities—comes to mind, but examples like this are few and far between. Scholars who write about ethnic humor have followed suit and tend to restrict their discussions to only one ethnic group at a time. For this reason, there are numerous books about Jewish American or African American humor, but very little scholarship about the ways in which ethnic humorists from multiple groups respond to or influence each other. In contrast, this book proposes that a trend is emerging in contemporary American ethnic humor, in which many humorists (white and nonwhite alike) are finding it necessary to articulate their identities within a much larger multiethnic context. Of course the old ways of ethnic humor are not going anywhere, but the most sophisticated humorists are finding it impossible, in light of the institutionalization of multiculturalism and the increasing diversity of the American population, to represent their ethnicity in isolation or only in relation to the majority group.

AMERICAN ETHNICITY IN THE TWENTY-FIRST CENTURY

At the turn of the twentieth century, W.E.B. Du Bois stated that the "color line" between black and white would define the coming century. And for the most part it did. American culture has long viewed itself as primarily a two-race country with a white majority and a sizable, vocal black minority. As I suggest above, however, this model no longer describes the America in which we live. The humorists discussed in this book are influenced by a score of changes that we can trace back, at least, to the 1960s. In particular, the civil-rights inspired 1965 Immigration Reform Act abolished exclusionist quotas placed on non-European immigrants and opened the door to unprecedented waves of immigration from Asia and Latin America.[23] Political turmoil throughout much of South America and the Caribbean and the political ramifications of the Korean and Vietnam wars (which led to many marriages between U.S. servicemen and Korean or Vietnamese women) further added to the rise in immigration from non-European countries.[24] As J. Eric Oliver asserts, these immigration changes "are rapidly turning America from a country monochromatically divided between blacks and whites into a multiethnic society composed of at least four sizable ethnic groups."[25]

Closely tied to the demographic changes brought about by immigration, the 1960s civil rights movements also gave rise to an identity politics that celebrated cultural pluralism over assimilation. The Black Power and feminist movements were the most visible during this era, but Latino, Asian American, and Native American groups also gained a stronger foothold in the national conversation. As nonwhite groups demanded more equal representation, colleges and universities created ethnic studies programs to accommodate these requests.[26] Furthermore, ethnic interest groups began to demand more control over their representations in mainstream media. As a response, many European Americans also began to rethink their ethnic affiliations, often choosing to be identified as "Irish American" or "German American" rather than simply "white."[27] As we saw in the above history of ethnic humor, this increase in ethnic consciousness enabled ethnic humorists to talk more openly about their ethnicity in mainstream venues. In the 1960s and 1970s, the vast majority of commercially successful ethnic humorists were Jewish and African American men, but by the 1990s and early 2000s, significant numbers of second- and third-generation Asian American and Latino humorists had claimed their own portion of the comedy market.

While the identity politics movements gave more freedom to ethnic humorists to joke openly about racism and ethnic difference, those same movements also created an environment in which each ethnic group tended to be viewed, and often to view itself, in a homogenous and circumscribed manner. Today, ethnically marked comic performers are still often expected to adhere to a specific brand of ethnically driven humor, and—owing to the increasing fragmentation of contemporary media brought about by the "narrowcasting" and niche markets of cable television and streaming services such as Hulu and Netflix Instant—they are often expected to create works primarily for their own ethnic group, as evidenced by an array of stand-up comedy specials focusing on a specific ethnic affiliation. In the past decade, however, there have also been signs of resistance against this rigid pluralism. In particular, those groups who have traditionally been associated with ethnic humor (Jewish and African Americans, as well as ethnically generic whites) are looking outside of their own mass-mediated ethnic enclaves and reconsidering how their specific ethnic identity fits in to multiethnic America. This recent trend is in no way replacing the pluralist model of ethnic humor that has been dominant since the late 1960s, but it is significant and widespread enough to warrant a study of its own, particularly for what it can tell us about ethnic attitudes *among* members of multiple ethnic affiliations.

There is a significant gap, in nearly all disciplines, in scholarly works that consider the relationships among multiple ethnicities. As Oliver explains, "almost nothing is known about the ways that social environments shape the racial attitudes among Asian Americans, blacks, and Latinos."[28] Most of the work that has been done exploring these relationships occur in the fields of sociology and political science and rely on extensive surveys and statistical analyses of population growth. What these studies have found reveals a complex web of multiethnic anxiety and ambivalence. Jennifer Hochschild and Reuel Rogers summarize a series of surveys exploring how multiple ethnic groups view themselves in relation to each other. The results could be an ethnic joke itself: "Whites feel most in common with African Americans, who feel little in common with Whites. African Americans feel most in common with Latinos, who feel least in common with them. Latinos feel most in common with Whites, who feel little in common with them. Asian Americans feel most in common with Whites, who feel least in common with them. Each group is chasing another that is running from it."[29] These puzzling emotions, I argue, frequently manifest themselves in contemporary ethnic humor. A study of America's ethnic humor thus contributes to a better understanding of the ways in which diverse ethnic populations relate to and understand each other. And more sophisticated ethnic humorists do more than simply reflect ethnic anxiety; they critique it and challenge audience members to consider their ethnic identification in relation to other ethnic positions.

My analyses of American ethnic humor draw heavily on the work of a handful of scholars who have offered various suggestions about how we should understand our multiethnic society and how we should live in it. Chief among these scholars is David Hollinger, who provides an insightful discussion of America's "ethno-racial pentagon," which is the product of the common practice in our culture to assign Americans to one of five ethno-racial groups: white, African American, Latino, Asian American, and Native American. Nearly everyone has seen these distinctions on various surveys. Academics, for instance, see some manifestation of these categories in the "equal opportunity" forms that we are asked (but not required) to fill out every time we apply for an academic position. A quick glance at the five groups signals a multitude of problems. For example, the categories of Asian American and Latino both conflate the individuals from a variety of national and ethnic backgrounds into single groups. According to this pentagon—and as Russell Peters critiques in his above discussion of Asian ethnicity—an Indian and a South Korean share the same ethnic affiliation. Likewise, the category of white (sometimes listed as Caucasian or Euro-American) combines a variety of backgrounds that less than a century ago were considered distinct ethnic positions in their own right, such as Italian American, Irish American, or Jewish American. And what of mixed-race individuals? Clearly, the actual ethnic makeup of American society is much more diverse than the ethno-racial pentagon will allow. Hollinger's primary criticism of the pentagon, though, is in the ways in which it encourages us to view ethnicity through a fixed lens of historical oppression rather than through the contemporary cultural practices and affiliations of individuals. Hollinger states that the "tendency to treat the blocs of the pentagon as cultural rather than political categories risks saddling us with a sense of diversity grounded in an analysis not of cultural difference but of the history of victimization justified largely by what we now recognize to be biologically superficial differentiators of human groups."[30] In contrast to this tendency, Hollinger argues for a "postethnic" perspective that "promotes solidarities of wide scope that incorporate people with different ethnic and racial backgrounds."[31]

It is of course difficult to envision how these "solidarities of broad scope" might be formed or what they might look like. Kwame Anthony Appiah, Paul Gilroy, and Hollinger himself, among others, have suggested that *cosmopolitanism* may offer insight for how individuals from diverse backgrounds may live among each other. Like Hollinger, Appiah and Gilroy eschew rigid group boundaries formed by ancestry or victimization. Gilroy, for instance, notes that "the defense of communal interests has often mobilized the fantasy of a frozen culture, of arrested cultural development. Particularity can be maintained and communal interests protected if they are fixed in their most authentic and glorious postures of resistance."[32] Put more simply, Appiah refuses to view ethnic difference as "a celebration of the beauty of a collection of closed boxes."[33] In contrast to these closed and frozen cultures, cosmopolitanism offers ways for individuals to speak across traditional ethnic and cultural barriers. Gilroy endorses what he calls a "vulgar" cosmopolitanism, which "finds a civic and ethical value in the process of exposure to otherness. It glories in the ordinary virtues and ironies—listening, looking, discretion, friendship—that can be cultivated when mundane encounters with difference become rewarding."[34] Along similar lines, Appiah asserts that cosmopolitan conversation should "begin with the sort of imaginative engagement you get when you read a novel or watch a movie or attend to a work of art that speaks from some place other than your own."[35] In essence, both scholars argue that an active engagement with other cultures—whether this be through actual conversation or through exposure to works of art—is necessary to live in a multicultural society.

Despite the critical recognition that Hollinger, Appiah, and Gilroy receive, in practice ethnic studies does not always reflect their influence. Rather, a large number of critics continue to view ethnic cultures singularly and to discuss ethnic cultural productions primarily in relation to the dominant white culture. Academic departments and courses are similarly built around the subdivisions of the ethno-racial pentagon: African American studies, Latino studies, and so forth. Some of this is undoubtedly necessary. Ethnic cultural productions arise out of particular ethnic histories and are deserving of close scrutiny on an individual level. Furthermore, without these divisions, we might run the risk of conflating different ethnic groups or falling back on the even more reductive categories of White and Other. But people do not exist in an ethnic vacuum; we live in a world in which every day we come into contact with people who emerge from different backgrounds, and these interactions undoubtedly influence the ways in which we view ourselves. There is also a need, then, for scholarship that addresses the manner in which different ethnic groups compete with and influence each other, particularly in media studies. Ethnic humorists, I argue, offer a series of primary texts that can help us understand intercultural dialogue on the ground level.

The ethnic humor discussed in the coming chapters does not usually depict the sort of broad solidarities described by Hollinger or the ideal cosmopolitan societies endorsed by Appiah and Gilroy, but it often does focus on interactions among people from different backgrounds and encourage an environment of multiethnic conversation. More important, ethnic humor also dramatizes the struggle, the awkwardness, and indeed the humor created by cross-cultural conversation. Ethnic humor can do this in part because it is the area of popular culture in which artists tend to speak the most frankly about ethnic identification and conflict. As Freud suggests, humor provides ways of articulating taboo emotions in a socially acceptable manner. Maybe it is only by wrapping our ethnic anxieties in layers of irony or by placing those anxieties in the mouths of buffoonish personas that we are able to express them at all. In his seminal work *Ethnic Humor around the World*, Christie Davies asserts that ethnic jokes "are social thermometers that measure, record, and indicate what is going on."[36] While Davies's work is specifically about "people's humor" (aka jokes), his assertion is equally true about the humor created by professional artists and performers, with the addition that these professionals have more opportunities and ability to dig deeply into ethnic issues and explore or critique ethnic preconceptions. Contemporary ethnic humor does not tell us one single thing about the state of ethnic relations in America; rather it reveals a web of ambivalence, cooperation, and anxiety. Taking a look at the humor itself is a way of navigating this maze.

THE STRUCTURE OF THIS BOOK

The organization of multicultural content is always problematic. I briefly considered a structure that would divide the entire book into chapters focusing on the humor of particular ethnic groups: African American, Jewish American, white, Latino, and Asian American. This format, though, too closely resembled the ethno-racial pentagon that I am working against. Furthermore, with some key exceptions such as Russell Peters and the *Harold and Kumar* films, Asian American and Latino humor did not readily lend itself to the multiethnic scope of this project, in which the emphasis is on conversation *across* cultural lines. A key concept in this book is that the humor of a particular ethnic group changes over time and that it is only in the past ten to fifteen years that some ethnic humorists have begun to construct their ethnic identity in relation to other groups. Asian American and Latino humor are still emerging into the mainstream and are thus not, at this point, fully engaged in intercultural dialogue. Moreover, because Latino and especially Asian American humorists emerge from a wide range of drastically different cultural backgrounds (as Hollinger's critique of the ethno-racial pentagon points out), it would be problematic to force them into singular comic traditions. These difficulties are reflected in a lack of critical literature (as exists with Jewish and African American humor) to which I could turn. My own discussions of Latino and Asian American humor are therefore relegated to a comparatively brief discussion of "emerging ethnic humors" in the conclusion.

Although I wished to avoid creating my own "ethno-comic" pentagon, it was impossible to avoid chapters based on ethnic groupings all together. African American and Jewish American humor are too central to the American comic landscape to avoid focusing on them specifically, and whites, who serve as both foils for other ethnic comics and, recently, as ethnic humorists in their own right, are impossible to ignore either. This book thus has a structure in which the first three chapters focus on particular ethnic groups and the ways in which those groups influence and respond to the diversity of the American population. The last two chapters, though, are not based on singular ethnic identifications at all but rather focus on those works of popular culture that attempt to represent the full diversity of American culture. Some works do this with remarkable insight, and others do not. In its entirety, the book thus constructs a narrative that begins with those groups who have historically been most central to American ethnic humor and then shifts to how mainstream and/or white Americans have reacted to, borrowed from, or utilized these traditions in various ways. Chapter 5 provides discussions of works that eschew rigid ethnic identification altogether in favor of a more complex and fluid *multi*ethnic affiliation.

The first chapter is devoted to recent developments in African American comedy. Most contemporary African American humor, inspired by Richard Pryor and exemplified by the HBO series *Def Comedy Jam* (1992–1996; 2006–2008), is influenced by a "double consciousness" model and is thus rooted in comic comparisons between black and white cultures. This "double consciousness" model is difficult to sustain in light of the massive growth of Latino and Asian American populations. Many African American artists have found it necessary to rethink black identity in relation to these other marginalized groups. I provide a discussion of the comedians Paul Mooney and Chris Rock, who often consider the diversity of the American ethnic landscape. Yet Mooney and Rock still attempt to reconfigure the complex American ethnic spectrum into a binary model: their humor, I suggest, reflects a resistance to seeing beyond the reductive white/black vision of American race relations. Dave Chappelle's comedy contrasts sharply with this approach. Through an analysis of both Chappelle's stand-up and his sketch comedy show, I assert that Chappelle looks past the simplistic white/black dichotomy and uses his humor to place blackness within a much wider multiethnic context. Finally, I consider the abrupt manner in which Chappelle left his lucrative series and discuss the ramifications of his absence on the future of African American humor.

Chapter 2 focuses primarily on the Jewish humorists Sarah Silverman, Larry David, and Sacha Baron Cohen.[37] The humorists under discussion reflect an anxiety in the Jewish American community about the position of Jews in the multiethnic American landscape. In the early twentieth century, Jewish entertainers participated in discrimination against African Americans as a means of assimilating into mainstream white culture. The contemporary Jewish humorists under discussion represent a backlash against the assimilationist motives of earlier generations. Having already achieved the status of whiteness, they attempt to assert their minority status by claiming affiliations with other ethnic groups, most often African Americans. Even as they claim affiliations with other groups, these humorists also work within the long tradition of Jewish culture and Jewish humor. Sarah Silverman, for example, builds her humor out of an extreme iteration of the Jewish American Princess (JAP) stereotype that became prominent after World War II. Larry David, in his series *Curb Your Enthusiasm*, reaches further back into the Jewish tradition and creates a contemporary manifestation of the *schlemiel* figure from Eastern European culture. As Borat, Sacha Baron Cohen parodies very old forms of anti-Semitism, which view Jews as evil, shape-shifting sorcerers. Through his wannabe gangsta persona Ali G, Baron Cohen places this version of anti-Semitism in conversation with contemporary stereotypes about African Americans. All three artists use their personas to explore the peculiar position of contemporary Jews, who exist in a sort of middle-space between white and other.

In chapter 3, I argue that the increased diversity of the American population has prompted many white humorists to articulate their own ethnic identity in ways that parallel traditional ethnic American humor. Without the legacy of oppression, this white ethnic humor has less potential to be genuinely transgressive; nonetheless, the rise of a white ethnic humor is indicative of the ways in which many whites in contemporary American culture are beginning to articulate their identity in more specific ways. Typically, whiteness remains an unmarked norm, but white ethnic humor offers an opportunity to view whiteness as a specific ethnic position rather than a raceless universal. I illustrate how nonwhite ethnic humorists—particularly African Americans—often critique white culture and present whites as bland, uptight, or nervous. Some white humorists, such as Mike Birbiglia and the late George Carlin, work these white stereotypes into their own acts. Next, I use various examples to show how the term "white," like all ethnic signifiers, is much too broad to account for the full spectrum of whiteness. To this end, I discuss different humorous constructions of whiteness, ranging from the rise of working-class "Blue Collar Comedy" to the blog *Stuff White People Like*, which mocks the stereotypical cultural preferences of educated, upper-middle-class, white liberals. Finally, I provide a detailed analysis of the Comedy Central animated series *South Park*. This show, I argue, offers an overt exploration and critique of white privilege. Furthermore, *South Park* does not represent a single homogenous whiteness but rather explores a larger spectrum of white culture, demonstrating the ways that class, education, and regional affiliation guide the construction of whiteness.

Chapter 4 analyzes some of the most commercially successful iterations of ethnic humor. It builds on Paul Gilroy's conception of a "corporate multiculturalism," in which token representations of diversity can be seen to increase the marketability of mainstream cultural productions. Gilroy's term offers a compelling approach to two commercially popular genres: the animated children's film and the network situation comedy. I focus on these genres primarily for their long, problematic history of ethnic representation and for their mainstream appeal. Both genres remain tied to their generic conventions and thus serve as, at best, one-dimensional vehicles for exploring issues of ethnic relations. I argue that contemporary iterations of these genres package and market the idea of diversity without really engaging with issues of ethnic conflict, inequality, or racism. In my discussion of children's films, I focus specifically on films that use the voices of well-known ethnic humorists in order to ethnicize animals and inanimate objects. Films such as *Madagascar* (2005), *Cars* (2006), and *Shark Tale* (2004) often reinforce broad ethnic stereotypes even as they make overtures toward an idealized multiculturalism. Overall, their representation of diversity is decidedly muddled. Likewise, sitcoms such as *The Office* (2005–), *Modern Family* (2009–), and *Community* (2009–) offer representations of diverse family units or multicultural workplaces. In keeping with sitcom conventions, however, these series sidestep issues of genuine ethnic conflict. Rather, they project a fantasy world in which systemic inequality does not exist and diverse ethnic characters live together in a rarely disrupted harmony. Both genres display the ways in which ethnic humor—often a vehicle for cultural critique—can be neutralized and contained in mainstream cultural productions.

In contrast to the "corporate multiculturalism" discussed in chapter 4, chapter 5 considers comic works that use ethnic humor to engage with diversity in more productive ways. I begin with an analysis of the Showtime series *Weeds* (2005–) and the film *Harold and Kumar Go to White Castle* (2004). These works create a *multiethnic humor*, which focuses on how individuals might reexamine their own ethnicity through interactions with other groups. While ethnic humor delineates rigid group boundaries and is often driven by conflicts between white and other, multiethnic humor focuses on interactions *among* members of many different ethnic identifications and blurs the lines between marginalized and mainstream cultures. This humor does not represent the point of view of any one ethnic group but is willing to engage with the full complexity of the American ethnic spectrum. Finally, I return to Russell Peters in order to offer a fuller analysis of his transnational approach to ethnic humor. Peters has achieved a global following and is particularly popular in Asia and the Middle East. As host of the Showtime series *Comics without Borders* (2008)—a showcase for stand-up comedians from all over the world—he has helped to generate an international comedy movement. I argue that Peters creates a cosmopolitan humor, which is based on his knowledge of other cultures and dialects and often involves humorous stories from his travels throughout the world. Peters ultimately encourages intercultural dialogue without relying on idealized and simplistic notions of diversity.

Lurking throughout this book is Werner Sollors, reminding us that ethnic humor is "a form of boundary construction." In this study, I examine ethnic humorists who go to great lengths to build ethnic boundaries and then use their comic skills to defend them, often ingeniously, against real or imagined invaders. Others work equally hard to tear those traditional boundaries down or, at the very least, to expose their weak spots. These latter humorists, I suppose, are the heroes of this book. They challenge their audiences to think deeply about the ways in which ethnicity is defined and/or performed, and while they acknowledge that ethnicity and historical oppression are often inextricably linked, they are willing to view contemporary ethnic identity as malleable, not as a frozen artifact of historical trauma. They can also be very funny.

1 • "JUST US"

African American Humor in Multiethnic America

ON HIS 1975 GRAMMY-WINNING comedy album, *. . . Is It Something I Said?*, Richard Pryor comments on the disproportionate number of African Americans in prison: "You go down there looking for justice," Pryor quips, "and that's what you find: just us."[1] The joke itself is a fairly simple pun addressing racial inequality in the American justice system, but it also speaks to Pryor's position (and by extension, the position of African American humor in general) in American culture. The "us" of Pryor's joke of course refers to African Americans. By this point in his career, however, Pryor was already a crossover comedian, and his audiences were racially mixed. In fact, Pryor is generally credited with bringing genuine African American folk humor to the attention of mainstream white audiences. According to Mel Watkins, Pryor "was the first African-American stand-up comedian to speak candidly and successfully to integrated audiences the way black people joked among themselves."[2] Given the heterogeneous racial makeup of his fans, Pryor's "just us" strategically excluded a large portion of his live audience and probably an even larger portion of the listeners who bought his albums. Ironically, this exclusion only increased Pryor's popularity with white audiences. In a cultural landscape where blackness itself is a commodity, the rhetorical exclusion of whites most likely served to make white audience members feel as if they were "down" with black culture. Siva Vaidhyanathan addresses this phenomenon, suggesting that if "white audience members got more than half the jokes at a Pryor concert, they could feel included. . . . White America desired an avenue into black oral tradition, and Pryor offered it on a large scale."[3]

Pryor's comedy was therefore a delicate balancing act between an authentically black "just us" aesthetic and mainstream crossover appeal. Even as whites flocked to his shows and purchased his albums in droves, Pryor used various rhetorical strategies, such as his "just us" joke, to delineate his performances as a black space. One of the most famous of these strategies is the comic comparison between white and black cultures. For example, in his most famous performance, the 1979 film *Richard Pryor: Live in Concert*, Pryor opens by joking about whites in the audience who, upon returning from the bathroom, find that blacks have taken their seats. Pryor uses this scenario to launch into an extended critique of white culture, in which he skillfully impersonates a series of nervous, uptight, and decidedly unhip white characters and contrasts them with looser, more relaxed, and cooler African American voices. Pryor, for example, impersonates a black man walking through the woods who, thanks to his natural rhythm, dodges a poisonous snake. An oblivious white man on a similar hike is not so attuned to Mother Nature and inevitably gets bitten. These sorts of black/white comparisons have since become staples of contemporary American humor. Indeed, the specter of Pryor's "just us" aesthetic, as well as his black/white comparisons, presides over the history of African American humor since the 1970s, and it provides a salient example of Werner Sollors's assertion that ethnic humor "is a form of boundary construction."[4]

A large portion of post-Pryor African American humor, however, has kept Pryor's comic attitude, especially his "blue" language, but lost his subversive edge. And very often, any progressive critiques in the realm of race relations are undermined by a regressive gender politics. This is seen most clearly in the early work of Pryor's heir apparent, at least in terms of mass appeal, Eddie Murphy. Murphy does occasionally critique American race relations, especially in his *Saturday Night Live* sketch "White Like Me," in which Murphy dons whiteface in order to learn the true nature of "white America," but his stand-up is often driven by homophobia and misogyny. Bambi Haggins asserts that Murphy's stand-up "reaffirms [the status quo] by reasserting black masculinity through the degradation of black women (and women in general) and annunciating the beginnings of a backlash against feminism."[5] For Haggins, the most disturbing aspect of this conservative gender politics is the way that it has been "embraced by the male and female comics of the Def Jam generation."[6] Indeed, there is little difference in the conservative visions of gender espoused in the *Def Comedy Jam*–inspired *The Original Kings of Comedy* (2000) or its 2001 female spin-off *The Queens of Comedy*.

Contemporary African American humorists, male and female, are more nuanced in their discussion of race than of gender, but even here the humor is most often driven by a traditional black/white vision of American ethnicity, in which humorists give scant attention to other ethnic groups. Despite growing numbers of Latinos, Asian Americans, and Arab Americans, most black comedians maintain a "just us" worldview. This is not to suggest that African American humorists never make jokes about Latinos or Asian Americans; they often

The influence of Richard Pryor can still be felt in contemporary African American humor. (Credit: ©Columbia Pictures. Courtesy of Photofest.)

do. Most of the time, however, this humor is fleeting and broad. Jokes about other ethnic positions rarely receive the sustained scrutiny that African American comics reserve for black/white race relations. In her stand-up special *I'ma Be Me* (2009), for example, Wanda Sykes provides a short routine about how a Mexican man can go anywhere as long as he is carrying a leaf blower. The jokes suggests the ways in which Latino laborers often remain invisible to mainstream America, but Sykes—who in the same act provides very insightful discussions of race and sexuality—offers little commentary past the initial observation. A more startling example can be found in the late Patrice O'Neal's assertion, in his *Comedy Central Presents* special, that Asian and Arab groups need to "pick a color" because it is too difficult for outsiders to understand their ethnic backgrounds.[7] The joke displays a strict adherence to the black/white racial lens. Some of the most sophisticated black comedians, like Chris Rock and Paul Mooney, address America's multiethnic demographic at more length, but even they do so in a way that ultimately reinforces the white/black binary and avoids discussions of the relationships between African Americans and other nonwhite groups. In contrast to this majority of African American humorists, Dave Chappelle has offered an in-depth exploration of African American culture in relation to multiethnic America. Chappelle's humor does not propose a consistent ethnic ideology, but it does suggest that a rigid "just us" aesthetic is no longer tenable for a full exploration of African American life and culture.

AFRICAN AMERICAN HUMOR AND BLACK COMMUNAL SPACE

Making humor out of the black/white divide, of course, goes back much further than Pryor. At the turn of the twentieth century, W.E.B. Du Bois articulated his well-known theory of "double consciousness" to explain the struggle of the African American: "One ever feels his two-ness,—an American, a Negro; two souls, two thoughts, two unreconciled strivings; two warring ideals in one dark body."[8] Watkins asserts that "Du Bois's eloquent description of African America's psychological predicament provides a salient clue to the source and special tenor of black American humor."[9] He goes on to explain that from the time of slavery until the civil rights movement, this double consciousness manifested itself in "a dual mode of behavior and expression—one for whites and another for themselves."[10] A prime example of this "dual mode of behavior" can be found in the oft-quoted African American folk saying, "Got one mind for white folk to see / 'Nother for what I know is me."[11] This imposed dichotomous worldview fostered the type of comparative black-versus-white humor that is a staple for black comics, and it simultaneously created the need for black communal spaces in which African Americans could express their criticisms of the dominant culture freely.

Christine Acham explains the genesis of such communal spaces, arguing that this sort of boundary construction was

> dictated by law from the days of slavery, through slave codes, the black codes in the post-Reconstruction era, and eventually Jim Crow laws, which enforced segregation. However, considering the antagonistic and destructive atmosphere created by the enslavement of black people and the cultural differences in American society, we need not wonder why reprieve was to be found within these black communal sites. It was here that many black people found a sense of self-affirmation. They garnered the strength to cope with the harsh reality of their public life and critiqued the white society that enslaved them and refused to acknowledge their status as human beings. They also celebrated, relaxed, and enjoyed themselves away from the critical eyes of white society.[12]

Black communal spaces were essential to African American humor as forums where it could be practiced, but over time, the spaces themselves became necessary components of the humor, part of its content. Thus in her book of folklore *Mules and Men* (1935), Zora Neale Hurston not only relates a series of often humorous African American folk tales, but she also painstakingly re-creates the front-porch setting in which the stories are told. Pryor and other late-twentieth-century black comics attempt to maintain the black communal aspects of this front-porch culture, but by doing so, black communal culture itself has become increasingly commodified and attractive to nonblack audiences. In recent years, the marketability of black communal culture has become increasingly apparent. Extreme examples are the *Barbershop* films (2002 and 2004) and the spin-off film *Beauty Shop* (2005), which celebrate the spaces named as being more than businesses but as community centers where African Americans can relax, talk, and joke. Similar examples can be found in the series of *Friday* films and in the seemingly never-ending stream of Tyler Perry vehicles.

Despite their mainstream appeal, these works use various rhetorical devices to maintain a semblance of communal black culture. Like Pryor's "just us" joke, black humorists repeatedly suggest that while white audiences are free to listen in—especially if they are willing to pay the cost of a ticket—the humor itself, and the spaces in which it is performed, are the cultural property of African Americans. This is extremely evident in a stand-up series such as HBO's *Def Comedy Jam*, produced by media mogul Russell Simmons. The series establishes itself as not only a comedy show but also as a black communal space. *Def Comedy Jam* helped launch the careers of dozens of successful African American comics, including Dave Chappelle, Chris Rock, Bernie Mac, Cedric the Entertainer, Martin Lawrence, and D. L. Hughley. Each episode features an emcee who playfully banters with the small studio audience before introducing the individual comics, thus establishing a relaxed and intimate atmosphere. Like Pryor, more than twenty years before them, the emcees and comics often make a point of singling out white audience members. By demonstrating white spectators as an anomaly, the show further establishes itself as a black space.

Spike Lee's concert documentary *The Original Kings of Comedy* is another important and extremely influential work of African American humor that deliberately creates a black space. The film records the acts of four *Def Comedy Jam* veterans—Steve Harvey, D. L. Hughley, Cedric the Entertainer, and the late Bernie Mac—for a primarily black audience in Charlotte, North Carolina. It also takes great pains to demonstrate that the live show is an African American community event. The comedy itself continues the "just us" tradition of African American humor: the comics make good-natured, self-deprecating jokes about perceived idiosyncrasies within black culture, and they offer a series of comic critiques of whites. Steve Harvey, for example, describes what the film *Titanic* would have been like if it had been about black people, and D. L. Hughley jokes about white people's love for extreme sports, asserting that bungee jumping is "too much like lynching" for him. Cedric the Entertainer repeats almost verbatim Pryor's joke about white audience members having their seats taken by blacks. The humor in the film is thus fairly conventional and offers exactly what audience members have come to expect from African American comedians. However, *The Original Kings of Comedy* is noteworthy in the way that it emphasizes the concert's black communal aspects. Steve Harvey, acting as master of ceremonies, leads the audience in a sing along to a series of classic R&B songs. In the film, the editing drives home the black communal aspects as the camera pans wide and shows a large auditorium full of primarily African American audience members dancing and singing together. Spike Lee's direction further highlights the importance of the concert for the black community by frequently cutting from the comedian performing to a shot of the audience's reaction. The visual rhetoric reinforces the black/white binary that is created by the humor itself: it includes black viewers while excluding whites.

Def Comedy Jam and *The Original Kings of Comedy* both succeed at creating black performance venues that continue the tradition of a communal African American folk humor. They are both, however, ultimately reductive in the ways that they represent and/or critique race relations in present-day America. By relying on a primarily black/white worldview, these works overlook contemporary changes in the American population and offer little consideration of how other ethnic groups, especially Latinos and Asian Americans, influence and are influenced by black culture. Ironically, despite its insularity, *The Original Kings* has had an enormous impact on the landscape of contemporary ethnic American humor, for it has inspired a series of imitation comedy tours and films that are built around celebrating a specific ethnicity, such as *The Original Latin Kings of Comedy* (2002) and *The Kims of Comedy* (2005).[13]

These various ethnocentric comedy programs suggest a pluralist model of contemporary American humor, which bears a striking resemblance to the fixed and rigid boundaries of David Hollinger's ethno-racial pentagon, discussed in the introduction to this book. In this model, each ethnic group has its own comedians and its own ethnic stereotypes to either overturn or self-deprecatingly reinforce. People of other ethnicities are free to watch as well, but it is understood that the comedy is not for them and that they will not fully "get" it. This comedy relies on what Paul Gilroy describes as an "emphasis on culture as a form of property to be owned."[14] This comic landscape further suggests that not only do many African Americans police their ethnic boundaries with anxiety but that they do so in ways that serve as a model for other ethnic groups. The influence of African American humor on the humor of other ethnic affiliations is in line with the ways that race in America is traditionally constructed. Gary Segura and Helena Alves Rodrigues note that "scholarly understandings of race and its consequences for American politics have been achieved largely through the analytic lens of a black-white dynamic. . . . When discussions move beyond these groups, political scientists often mistakenly presume that arguments and findings with respect to African-Americans extend to other racial and ethnic groups. Moreover, racial and ethnic interactions between Anglos and other minority groups are assumed to mimic—to some degree—the black-white experience."[15] The actual ethnic landscape in America is of course significantly more complex and consists of a tangled web of multiethnic cooperation, conflict, anxiety, and influence. For instance, most studies seem to indicate that blacks feel somewhat threatened by the increasing numbers of other minority groups (especially Latinos) and the claims that they might make on jobs and resources that would otherwise help black communities.

According to Hollinger, these feelings of anxiety are well-founded. He explains that when the African American experience is used as a lens through which to understand all nonwhite groups, that nonblack minorities often end up benefiting from resources that were intended as reparations for the *specific* history of black enslavement and segregation.[16] There is not necessarily a direct connection between such concerns and the insular nature of most African American humor, but the fact that many African Americans are aware of these issues may help explain the reluctance of contemporary black comics to discuss the relationships between African Americans and other nonwhite groups. The rigidly delineated humor of *Def Comedy Jam* and *The Original Kings of Comedy*, however, does not represent the entire range of African American humor. There are contemporary black humorists who display more willingness to explore blackness in a larger multiethnic context, and discussions of this sort may illuminate more fully the complex relationships between African Americans and other groups. Paul Mooney and Chris Rock, for example, occasionally discuss African American culture in relation to other ethnicities, but they do so in a manner that ultimately reinforces a traditional "just us" black comic aesthetic.

MOONEY AND ROCK: ENFORCING THE BINARY

African American humorist Paul Mooney has spent most of his career relatively unknown by mainstream audiences and ignored by humor scholars. In his foreword to Mooney's memoir, *Black Is the New White* (2010), Dave Chappelle addresses this obscurity, arguing that Mooney is "*too black for Hollywood!*"[17] Despite his lack of fame, Mooney has been a constant presence in African American humor for the past forty years. He was a writer for, and close friend of, Richard Pryor, and he served as head writer for Pryor's short-lived variety program *The Richard Pryor Show* (1977). With Pryor, he also wrote occasionally for Norman Lear's sitcom *Sanford and Son* (1972–1977).[18] In the 1990s, Mooney worked as a writer for the African American–centered sketch comedy show *In Living Color* (1990–1994), where he created one of the series's most popular characters, the angry black children's entertainer, Homey D. Clown, portrayed on the show by Damon Wayans.[19] In the twenty-first century, Mooney worked as a writer for, and appeared in various sketches on, *Chappelle's Show*. Mooney has also had an active and prolific stand-up career, having produced two comedy albums and three concert films. His résumé shows he has been a major part of African American humor since it became mainstream in the 1970s. A consideration of Mooney's work can thus be useful in tracking the history of African American humor. As part of this history, Mooney, even more so than Pryor and the *Def Comedy Jam* comics, fiercely enforces a "just us" comic aesthetic. In fact, on the liner notes to *. . . Is It Something I Said?*, Pryor claims to have stolen the "just us" joke from Mooney.

Mooney's humor is a mixture of indignation and racial pride and, when it is unmitigated by the more easygoing comic personas of Pryor, the Wayans brothers, or Dave Chappelle, it can come across (as does much of the late Lenny Bruce material) as more like enraged social commentary than actual comedy. Unlike most African American comics, Mooney's critique of black/white race relations does not rely on comic impersonations of whites. Rather, Mooney draws on his experiences of living through segregation and the civil rights movement, and he interprets the world through a narrow black lens. This concern with blackness is evinced in the title of his most famous stand-up film: *Know Your History: Jesus Was Black . . . So Was Cleopatra* (2007). In his memoir, Mooney provides a series of similar historical revisions, arguing, for example, that rice comes from Africa not China: "*Uncle Ben's black ass belongs on the rice box, because we introduced rice to Chinese people."*[20] Mooney's revisionist history, however, serves as a telling example of the extent of his "just us" comic worldview. While other black comics may maintain black exclusivity through the use of African American slang or references to black popular culture, Mooney paints his picture of blackness on a much larger canvas, asserting the importance of black culture throughout world history.

While Mooney may express an overriding concern with blackness as a sweeping historical category, he still reserves the most attention for specifically African American concerns, and more specifically, his humor embodies the dominant strain of conservative gender ideology that typifies most African American humor. Mooney writes that he is "not intending any disrespect to Africans. I know what the game is. But the American black man is a unique kind of black person. All over the world, people copy us. . . . We are the most imitated people on earth."[21] Mooney goes on to explain, however, that despite this imitation, African Americans are still hated and feared. He wraps this thought up with the maxim: "Everybody wants to be a nigger, but nobody wants to be a nigger. It's complicated that way."[22] This routine is in keeping with Haggins's comment that African American humor is driven by both regressive and progressive impulses. Mooney's specific focus on African American men problematically removes African American women from the equation but provides an insightful critique of the paradoxical position that black men hold in contemporary America, in which mainstream society is simultaneously fascinated with black cultural productions and afraid of black cultural influence. It also suggests Mooney's attention to the multiple ways in which African American culture, or "blackness," can be seen. Mooney points out that black culture is not simply a set of values or practices created within African American communities, but that, as Herman Gray asserts, it is "open to multiple and competing claims."[23] Mooney, whose thinking here is in line with Eric Lott's discussion of minstrelsy in *Love and Theft* (see introduction), understands that blackness is a commodity forever subject to being co-opted and revised by the larger surrounding culture. Mooney's racial commentary clearly adheres to a "just us" African American aesthetic, but unlike most of his *Def Jam* peers, he is more fully aware of the wider cultural context in which African American humor participates.

This wider cultural awareness also allows Mooney to discuss other ethnic groups in more detail than most African American comics. The way he does so, however, does not encourage intercultural dialogue; rather, it reshapes the diverse American ethnic demographic into a binary model in which African Americans retain primacy as the country's principal other. For example, one of Mooney's more famous routines is "The Nigga Wake-up Call," which he first developed as a means of critiquing African American celebrities, such as

Tiger Woods, Diana Ross, or Oprah Winfrey, who—according to Mooney—believe that they are accepted unequivocally by whites but who eventually get their "wake-up call" when whites remind them that they will never be wholly accepted.[24] In *Know Your History,* Mooney adapts this routine to include other nonwhite ethnic groups. Speaking of the push for immigration reform in California, Mooney says, "I am so happy because the Mexicans got their nigger wake-up call . . . they was running around here thinking they was white folks."[25] The comment is richly ambivalent. First, it should be pointed out that poor and working-class Mexican immigrants are in a drastically different position from the wealthy black celebrities who were the original inspiration for Mooney's "wake-up call" routine. On the surface, his happiness at the discrimination against Mexican Americans is derogatory and mean-spirited. At the same time, though, it could be argued that the satire is mainly directed at a mainstream white American culture that refuses to make concessions to ethnic outsiders. The use of the word "nigger" to describe Mexicans can also be read in different ways. On the one hand, it appears that Mooney may be suggesting a coalition of sorts between Mexican and African Americans as they both face discrimination, for black comics often use the word as a term for friends and community members. On the other hand, though, Mooney forces Mexican Americans into a black/white paradigm and thus strips them of their ethnic specificity.

Later in the same performance, Mooney returns to this theme and treats a variety of other ethnic groups in a similar manner. Addressing hypothetical Puerto Ricans who claim to be Spanish, Mooney says, "I know a nigger when I see one. . . . You speak Spanish; you have Spanish blood, but you are a nigger." Mooney goes on to make similar jokes about Filipinos and Dominicans. He also explains that Samoans are just "some mo' niggers" and that Cubans are "niggers that can swim." The routine is a fascinating display of ethnic anxiety, especially considering Mooney's preoccupation with Latino ethnicities, who, according to Hollinger and other critics cited above, provide the most direct threat to African Americans' status as the country's major minority group.[26] Mooney invokes diversity by cataloging ethnic groups, but he immediately dismisses it by lumping everyone together as a "nigger." The bit not only reinforces a traditional black/white ethnic binary, but its repeated use of the word "nigger" aggressively asserts that the African American experience provides the standard for discrimination, oppression, and general "otherness" by which all other ethnic groups will be measured. One could argue, I suppose, that Mooney's bit is actually an ironic satire of a white culture that refuses to see a nonwhite as anything but a "nigger," but this reading strikes me as a subtext. Unlike, say, Sarah Silverman, who is well known for wrapping her humor in layers of sarcasm and knowing irony, Mooney tends to present his humor in a more direct "tell it like it is" fashion. As he himself states in his memoir, "I am who I am."[27]

Another African American comedian who approaches diversity in a similar way is former *Saturday Night Live* cast member Chris Rock. Unlike Mooney, Rock has earned international fame and has perhaps achieved more crossover success than any black comic since Eddie Murphy. His stand-up specials and the HBO series *The Chris Rock Show* (1997–2000) root themselves firmly in African American culture, but he is also a presence in wholly mainstream media venues. He hosted the Academy Awards in 2008; he provides the voice of the zebra in the popular animated *Madagascar* films (discussed in chapter 4), and he occasionally appears as the "token black guy" in otherwise white films, such as the Adam Sandler vehicle *Grown Ups* (2010). While Rock's humor mostly adheres to a "just us" aesthetic and embraces a traditional gender politics, he is much more critical of African American culture than his peers. This is evident in his most infamous routine, "Niggas vs. Black People," which appears in his concert film *Bring the Pain* (1996). Here Rock laments "niggas," those segments of the black population who Rock argues adhere to negative black stereotypes and tarnish the image of the African American community. Rock explains that "there's some shit going on with black people right now. There's like a civil war going on with black people, and there's two sides. There's black people, and there's niggas, and niggas have got to go." By splitting African Americans into two distinct groups, Rock clearly refuses to see blackness as a homogenous category. Furthermore, by voicing criticism of certain segments of the African American community, he avoids the easy celebrations of black culture that are offered by *The Original Kings* and the *Def Comedy Jam* comics. His critique destabilizes his performance as a communal black space and undermines the typical "just us" worldview.

Interestingly, however, Rock refuses to see whiteness in a similarly complex way. In *Bigger and Blacker* (1999), Rock argues against Louis Farrakhan's anti-Semitic comments: "I never been in a barbershop and heard a bunch of brothers talking about Jews. Black people don't hate Jews. Black people hate white people! We don't got time to dice white people up into little groups. I hate everybody. I don't care if you just got here. 'Hey, I'm Romanian.' You Romanian cracker!"[28] This routine follows the same impulse, albeit from a different direction, as Mooney's use of the word "nigger" to apply to various ethnic groups. Both comics acknowledge a more complex view of the American ethnic demographic, but they both ultimately reject a vision of multiplicity and revert to the black/white binary. Mooney and Rock are certainly more astute than the *Def Jam* comics or *The Original Kings*, but they ultimately reinforce a static image of American racial politics. The long history of oppression at the hands of whites, the larger culture's tendency to view American race-relations through a black/white lens, and the enduring power of Du Bois's "color line" in African American self-definition all manifest themselves in an African American humor that is strongly resistant (even in the hands of some of the most sophisticated comics) to looking beyond white and black.

An exception to this trend may be found in Mooney's and Rock's treatment of Native Americans. Surprisingly, they are the one group that both Mooney and Rock agree are deserving of real sympathy. In his memoir, Mooney writes that "racism is . . . the country's original sin—that and the shit the Europeans pull on the Indians, which is part of the same trip."[29] And in *Know Your History*, Mooney asks "Why does white folks hate the Indians so much? There ain't but two of them left." In *Bigger and Blacker*, Rock tackles the Native plight even more directly: "Black people yelling 'racism!' White people yelling 'reverse racism!' Chinese people yelling 'sideways racism!' And the Indians ain't yelling shit, 'cause they dead. So everybody bitching about how bad their people got it: *nobody* got it worse than the American Indian." At first glance, it appears that Mooney and Rock are genuinely stepping out of the black/white binary and considering the conditions of another ethnic group. Not only that, but Mooney gives the Native American genocide equal stature with slavery, calling it "part of the same trip," and Rock (in addition to literally placing Chinese Americans on the racial sidelines) goes so far as to assert that Native Americans suffered even worse than blacks. Both Mooney and Rock, however, couch their analysis in the myth of the vanishing Indian: they are careful to structure their depiction of Native Americans as an absence, Mooney joking that there are only two Natives left and Rock stating plainly that "they dead" and thus cannot complain. Of course, Mooney and Rock are relying on comic hyperbole, and I am sure that both men are well aware of the many still-living Native populations. Nonetheless, both jokes point to a truth in American race relations: Native Americans do not have a voice in the national conversation to the same degree as Latinos, whose growing numbers continue to threaten African Americans' place in the American ethnic imagination, or Asian Americans, so-called model minorities whose successes are often erroneously presented as an example that blacks could improve their situation if they worked hard enough. Native Americans therefore pose little or no threat to African Americans, and Mooney and Rock can talk about their suffering openly without undermining the black/white dichotomy with which they feel most comfortable.

TOWARD A BLACK MULTIETHNIC HUMOR: DAVE CHAPPELLE

While Mooney, Rock, and dozens of other more conventional black comics derive their humor from comparisons between black and white cultures, Dave Chappelle is unique in his willingness and ability to place blackness within a larger multiethnic context. Mainly for his work on *Chappelle's Show*, Chappelle

Dave Chappelle is unique in his ability to situate African American concerns in a wider, multiethnic context. (Credit: ©Showtime. Photographer: Greg Gorman. Courtesy of Photofest.)

has received a level of critical recognition and scholarly attention that is rarely afforded to contemporary comedians, and he is well on his way to canonization. Haggins, for example, places Chappelle's work as the most recent step in a trajectory of black humor that she traces back to crossover pioneers like Richard Pryor, Bill Cosby, and Dick Gregory. Glenda Carpio reads Chappelle alongside not only Pryor but also revered black writers like William Wells Brown, Charles Chesnutt, and Ishmael Reed.[30] Owing to the critical tendency to place Chappelle's work within the larger history of African American culture, its significance in relation to other nonwhite ethnic groups has received far less attention. A handful of critics have noted Chappelle's interest in collapsing or expanding the traditional black/white binary. K. A. Wisniewski, for instance, describes Chappelle as the "voice for an emerging culture," which Wisniewski describes as a "polyethnic society."[31] And in an excellent essay focusing on Afro-Asian motifs on *Chappelle's Show*, Graham Chia-Hui Preston notes that "*Chappelle's Show* speaks to and with a diverse, nuanced and complex American cultural and racial landscape."[32] This section builds on such assertions and places Chappelle more explicitly within a multiethnic context.

Chappelle's work is deeply rooted in the tradition of African American humor, and like most African American comedians, his gender politics are unfortunately less nuanced than his racial material. Haggins defines Chappelle's treatment of gender as "sexism by omission," stating that "[w]omen, in general, don't occupy a significant space in Chappelle's comedy except as occasional foils and punch lines."[33] Novotny Lawrence goes further in his critique, asserting that Chappelle's often juvenile gender-based humor "devalue[s] the significance of his more relevant material."[34] Indeed, breast-obsessed sketches like "New York Boobs" or "It's a Wonderful Chest"—in which the female body is celebrated primarily as an object for the male gaze—are fairly sophomoric, potentially offensive, and definitely less sophisticated than his racial humor. To his credit, though, Chappelle's treatment of masculinity is more fluid than that of most African American humorists. Chappelle embodies a laid-back "stoner" persona that does not celebrate an aggressive black masculinity to the same degree as Mooney, Rock, or even Pryor, and it is a far cry from the overt misogyny of a figure like Murphy. Chappelle's primary contribution to contemporary humor, however, lies in his ability to see blackness not as part of a fixed black/white binary but rather as a fluid yet integral facet of America's multiethnic landscape.

In contrast to the "just us" aesthetic, Chappelle displays a remarkable willingness to talk about and talk to members of other ethnic groups. In his standup special *Dave Chappelle: For What It's Worth* (2004), for example, Chappelle performs a routine that usefully contrasts his outlook with that of Mooney and Rock. In fact, the opening lines of the bit sound as if they could be replying directly to Mooney's and Rock's own jokes about Native Americans, discussed above. Chappelle says, "You know who I feel real bad for is Indians. They get dogged openly because everybody thinks they're dead. These motherfuckers are not all dead, all right." Chappelle then proceeds to tell a story about meeting a Native American named Running Coyote in a Walmart in New Mexico. After a brief conversation, Chappelle goes home with Running Coyote and smokes marijuana with him and a group of other Natives. Chappelle gets so high that he has to spend the night. The differences between this routine and Mooney's and Rock's routines are clear. Chappelle deliberately constructs Native American identity as a presence rather than an absence. Furthermore, Chappelle builds the bit on personal interactions (probably fictional or largely imagined) rather than broad strokes. And finally, the fact that Chappelle smokes marijuana with the group—a "breaking bread" type symbol of forging a common ground—suggests that he is open to intercultural dialogue. While the bit is rooted in the devices of ethnic humor, it also works toward a sort of cosmopolitan understanding, or what Kwame Anthony Appiah calls "debate and conversation across nations."[35]

The routine, however, is not quite as idyllic as I have so far described it. Chappelle's depiction of Running Coyote is deliberately rife with exaggerated stereotypes. For example, when Chappelle first comes upon Running Coyote, he is in the sporting goods section at Walmart, shopping for bows and arrows. Also, Chappelle does not initially believe that he has met a "real Indian," so he throws a gum wrapper on the floor and is only convinced once Running Coyote has cried a single tear. The latter example, referencing the crying Indian in the 1970s "Keep America Beautiful" commercials, speaks directly to the co-opted image of the Native American—an issue that Chappelle is extremely perceptive of in regards to African American images. This point is also apparent when Chappelle learns that Running Coyote is a Navajo. Chappelle replies, "I studied you in social studies. You're a hunter/gatherer, correct?" Chappelle's reply shows a more complex understanding of the Native American experience than Mooney or Rock, for Chappelle mocks most Americans' (including his own) ignorance of Native cultures by suggesting that their understanding is gleaned from pop-cultural representations and elementary school textbooks, which reduce tribal cultures to facile categories like "hunter/gatherer." Throughout most of this routine, Chappelle depends on outlandish Native stereotypes, but in the last moment he switches gears. He explains that when it was time for bed, the Natives gave him his "own teepee to sleep in, which sounds nice. I personally think it was a little fucked up, 'cause you know, they all had houses." The comment subverts expectations, for his audience has become acquainted with a routine that derives its humor from stereotypes, but in the last line, Chappelle doubles back on himself. The reversal further highlights the ridiculousness of the stereotypes he has been critiquing throughout.

On his Comedy Central program *Chappelle's Show* (2002–2006), in which Chappelle appears before a studio audience and introduces previously filmed sketches, he utilizes a multiethnic cast in order to explore America's diverse ethnic landscape even more explicitly than in his stand-up. This is not to say that *Chappelle's Show*'s primary theme is multiculturalism. Many of the sketches are built on standard comparisons between black and white culture, such as "Black Bush," which envisions the high jinks that would ensue if George W. Bush were an African American, and "The Mad Real World," which inverts the "token black guy" scenario that is found in most reality shows by imagining a program in which one white man lives in a house with six African Americans. Furthermore, the show frequently features African American musical guests such as Mos Def, Kanye West, and the Wu-Tang Clan, suggesting a certain level of adherence to a "just us" perspective—although all three of those musical acts have achieved crossover success. Chappelle has also chosen African American cast members who help to place him within the larger history of African American humor. Eddie Murphy's older brother Charlie Murphy is a regular player and figures in some of the most popular sketches, and Paul Mooney often appears in Afrocentric segments like "Ask a Black Dude" and "Negrodamus." By placing himself alongside Eddie Murphy's brother and Richard Pryor's friend/writing partner, Chappelle suggests that he has deep ties to the tradition of African American humor.

At the same time, though, Chappelle distances his humor from an unbending "just us" aesthetic. This can be seen in the manner in which he positions himself in relation to Paul Mooney. The first time Mooney appears on the program (in the season 1, episode 5 sketch, "Ask a Black Dude"), Chappelle introduces the sketch by invoking cross-cultural dialogue. He says that viewers at home might assume that everyone in the studio audience is black, but that the onlookers are actually a "multiethnic, multicultural patchwork." Chappelle asserts, somewhat ironically, that this diverse audience probably has questions that they would like answered about black culture and that Mooney will answer them in the service of cross-cultural understanding. Chappelle's overture to diversity is certainly sarcastic, but at the same time, his easygoing persona really *does* make his show appealing to multiple ethnic groups. In the sketch that follows, Chappelle's laid-back attitude is placed in sharp contrast with Mooney.

In the "Ask a Black Dude" segment, Mooney appears solemn-faced and responds to a series of prerecorded "person-on-the-street"-style questions about black culture. The queries asked are largely superficial, and Mooney often ridicules the person asking the question or sidesteps it altogether to discuss a tangential issue. When a man asks Mooney why black people walk the way they do, Mooney, justifiably annoyed by the question, launches into his bit about African Americans being the most imitated people in the world and ends with the previously cited maxim, "Everybody wants to be a nigger, but nobody wants to be a nigger." After the sketch closes, Chappelle appears laughing before the camera, seemingly surprised and amused by Mooney's comments. He then provides a brief imitation of Mooney, repeating in a mock stern voice the "everybody wants to be a nigger" line before laughing some more. Chappelle's introduction and response to the sketch highlights the differences between himself and Mooney. Chappelle appears to be relaxed and fun while Mooney comes across as angry and unyielding. Throughout the series, Mooney's segments are handled in a similar way, and significantly, Mooney and Chappelle never appear in any sketches together. This method of framing Mooney's segments suggests that while *Chappelle's Show* provides a space for Mooney's brand of aggressive "just us" humor, the show itself is ultimately more fluid.

In fact, *Chappelle's Show* offers some ethnic sketches that eschew the black/white binary all together in favor of a more complex multiethnic humor. For example, in the fifth episode of season 1, a very brief sketch appears in between a commercial break and the official resumption of the show. The segment takes place on an airplane, and the camera slowly moves up the aisles, showing the different people in each row. In the first row, we see two Arabs wearing traditional cloaks and headdresses and speaking to each other in Arabic; their clothes and language suggest that they are Arab, not Arab American. However, the subtitles tell us that they are arguing about the results of *American Idol.* In the next row are two African Americans looking uneasily at the Arabs in front of them. In a voice-over, we hear that one of the men is thinking of the Arabs as "terrorist sons of bitches." Behind them, is a middle-aged white man with his daughter; the man wonders, "What are those negroes doing in first class?" He then grasps his daughter's hand protectively and thinks, "I had better keep my eye on Sarah." The next row seats two Native Americans wearing ponchos and feather headdresses and looking like extras in a John Ford movie. One of them thinks, "Me better not go to bathroom. White man will steal my seat and call it manifest destiny." Behind them, outrageously, we find two buffalo who think, via subtitles, "At least you Indians got casinos. You corn-eating bastards." And finally, at the very back of the plane, we find Chappelle, asleep with a newspaper—*The Daily Truth*—laid across his chest. The headline reads "America United."

The humor of this sketch is based on a series of ethnic stereotypes, but Chappelle uses these stereotypes in a versatile and disorienting manner. The image of traditionally dressed Arabs on an airplane is politically charged in and of itself, especially when the episode originally aired in February 2003. The fact that they are discussing *American Idol* subverts audience expectations and speaks more directly to the far-reaching influence of American popular culture than it does to the "War on Terror." On the other hand, the white man fearing for his daughter's well-being in the presence of two African American men is an easily recognizable stereotype that appears frequently in both white and African American cultural productions. That the same short sketch seems at times to undermine stereotypes and at other times to reinforce them contributes to the overall effect of disorienting the audience. By the time we see the buffalo, however, it becomes clear that the sketch is driven by an absurd logic that cannot be easily applied to a real-world corollary.

The most striking component of this sketch is the way that it constructs ethnicity not through the binary lens of oppressed/oppressor but in a manner closer to what Susan Stanford Friedman has called "relational positionality," which views "identity as situationally constructed and defined and at the crossroads of different systems of alterity and stratification."[36] The seating placement on an airplane serves as a useful metaphor for an exploration into ethnic attitudes that are "situationally constructed." We see a traditional victim/victimizer model in the white man's reaction to the African Americans and in the Natives reaction to the white man, but the African American who both stereotypes and fears the two Arabs complicates matters. While both groups can be viewed as minorities in the American ethnic landscape, the sketch also suggests that they are equally subject to the problematic values of the dominant cultural framework. The bigoted African American, while still an "other" in the eyes of the white man behind him, has clearly been influenced by negative rhetoric about Arabs and is as equally capable of participating in prejudiced thought. And the Arabs themselves, immersed in an impassioned debate about *American Idol,* demonstrate that they are not immune either to the spectacle of American culture.

It is interesting that Chappelle does not play the African American man sitting behind the two Arabs. If we read, as I think we are invited to, each passenger as a representative member of his or her respective racial or ethnic category, then Chappelle, in this sketch at least, deliberately places himself *outside* of the African American position. In fact, Chappelle's placement at the back of the plane (in conjunction with the ironic "America United" headline) suggests that he is either above all of the ethnic strife (and buffalo) around him, or that he is oblivious to it. The fact that he is sleeping seems to suggest the latter. But while Chappelle's laid-back persona may be able to sleep through this racial tension, viewers understand that Chappelle and the other *Chappelle's Show* writers created this segment. In this light, the sketch is telling about the program's general attitude toward American ethnic politics. It suggests that *Chappelle's Show,* in contrast to the mainstream media as represented in *The Daily Truth,* is well aware of the complexity of American racism and is thus taking upon itself the task of representing and commenting on it in its myriad forms.

A longer sketch that takes up this mantle of commenting on big-picture American race relations is "Racial Draft," from the first episode of season 2. In his introduction, Chappelle begins by celebrating American diversity, saying, "You know what's cool about being an American? We all mixed up . . . genetically. We all got a little something else." Chappelle goes on to explain, though, that this sort of racial mixing can get confusing or cause arguments and that he and his Asian American wife, for example, often disagree about which part of mixed-race golfer Tiger Woods plays golf so well. Chappelle then segues into a prerecorded sketch that sets out to settle racial confusion once and for all. The skit imagines a "racial draft," in which delegates from all of the major American ethnic groups choose ethnically indeterminate celebrities to become permanent members of one specific ethnicity. The sketch mocks, in Katrina Bell-Jordan's words, "our overt concern with the racial and ethnic categories that are thought to define us."[37] It also suggests, through humorous exaggeration, American culture's often extreme discomfort with ethnic ambiguity.

As the sketch moves forward, it becomes an extended exploration of the various ways in which ethnicity can be formed and goes well beyond Werner Sollors's "consent/descent" model of ethnic identification. The first two celebrities drafted—Tiger Woods by the African American delegation and Lenny Kravitz by the Jewish delegation—are simple enough (although the Jewish choice of half-black/half-Jewish musician Lenny Kravitz demonstrates Chappelle's awareness of the Jewish American tendency to identify with aspects of African American culture, discussed in more detail in the next chapter). Both choices deal with mixed-race celebrities and satirize the culture's tendency to view ethnicity in the simplest manner possible, but these draft picks also accept the premise that ethnic identification is formed, at least in part, by genetics or descent. Things get more complicated, however, when the Latinos choose Elian Gonzalez, explaining that "we wanted to do this before the white people try to adopt him as one of their own, again." The choice is an odd one, considering that in terms of ethnicity, all of the relatives who made a claim on Elian Gonzalez in the 2000 Cuban/American diplomacy affair were, strictly speaking, Latino. The Latino delegate's claim that white people tried to adopt him, then, speaks most likely to the media coverage of the Gonzalez affair, in which the young boy became the center, for a few weeks, of the national—read white—imagination. The choice also brings into question the relationship between national citizenship and ethnic identification. For if Gonzalez were to become "American," the sketch suggests, then "whiteness" may not be far behind.

White people's ability to simply take or "adopt" ethnic minorities whom they like is suggested again in the next pick when the white delegate drafts Colin Powell.[38] Since Powell is, in the words of the announcer, "not even an eighth white," the choice is subject to approval by the African American delegation, who eventually agrees, on the condition that the whites also accept Condoleezza Rice. The screen then shows a picture of Rice with the caption "given away by blacks" beneath it. Then, in a last-minute move, the black delegation makes a failed attempt to claim white rapper Eminem as part of the bargain. This turn of events, as Haggins points out, "raises questions about race by affiliation rather than lineage," for Powell and Rice are ultimately deemed "white" because of both their conservative politics and the fact that they have each achieved popularity with whites.[39] Eminem, on the other hand, is an obvious candidate for blackness because of his success in hip-hop and the respect he has earned from African American music moguls like Dr. Dre. The concept of ethnicity by affiliation is taken to humorous extremes when the Asian delegation chooses the entire Eastern-influenced hip-hop group the Wu-Tang Clan. For years, scholars in the humanities and the social sciences have been pointing out that race and ethnicity are actually social constructs rather than biological categories, but rarely do we see this sort of thinking manifested in popular culture. This sketch, however, playfully literalizes the concept.

In its undermining of inflexible ethnic classifications, "Racial Draft" also problematizes the strict "just us" worldview of most African American humor. African American ethnicity certainly plays a large part in this sketch, as it is connected in some manner to every draft pick except for the Latinos' choice of Elian Gonzales. "Racial Draft" constructs blackness, however, not as an essential category but as a concept that, like all of the other ethnicities considered, is fluid and debatable. Even more important is the manner in which this sketch positions blackness in relation to the larger American culture. The "racial draft" itself is actually a cynical vision of American ethnic relations cast as competition. This competition, however, is not over votes, resources, or funding but is rather about cultural capital, hence the ethnic delegates' preoccupation with high-profile celebrities. In this quest for cultural capital, the sketch makes clear that the products of black culture are highly prized by nearly every group. It recalls Mooney's statement that "Everybody wants to be a nigger," but it represents the idea in a more complex manner by placing blackness in relation to other ethnic positions. This sketch represents blackness not as closed off or fixed but as endlessly negotiable and situated at the nexus of America's multiethnic society.

Blackness is treated in a similar manner in the sketch "I Know Black People," from season 2, episode 8. Chappelle sets up the segment with an anecdote about a white man telling him recently that his show was offensive to black people. Chappelle says that he was initially puzzled by the comment, but that he had to concede that "some people just know black people." This comment is then used to transition into a game show parody that attempts to determine who really knows the most about black people. Chappelle assures the audience that the competition is unstaged. The contestants include a white male professor of African American studies, a white female New York city police officer, a white female social worker, a Korean male grocery store worker, a white male television writer who has worked on both *The Chris Rock Show* and *Chappelle's Show*, a black male

Brooklyn barber, a white male high school student who embraces black culture (i.e., a "wigger"), and a light-skinned yet racially indeterminate male DJ who claims to have many black friends.[40]

This list of participants forms a series of ethnic jokes on its own, for the chosen contestants point to a variety of stereotypes about African Americans, but they also suggest some genuine truths about both systemic inequality and the cooptation of black culture. The notion that a white police officer or social worker, for example, might have expertise on black people draws on the stereotype of the African American as being either lazy or criminal, but it also harks back to the original context of Pryor's "just us" joke about the disproportionate number of black people being pushed through the American justice system. The African American studies professor and the "wigger" high school student, on the other hand, point to the power that black cultural productions hold in the white imagination and the co-optation of black culture by a mainstream white majority. The white television writer, however, questions what we even mean when we say things like "black culture," for his presence suggests that while African American artists like Rock and Chappelle are in the spotlight, that behind the scenes there are whites who are also contributing to the cultural production of so-called blackness. The Brooklyn barber, though, points to the long tradition of black communal spaces and suggests that, unlike the co-opted black culture found in popular music and television venues, there is a more authentic version of blackness that remains inaccessible to those outside of the black community. But then again, owing to mainstream films like *Barbershop*, the black barber has also become a stereotype in its own right. The contestants thus point to multiple, competing versions of blackness, and—like the racial draft sketch—position black culture in relation to multiple interested parties.

As the sketch moves forward, Chappelle plays the game show host, and the questions that he puts to the competitors similarly suggest a multiplicity of ways that blackness can be defined. There are questions, for example, about well-known staples of black pop culture, many of which deal with the Norman Lear sitcom *Good Times* (1974–1979). There are also a series of questions asking for definitions of terms from African American street vernacular, such as "badonkadonk," "loosey," and "chickenhead."[41] The sketch, however, also takes time to illustrate black disillusionment with mainstream American culture. For example, one question asks, "Why did black people distrust Ronald Reagan?" The correct answers include "because he was white," "because he was a Republican," and "because he took all [their] money." Along similar lines, the final question of the competition asks, "How can black people rise up and overcome?" Correct answers here range from "Can they?" to "reparations" to "stop cuttin' each other's throat." The only answer submitted to this question deemed incorrect is "Get out and vote." In light of this last question, it is perhaps relevant to point out that this sketch aired four years prior to President

Barack Obama's campaign, which brought out record numbers of African American voters. Nevertheless, while "Racial Draft" and "I Know Black People" situate blackness at the center of American popular culture, the latter sketch also makes a point of suggesting that black culture is still at the margins of mainstream American politics.

Given the conflicting versions of blackness that "I Know Black People" constructs, it is probably irrelevant who actually wins the competition. The Korean grocer, unsurprisingly, answers very few questions correctly, suggesting that a place of business in a low-income black neighborhood is an insufficient gateway into black culture. Similarly, the police officer and the social worker only do slightly better. The black Brooklyn barber and the white television writer, however, both demonstrate a far-reaching knowledge of African American slang and pop culture. The winner, though, is DJ Rob, who is light-skinned enough to be considered white but appears to be of possibly Asian and perhaps African descent as well. It is apt that an ethnically ambiguous man is the ultimate winner of the show, for his prominence helps to place "I Know Black People" in conversation with the anxiety over ethnic ambiguity represented in "Racial Draft," and it also drives home the sketch's suggestion that blackness is an unfixed yet inextricable part of a much larger multiethnic web.

Perhaps Chappelle's most famous multiethnic sketch is "White People Dancing," from the third episode of season 2. Blackness here plays an integral role, but the segment is really more of an extended exploration into white culture, albeit a more complex one than those found in "the litany of 'white people be like'" jokes articulated by many African American humorists.[42] In his introduction to the sketch, Chappelle explores the role of ethnic humor more directly than usual, asserting that "when you do stereotypical kinds of jokes, there's no room for subtlety. People always say things, for instance, white people can't dance. . . . Let's explore this." The sketch that follows is set up as a sort of ethnographic experiment in which Chappelle puts to the test his hypothesis that "it's not that white people can't dance, it's just that they like certain instruments." Accompanied by white musician John Mayer, Chappelle then visits a variety of "white" venues, such as a corporate office and a fancy restaurant. In each setting, John Mayer plays the electric guitar, which is, Chappelle guesses, white people's instrument of choice. The white people respond in a categorically uniform manner: in the corporate office, they dance in a slow trance as Mayer plays a "smooth jazz" guitar solo. In the restaurant, Mayer plays a loud heavy metal riff, and the white people, all very well dressed and sober before the music begins, form an impromptu mosh pit and begin tearing the restaurant apart. These Pavlovian responses to the electric guitar comically invert Chappelle's earlier assertion that he would explore white ethnicity with more subtlety, for whiteness thus far is presented as an homogenous entity. The sketch draws no distinction between white corporate executives and the white waiters and waitresses who serve them. Of course, this is all presented with such comic exaggeration that it is impossible to take seriously.

Chappelle then applies the same test to other ethnicities. He goes to a barbershop in Harlem where there are only blacks and Latinos present. First, John Mayer plays the electric guitar and is met with hostility by both blacks and Latinos. Chappelle then brings out a drummer; when the drums start, the African Americans (including Chappelle) begin dancing, but the Latinos only nod their heads. Chappelle produces an electric piano player to play along with the drummer, and the Latinos immediately begin salsa dancing in the middle of the barbershop. Chappelle adds to the ethnic stereotype by screaming what he calls "Spanish gibberish" through a bull horn. At first glance, this routine in the barbershop simply restates the same joke that Chappelle had made earlier in the sketch about whites, only with different music. However, it is important to note the ways that this sketch places blacks and Latinos in relation to whites and to each other. The barbershop, as we have seen, is a well-known symbol of a black communal space, and the word "Harlem" still reads as exclusively black in the minds of many Americans. That Chappelle places both African Americans and Latinos in the same barbershop together suggests that they form a community of their own, separate from white culture. This is driven home when both groups share equal disdain for "white" music in the form of electric guitar. To a certain extent, then, the sketch reinforces a white/other dichotomy in which so-called persons of color (or at least blacks and Latinos) form their own group. At the same time, though, the sketch complicates this white/other binary by insisting on differences (albeit stereotypical ones) within the category of "other." The sketch is also significant in that it evinces no anxiety or hostility between blacks and Latinos. In its reliance on humorous cultural comparisons, the sketch could be seen to adhere to a "just us" comic vision, but at the same time, it both broadens and complicates the traditionally rigid definition of "us."

In the final moments of "White People Dancing," Chappelle provides one last joke that further complicates the sketch's construction of ethnic stereotypes. Chappelle and Mayer are approached by two male police officers, one black and one white, who tell them that they need a permit to film on the street. Chappelle tells Mayer to "do something quick," and Mayer begins playing guitar and singing the band Poison's heavy metal ballad "Every Rose Has Its Thorn." Both the white and the black police officers begin to dance and sing along. Chappelle asks the black officer how he knows the song, and the man replies, "I'm from the suburbs. I can't help it." Novotny Lawrence asserts that this last joke "deconstructs the entire sketch . . . because it highlights the importance of individual experience. Hence, the sketch demonstrates that ethnic groups are not monolithic and, therefore, should not be characterized by narrow stereotypes."[43] I agree with regard to ethnic stereotypes, but it is also important to note that the joke is humorous because it supplants an ethnic stereotype with a regional/economic one. Suggesting that everyone who grows up in the suburbs likes the band Poison is just as ridiculous as suggesting that all white people must dance to the electric guitar. The important point, though, is that by placing these two types of stereotypes in conversation with each other, Chappelle challenges his audience to view ethnic/cultural identification as part of a matrix of overlapping factors.

The *Chappelle's Show* segments discussed above constitute the series's most explicit multiethnic strain; there are many other skits that rely on a more a traditional black/white binary, just as there are a number of sketches that are not overtly about race at all. Once Chappelle's commitment to complicating inflexible representations of blackness has been established, though, it is easier to see it working in other parts of the series that seem to be purely about black/white relations. For example, the most discussed *Chappelle's Show* segment, "Blind Supremacy," from the first episode of season 1, makes a point of acknowledging a more complex ethnic landscape than the black versus white construction typically allows. "Blind Supremacy" posits Clayton Bigsby, a blind, black, white supremacist, who is unaware of his actual race. The diversity of American ethnicity is established early on in the sketch when Bigsby, played by Chappelle, explains his philosophy: "Niggers, Jews, homosexuals, Mexicans, Arabs, and all different kinds of chinks stink, and I hate 'em!" While this list is couched in the language of stereotypical southern bigotry, its inclusivity acknowledges Chappelle's awareness that African Americans are not the sole target of prejudiced thought. The inclusion of homosexuals acknowledges oppression that goes beyond mere ethnicity, and the label "all different kinds of chinks" forces viewers to look past the all-encompassing label of "Asian American," even as Bigsby himself refuses to do so.

Despite this list, the segment still relies on a primarily black/white dichotomy, but its humor is not driven by the sort of cultural comparisons found in most African American comedy. Rather than relying on essentialist stereotypes for what is "black" and "white" culture, the sketch reveals each category to be situationally constructed. Like the black police officer in the last scene of "White People Dancing," Bigsby acts in ways that are coded white because he was raised white. Whiteness thus emerges as an ideology rather than a biological fact. The sketch treats blackness in a similarly complex manner when Bigsby's car pulls up next to two white teenagers listening to hip-hop music. Upon hearing the music, Bigsby assumes that the two teenagers are black and yells, "Why don't you jungle bunnies turn that music down? You niggers make me sick." After Bigsby's car drives away, the two white teenagers congratulate each other on being called "nigger" by a black man. As in "I Know Black People," the moment acknowledges that blackness is a commodity as much as it is a set of cultural practices or values.

CHAPPELLE'S EXODUS AND THE UNCERTAIN FUTURE OF BLACK MULTIETHNIC HUMOR

Even though *Chappelle's Show* demonstrates a commitment to challenging the received logic of American race relations, questions still arise about whether or not the series perpetuates racist thought, and Chappelle himself clearly takes such questions very seriously. It is impossible to analyze the comedy of Chappelle at length without also discussing the abrupt manner in which he walked away from both his show and a fifty-million-dollar contract. As Chappelle later explained in a series of interviews, while filming a sketch for season 3 about "Racial Pixies," Chappelle, dressed in blackface, felt uncomfortable with the laughter of a white crew member, and he started to suspect that his humor was reinforcing negative black images rather than collapsing them.[44] While most fans were understandably disappointed with Chappelle's departure from the show, scholars largely applaud the decision. Lawrence, who chastises Chappelle for homophobia, misogyny, and use of the word "nigger," asserts that Chappelle's reasoning for leaving the show exhibited "the kind of recognition that leads to true change," and Kimberly Yates argues that "his walking away demonstrated his commitment to authenticity and black standards."[45] I have no desire to refute these assertions or to challenge Chappelle's reasoning. I find it unfortunate, however, that the image of a white man laughing at a blackfaced Chappelle became the centerpiece of discussions about his leaving, for this has caused many viewers to see *Chappelle's Show* retroactively through a lens of inflexible black versus white racial politics. As I hope to have demonstrated, his humor is much more multifaceted and his representations of blackness are much more fluid than black/white narratives typically allow.

Even the sketch that caused all of the controversy to begin with demonstrates Chappelle's commitment to looking past the black/white divide and at the larger multiethnic spectrum. The sketch, which aired in the second of three "Lost Episodes," features a series of characters who are taunted by tiny, stereotypical ethnic pixies (all played by Chappelle), who attempt to coerce the characters into acting in a stereotypical manner. For example, in the infamous blackface scene, Chappelle plays a man on an airplane who orders fish against the wishes of a tiny blackfaced minstrel who urges the man to order fried chicken. In a similar manner, a Latino pixie urges a Mexican American to buy leopard car seat covers and a plastic Jesus for his dashboard. A white pixie is overcome with outrage and anxiety when a white man dances with a black woman to a hip-hop song, and an Asian pixie attempts to convince an Asian American man to pronounce L-sounds as R-sounds. The sketch suggests that while ethnic stereotypes may be largely false, that the stereotypes themselves still hold power for the individuals who have internalized them. In each instance, however, the ethnic character resists the urging of his respective pixie and acts in a nonstereotypical manner. As Brian Gogan points out, this rejection "reveals the relationship between people, practices, and race to be conditional."[46] The most important aspect of this sketch, however, is the way in which Chappelle treats each ethnic group in the same manner, thus displacing whiteness as an unmarked given and dislodging blackness as the primary marker of "otherness."

While this sketch, along with general disillusionment about the Hollywood industry, propelled Chappelle away from his show and his lucrative contract, it is important to remember that Chappelle has *not* stopped being a comedian. As of this writing, he still performs regularly for live audiences throughout the country and internationally. Short clips of these performances frequently make their way on to YouTube and other online video sites. I want to briefly consider one bit from a show Chappelle performed at a small club in London in order to demonstrate that, even out of the pop-cultural limelight, Chappelle is still using his humor to interrogate multiethnic issues.[47] Throughout the performance, Chappelle talks with the audience, creating a cozy and intimate atmosphere. At one point, he asks individual audience members where they are from, and one replies initially that he is "mixed up" and then reluctantly reveals that he is Pakistani and Scottish. Chappelle says, "Hey man, my mother is half white, what do you think of that? I'm what they call the new Americans because my dad is all black, and my mom is half white, which makes me a 75 percenter. . . . My wife is Filipino, so my kids are Puerto Rican somehow. . . . That's how it's going to be in a little while. We're all just gonna be beige. Take a look at these black folks; we might be the last generation." Chappelle's joke about his kids being Puerto Rican recalls his "Racial Draft" sketch and mocks the need to categorize based on genealogy. His comments about Americans turning beige and about current blacks being the "last generation," however, may be his most explicit statement against a "just us" Afro-centric aesthetic. Rather than viewing African Americans as pure, authentic, and enclosed by unyielding boundaries, Chappelle constructs a blackness that is unfixed and malleable. More important, he suggests that these changes are a positive force, adding that "it's all good. We'll be one world soon." The routine makes it clear that, with or without a television show, Chappelle uses his humor to undermine reductive racial constructions.

Despite the fact that Chappelle still performs in small venues, there is no doubt that the ending of *Chappelle's Show* has left a gap in mainstream African American comedy, for most contemporary black humorists still adhere to a rigid "just us" aesthetic, as can be seen in stand-up specials like *Russell Simmons Presents: Stand Up at the El Rey* (2010) and *Shaquille O'Neal Presents: All Star Comedy Jam* (2010), both of which follow the *Def Comedy Jam* formula. Despite their unabashed manner of establishing blackness as a commodity, these sorts of shows serve an important role by keeping black culture as a main component of

American humor and by providing uncensored venues for aspiring black comics (Chappelle himself began on *Def Comedy Jam*). As long as we have ethnic categories, we will have this sort of humor. But it is also necessary to have comedians, like Chappelle, who are able to complicate their culture's received notions of race and look more deeply into contemporary ethnic politics.

At this point, Chappelle's humor is the most explicit iteration of a multiethnic black humor. Chappelle, however, may have had an influence on the black humorists that followed him. In particular, Aaron McGruder's animated series *The Boondocks* (2005–2010) presents a more complex vision of blackness than does most African American humor. The show, based on McGruder's serialized comic strip of the same name, is about two brothers, Huey and Riley, who move from inner-city Chicago to a predominantly white suburb to live with their wealthy grandfather. While the series deals almost exclusively with African American issues, it avoids a "just us" aesthetic and creates what Avi Santo has called "a differentiated black cultural citizenship," in which blackness is not monolithic but is rather a signifier for multiple subject positions.[48] This can be seen in the variety of black characters depicted on the show. Huey, perhaps named after Black Panther leader Huey Newton, is a well-read Afrocentrist and conspiracy theorist, whereas his younger brother is a wannabe gangsta' rapper steeped in hip-hop culture. Their grandfather is a wealthy curmudgeon who has moved to an upper-class, predominantly white suburb in order to have peace and quiet. Other notable black characters include the well-educated attorney Tom DuBois and the self-loathing, white worshiping Uncle Ruckus, a sort of aggressive Uncle Tom. This multifaceted collection of black voices makes it impossible to get a single reading of blackness from the show.

Furthermore, *The Boondocks* is ultimately more critical of black popular culture than most African American humorists, including Chappelle. While much of the series derives humor at the expense of whiteness, its object of ridicule is more often sites of black culture, such as BET and the popularity of gangsta' rap. For example, two episodes chronicle the life of the fictional gangsta' rapper Gangstalicious and satirize the often violent and misogynistic tendencies of mainstream hip-hop culture. The season 1 episode "The Story of Gangstalicious" relates a rivalry between Gangstalicious and another rapper; in the end, though, we learn that not only is Gangstalicious not from "the street" but that he is also a homosexual. The news causes Riley, Gangstalicious's biggest fan, to faint. The story is picked up again in the season 2 episode "The Story of Gangstalicious Part 2." Here, the theme of homosexuality is put in the forefront, as Gangstalicious sings homoerotic songs such as "Homies over Hoes" and promotes his own fashion label, which features decidedly feminized clothing. Both episodes openly mock the hypermasculinity of mainstream black culture and suggest that a fundamental insecurity lies behind much of the violent posturing. The series's most controversial episode, "The Return of the King" from season 1, critiques popular black culture even more scathingly. Here, Dr. Martin Luther King awakens from a coma into present-day America. In a moment that recalls Chris Rock's "Black People versus Niggas" bit, King chastises many contemporary blacks for being "ignorant niggas." While the series is certainly rooted in the tradition of African American humor, moments like this work against the rhetoric of shows like *Def Comedy Jam*, which primarily celebrate black culture.

In addition to its critique of popular representations of blackness, *The Boondocks* also follows in the footsteps of Chappelle and places blackness in conversation with other cultural groups. McGruder demonstrates an acute awareness of ethnicity beyond the simplistic black/white dichotomy. For example, the season 1 episode "The Itis" shows Granddad open his own "Soul Food" restaurant, which features menu items such as a bacon-cheeseburger with Krispy Kreme donuts as buns. The food is so unhealthy and addictive that the neighborhood around the restaurant turns into a slum. The episode critiques the stereotypically unhealthy black diet, but, interestingly, McGruder relates the most important point of the episode through the voice of a Mexican American cook who works at the restaurant. The cook explains that the history of African American cuisine is tied to the history of African American oppression because slave owners would give blacks only the cheapest and worst types of food. When the black characters look at the Latino man skeptically, he shrugs and says that he "took an African American studies class." The moment, in a manner similar to Chappelle sketches like "Racial Draft" and "I Know Black People," places blackness in a larger multiethnic context by asking to whom black culture really belongs.

These multiethnic concerns are apparent as much in the show's style and structure as it is in its content. The animation style draws heavily from Japanese anime, and the characters often erupt into extended martial arts battles. This Eastern influence further extends into other aspects of the series, for Huey is well-versed in Eastern philosophy, and his voice-overs often reflect this. Since Huey is otherwise seen as the show's staunchest proponent of Afrocentrism, this Eastern influence plays an important role in complicating its depiction of African American culture. McGruder, like Dave Chappelle, refuses to see view blackness in a vacuum; rather, he is well aware that African American culture exists at the crossroads of numerous other cultural positions. McGruder's humor is not as consistently multiethnic as Chappelle's, but *The Boondocks* is ultimately *not* a black communal space. Instead of using his humor to construct boundaries around an abstract and mythical blackness, McGruder interrogates the traditional boundaries of African American culture—the most famous of which is the color line between black and white—and encourages his viewers to understand blackness from multiple perspectives.

2 • THE NEW JEWISH BLACKFACE

Ethnic Anxiety in Contemporary Jewish Humor

IN LATE AUGUST 2005, as fans of *Chappelle's Show* were still scratching their heads over Chappelle's puzzling departure from his lucrative series, Sarah Silverman starred in a sketch on *Jimmy Kimmel Live!* titled "*Chappelle's Show:* Starring Sarah Silverman." The skit begins with an announcer proclaiming that "*Chappelle's Show* is back, and funnier than ever, with new host Sarah Silverman." Then we see a brief series of clips showing Silverman, a Jewish white female, performing a collection of Chappelle's most popular recurring characters, including Rick James, rapper Lil John, and the inner-city crack addict Tyrone Biggums. The humor here is driven by the unexpected discrepancy of seeing a recognizably white female perform characters who are black and male. Silverman reinforces this awkward juxtaposition, for even though she dresses in each character's costume, her skin remains white, and her voice is clearly female. The sketch also suggests that Silverman—who was, at the time, already well-known for her irreverent stand-up—might be able to assume Chappelle's position as the primary creator of hip, ironic, and controversial humor. In this sense, the sketch anticipated Silverman's own show, *The Sarah Silverman Program* (2007–2010), which also aired on Comedy Central. While it did not achieve the success of *Chappelle's Show, The Sarah Silverman Program* was a modest hit and ran for a full three seasons. In the larger context of contemporary ethnic humor, however, Silverman's *Chappelle's Show* sketch is indicative of a tendency among many Jewish humorists of turning toward blackness and other forms of alterity as a means of suggesting their own countercultural status and of asserting Jewishness as an ethnic category distinct from whiteness.

Jewish performers turning toward black culture is hardly a new phenomenon, nor are discussions of the relationship between Jewish and African Americans.[1] As Vincent Brook explains, "Jews' appropriation of blackness to mark yet disguise their own position as outsiders has a long history in American culture, from Al Jolson's blackface and Sophie Tucker's 'red hot mama' to George Gershwin's *Porgy and Bess* and Norman Mailer's 'White Negro.'"[2] This Jewish identification with blackness is also visible in the work of many canonical Jewish American humorists. The style of Lenny Bruce, for example, was inflected by the rhythms and structure of jazz, and his language was often infused with an African American vernacular; as Mel Watkins notes, Bruce "conveyed a comic *attitude* reflecting prominent aspects of genuine black American humor."[3] Additionally, Mel Brooks's comic western *Blazing Saddles* (1974)—for which Richard Pryor was a cowriter—suggests a Jewish and African American alliance and anticipates the series of black/Jewish buddy movies starring Pryor and Gene Wilder. While connections between Jewish and African Americans have been prominent throughout much of the twentieth century, the number of twenty-first-century works that rely on African American tropes in order to articulate Jewishness is startling. As historian Eric Goldstein asserts, many contemporary Jews "have turned to the African American community in unprecedented ways in order to validate their own minority consciousness."[4] We can find examples in the Hasidic reggae singer Matisyahu or in the popularity of the "Jewfro" hairstyle. Current Jewish humor, however, provides the most prominent manifestation of this move. Jewish American comic David Cross, for instance, named his most recent stand-up album *Bigger and Blackerer* (2010), ironically alluding to the famous Chris Rock special.

Another instance of the black/Jewish connection occurs in the film *The Hebrew Hammer* (2003), which is a Jewish rewriting of the 1970s blaxploitation genre; many of its scenes and the title song are based directly on the blaxploitation classic *Shaft* (1971). The film tells the story of a Jewish detective who seeks to save Chanukah from Santa Claus's evil son. It is basically a one-joke film that derives its humor from the awkward juxtaposition of Jewish and African American stereotypes. The jokes are often amusing, but the film remains superficial and relies on tired Jewish stereotypes, such as the overbearing Jewish mother and the Jewish desire to pursue a career in medicine. The premise of *The Hebrew Hammer*, then, is based not on any real identification between black and Jewish cultures but rather on their perceived incompatibility. Jews, the film tells us again and again, are weak and neurotic, whereas African Americans are cool and stylish. In reality, the film suggests, there is no connection between blacks and Jews. In contrast, the comedians discussed at length in this chapter—Sarah Silverman, Larry David, and the British comedian Sacha Baron Cohen—see blackness as an avenue through which to better understand

and articulate Jewish identity.[5] Rather than rely on surface-level comparisons of black and Jewish stereotypes, these humorists suggest real ties with blackness, even as they assert their own Jewishness.

In this sense, the comedians under discussion exemplify Brook's conception of a "post-Jewish" identity that became prominent in the American situation comedy in the late 1990s and early 2000s. Borrowing from David Hollinger's notion of "postethnicity," discussed briefly in the introduction to this book, Brook argues that in shows such as *Dharma and Greg* (1997–2002) and *Will and Grace* (1998–2006), the Jewish characters claim alterity through association with various marginalized individuals, including African Americans and homosexuals.[6] This claiming of alterity is a result, in part, of contemporary Jews' uneasy relationship to multiculturalism, in which Jews occupy a sort of middle-space between white and other (although they are closer to the white end of this spectrum). In particular, Silverman, David, and Baron Cohen adhere to what Brook describes as a *receptive* Jewish multiculturalism, in which Jews "engage multiculturalism mainly as a way to 'open up,' redirect, or reclaim Jewishness."[7] The primary difference between the humorists under discussion here and the sitcoms discussed by Brook is one of degree. The Jewish presence in the work of Silverman, David, and Baron Cohen is much more overt than in the late 1990s/early 2000s sitcoms, in which Jewishness is more often treated in passing or signified by a character's last name or parents. Furthermore, the claiming of blackness and/or alterity in general is also much more pronounced in the works under discussion here: Silverman and Baron Cohen literally dress up as black people, and David becomes an honorary member of an African American family named the Blacks. As opposed to the more subtle representations of black/Jewish alliances in most sitcoms, Silverman, David, and Baron Cohen opt for an "in-your-face" comic aesthetic.

It is important to note that, despite the suggested affinity with black culture, these Jewish humorists, unlike many other ethnic humorists, are not overtly influenced by the conventions of African American humor discussed in the previous chapter. While one will occasionally find Jewish comics—such as Lenny Bruce in the routine that opened this book—who base their humor on comparisons between WASP and Jewish culture, contemporary Jewish humor is not generally driven by a *double-consciousness* mode of thought, nor is it as concerned with the rigid boundary construction that typifies most "just us" ethnic humor. Unlike black, Latino, Asian American, or Arab American humorists, Jewish comics (despite, or perhaps because of, their overwhelming prominence in the comedy industry) have never had their own *Original Kings*–style special featuring all Jewish performers and intended for a primarily Jewish audience. Rather, even as they rhetorically align themselves with African Americans or other marginalized groups, contemporary Jewish comics continue to draw from the conventions of traditional Jewish humor that can be traced back, at least, to the nineteenth century shtetl (small village) humor of eastern European Jewry. These conventions include irony, self-deprecation, and a notorious sense of comic pessimism—in Sarah Blacher Cohen's words, the mingling of "laughter and trembling."[8] We can add to these a series of stock characters like the *schlemiel* and the *schlimazel* and a collection of stereotypical, American-made Jewish characters, like the overbearing Jewish mother or the spoiled JAP (Jewish American Princess). In addition to this rich heritage of Jewish wit, another key reason for the difference between Jewish American humor and other American ethnic humors is that Jews today, as suggested above, are largely considered white. They therefore have the privilege of being ethnically distinct (Jewish) or ethnically generic (white) at will. Some Jewish comics present themselves as primarily white and only use their Jewish backgrounds to add a sort of ethnic texture to their humor. *The Daily Show* host, Jon Stewart (originally Leibowitz), for example, often refers to his Jewishness in passing, but his persona ultimately reinforces his position as the champion of youthful white liberalism. In contrast, other humorists like Jackie Mason, Mel Brooks, and Woody Allen make Jewishness central to their comedy and inextricable from their personas.

An analysis of contemporary Jewish humor can therefore complicate the ways in which ethnic humor works as "a form of boundary construction." When Jewish humorists construct a Jewish identity, there is always a question over whether this identity will be subsumed by whiteness or will remain its own distinct ethnic category. The three humorists discussed in this chapter are well aware of this dilemma, and they use their humor to explore the tenuous ethnic position of modern American Jews. By embracing black culture, Silverman, David, and Baron Cohen thus construct Jewishness as an ethnic particularity. This is not done, however, in an obvious or straightforward manner. All three humorists approach blackness through a series of fictional personas. While the comedians themselves are well aware of the complex racial issues that their humor raises, their personas—which often share similarities with the artists themselves—are ignorant and insensitive to the nuances of racial and ethnic identity. Their humor, then, often comes across as shocking and politically incorrect, and locating stable or consistent racial commentary amid this humor proves problematic. Furthermore, even while these humorists assert Jewishness as an ethnic particularity, they also mock the desire of many American Jews to maintain their privileged position in American culture even as they claim ethnic difference from that culture. Contemporary Jewish humor projects and critiques a Jewish population that wishes to maintain the privileges of a white majority and the self-identification of a victimized minority.

BLACKFACE AND JEWISH AMERICAN IDENTITY

In order to understand the full cultural implications of contemporary Jewish humorists' overt return to blackness, it is necessary to consider the complex relationships that Jews—and particularly Jewish entertainers—have historically had with both African American culture and with the white, Christian majority. Most American Jews are descendants of eastern European immigrants who came to the United States to escape persecution between 1880 and 1910. In most eastern European countries, Jews were seen as the primary cultural other on which the Christian majority projected its fears and often inflicted violence. Therefore, in Goldstein's words, eastern European, or Ashkenazi, Jews "had come to see 'apartness' as one of the most salient aspects of Jewish identity."[9] It is only natural then that in America many Jews would come to identify with African Americans, who, especially in the late nineteenth and early twentieth centuries, were America's primary other. This identification between blacks and Jews occasionally resulted in cooperation between African American and Jewish activist groups and has caused, as Cheryl Lynn Greenberg notes, blacks and Jews to be "linked in the minds of bigots, mid-century progressives, and each other."[10]

Running alongside this story of Jewish and African American identification and cooperation, however, there is another narrative in which many American Jews recognized that America offered unique opportunities for Jewish assimilation and upward advancement. Two of the main reasons for these opportunities were the Jews' light skin and the presence of dark-skinned African Americans who already held the lowest position in the American racial hierarchy. Many American Jews therefore found it beneficial to distance themselves from African Americans in order to achieve an elevated social position within white America. One of the most fascinating and symbolically useful manifestations of Jews' simultaneous identification with and distancing from African Americans was the Jewish donning of blackface makeup. In the nineteenth century, blackface minstrelsy was among the most popular cultural expressions in the country, but at that time, most blackface performers were working-class Irish Americans.[11] In the twentieth century, however, blackface moved from concert halls and minstrel performances to vaudeville and motion pictures, where most of the entertainers to wear blackface were Jewish. The most famous Jew to black up was undoubtedly Al Jolson in the 1927 film *The Jazz Singer*, but George Burns, Sophie Tucker, Fanny Brice, Eddie Cantor, and the Marx Brothers all donned blackface as well. Michael Rogin argues that Jewish blackface in the first half of the twentieth century served as a cultural "rite of passage," transforming the immigrant Jew into an American.[12] By participating in the exclusion and stereotyping of blacks, American Jews made themselves white. Rogin asserts that for American Jewish entertainers, "[f]ocusing attention on blackness protects [their own] whiteness as the unexamined given."[13]

After World War II, there was no longer any symbolic need for Jews to don blackface: assimilation had been, for the most part, achieved, and American Jews were largely subsumed by the American middle class. While this entailed greater material success, it also destabilized "Jewishness" as a distinct ethnic position. Brook explains that "in the post–World War II era, the [blackface] mask began to wear thin. Less and less an aggrieved minority, more and more at one with the mainstream, Jews found their identification with blackness attacked as anachronistic at best, self-serving at worst."[14] In addition to criticisms from outside of the Jewish community, most significantly from African Americans, many Jews themselves began to feel uncomfortable with the fruits of assimilation. As Goldstein notes, many contemporary American Jews "seem particularly conscious of the way that being seen as white delegitimizes their claim to difference as Jews."[15] In light of this consciousness, many Jews today are attempting to reassert their ties to blackness. This return to blackness, I argue, represents a new brand of Jewish blackface, which suggests a backlash against the assimilationist motives of early Jewish entertainers. While Rogin argues that early Jewish entertainers donned blackface as a means to claim white identity, today Jews claim blackness in order to distance themselves from whiteness.

Some critics have noticed that recent Jewish humor suggests a reaction against the assimilation of Jewish entertainers of the past, but they generally tend to read this backlash as representative of a new sort of Jewish freedom or as indicative of a sense of Jewish pride and fearlessness. Simcha Weinstein, for example, argues that twenty-first-century "Jewish comics aren't afraid of proclaiming their ethnicity. Nor are they desperate to apologize for who they are. . . . The understated 'Jew-*ish*' flavor of *Seinfeld* and its predecessors has been replaced by a brutal matter-of-factness that would make earlier generations of Jewish comics cringe."[16]

Lawrence Epstein makes a similar point, asserting that recent Jewish comedians, such as Adam Sandler, who became famous for his prideful "Chanukah Song," do not "have to or want to hide being Jewish or feel any shame either. In this sense, there is a great irony. The earlier generations had a much more intimate relationship with their Jewishness; it enveloped and penetrated them. Yet, with all that, they were (often justifiably) reluctant to express their identity in a public forum. This new generation, with far more tenuous Jewish connections, has been freed to express just such an identity."[17] While Epstein's point about the precarious relationship that many contemporary Jewish comics have with Jewish culture and/or religion is an important one, both Weinstein and Epstein ultimately oversimplify the position of recent Jewish comics by failing to take into account the cultural context in which they are asserting their Jewishness and the often surprising ways in which these assertions manifest themselves. In an ethnic landscape that is often cast through a white/black or white/other lens, Jews—whether they assert their Jewishness or not—are largely considered white. Even in the more complex five-pronged vision of American ethnicity that Hollinger critiques in *Postethnic America* (see the introduction to this book), Jews are still considered white. Recall Chris Rock's joke, discussed in chapter 1, that a Jew is just another kind of white person and that blacks don't have time "to dice [whites] up in to little groups." Therefore, when Jewish comics assert their Jewishness, the main risk involved is whether they will be taken seriously as a specific ethnicity—not that they will be discriminated against for being Jewish. I am by no means suggesting that American anti-Semitism is over and done with; I am only pointing out that, by and large, American Jews occupy a position of white privilege in American culture. Furthermore, Jewish humorists will surprise very few audience members when they assert their Jewishness, for the notion of a Jewish comedian has become so commonplace that it borders on stereotype. This chapter is therefore not concerned with the fact that contemporary Jewish humorists proclaim their Jewish background but with the ways that they do so, the strategies they employ to present Jewishness as distinct from whiteness.

SARAH SILVERMAN: THE SPOILED JAP

In her best-selling memoir, *The Bedwetter: Stories of Courage, Redemption, and Pee* (2010), Sarah Silverman makes black/Jewish identification a foundational theme in her life. In the first chapter, Silverman explains the influence that her father (described as a "black-haired, dark-skinned Jew") had on her development as a humorist.[18] She tells an anecdote about her father making a powerful speech at a bar mitzvah, in which he explains the wonders of being Jewish. While the speech was met with wild acclaim by the guests at the bar mitzvah, Silverman reveals that her father actually plagiarized it from the play *Purlie Victorious* by Ossie Davis: "Other than changing all the instances of 'black' to 'Jew,' my father stole the passage pretty much word for word."[19] While the anecdote is provided primarily as a quintessential example of her father's tendency to steal other people's material for his speeches and jokes, it also speaks to a perceived connection between Jewish and African Americans. Not only does her father's successful plagiarism imply that, at least rhetorically, blacks and Jews are interchangeable, it also suggests that African American culture can literally prove useful in helping Jews define themselves.

Throughout her memoir, especially in the chapters detailing her early life, Silverman provides similar anecdotes that suggest the connection between blacks and Jews. In her early years as a comic in Boston, for example, Silverman formed friendships with two black drug dealers and with a homeless African American man named James. And her best friend in high school was a Nigerian girl named Kerry. These friendships are drastically different from the superficial juxtaposition of Jewish and African Americans found in a film like *The Hebrew Hammer*. Rather, Silverman places the black-Jewish connection on a personal level and suggests, like Kwame Anthony Appiah and Paul Gilroy (discussed in the introduction) that ethnic boundaries are best negotiated through intercultural conversations between individuals. In particular, Silverman's relationship with Kerry helps her to articulate her own Jewishness. Silverman explains that she and Kerry "were the black and the Jew in a sea of whiter-than-white preppy rich kids, and both from bleeding-heart liberal homes in a district of conservatives."[20] Here Silverman not only yokes together blacks and Jews, but she suggests a political affiliation between them and deliberately contrasts both groups with whites. The phrase "whiter-than-white" serves to darken Silverman herself and suggests that her own whiteness is a marginalized form in comparison with the mainstream whiteness of her classmates. This process of Silverman darkening herself recurs later in a photograph that shows a young Silverman sitting on a bench as part of what appears to be a softball team. All of the other children in the picture are fair-haired, and the dark-haired Silverman is thus easy to spot. The caption reads, "This is a game I like to call 'Find the Jew.'"[21]

Despite this tendency to highlight her Jewishness, Silverman also admits that her actual relationship with Jewish culture or religion is slight. Recalling Epstein's assertion that the new generation of Jewish comics have a tenuous connection to their heritage, Silverman explains that growing up "she knew almost nothing about being a Jew other than I *was* one."[22] In her comedy, Silverman transforms her unstable understanding of Jewishness and her identification with black culture into an outrageous form of politically incorrect humor. She accomplishes this by creating a crude, spoiled, and blissfully ignorant stage persona.[23] This persona is an extreme iteration and critique of the Jewish American Princess (JAP) stereotype, which gained prominence in the 1970s and 1980s. The JAP stereotype is the product of the increasing affluence of American Jews and the perceived indulgence of wealthy Jewish parents, particularly fathers, toward their daughters.[24] Folklorist Alan Dundes provides a useful definition: "The J.A.P. is spoiled rotten. She is excessively concerned with appearance. She diets. She may have had a nose job. . . . She worries about her fingernails. She is interested in money, shopping, and status . . . she refuses to cook (and eat). The J.A.P. is indifferent to sex, and is particularly disinclined to perform fellatio."[25] Silverman's persona embodies this stereotype in a number of ways, but she also deflates it by exaggerating its qualities to outrageous proportions. For example, in the stand-up film *Jesus Is Magic* (2005), Sarah admits to having JAP-like qualities when she expresses her fondness for a rare jewel that can only be found on "the tip of the tailbone of Ethiopian babies." And in the same film, the JAP's overwhelming concern for her appearance can be seen in Sarah's famous phrase: "I don't care if you think I'm racist, as long as you think I'm thin."

Sarah Silverman's persona is an outrageous exaggeration of the JAP (Jewish American Princess) stereotype. (Credit: ©Roadside Attractions. Courtesy of Photofest.)

Silverman's raunchy, politically incorrect humor and her utilization of the JAP stereotype place her in a tradition of what Sarah Blacher Cohen has called "unkosher comediennes." The figure of the Jewish comedian is most commonly associated with Jewish men, but a number of Jewish women have managed to secure a foothold in the popular culture landscape. Cohen asserts that female humorists such as Sophie Tucker, Belle Barth (often referred to as the female Lenny Bruce), and Joan Rivers create a humor that "violates the Torah's conception of *tzniut* or feminine modesty."[26] Cohen also sees in these humorists a revolt against the traditionally male-dominated world of comedy: "By invading the holy sphere of the Jewish male comic, they usurp his audience and so diminish his self-esteem."[27] Silverman shares with these "unkosher comediennes" a refusal to adhere to society's rules of female decorum. Her additional use of the JAP persona (and her ultimate challenging of it) also place her alongside Jewish female performers such as Gilda Radner, who starred in a JAP-inspired mock commercial for "Jewess jeans" on *Saturday Night Live,* and Fran Drescher, who transformed the upper-class asexual JAP into a working-class sexualized temptress on the sitcom *The Nanny* (1993–1999). Silverman is ultimately unique, though, in her ability to place the JAP stereotype in conversation with other ethnic groups. Her method of doing so reflects the anxiety that many contemporary Jews feel about their position in multiethnic America.

We can see Silverman place her JAP persona in a wider multiethnic context in *Jesus Is Magic.* Here, Sarah unexpectedly invokes blackness in relation to two hot-button moments in Jewish history: the crucifixion and the Holocaust. In the first instance, she says, "everybody blames the Jews for killing Christ, and then the Jews try to pass it off on the Romans. I'm one of the few people that believes it was the blacks." In the second instance, which occurs much later in the film, Sarah argues that "had there been black people in Germany, the Holocaust would have never happened—at least not to Jews." Both examples achieve their humor (if you find these examples humorous) by displaying the ignorance of the Sarah persona and by anachronistically transferring the American ethnic hierarchy into other historical situations. While Sarah's comments may be potentially offensive to Christians, blacks, and Jews, the jokes also reflect the complex relationship between Jewish and African Americans in contemporary culture. By invoking blackness in relation to two events that are inextricably tied to anti-Semitism (its supposed cause and its horrifying results), Sarah suggests a connection between the black and the Jewish plight. Both jokes, however, also depend on a contemporary American vision of ethnicity, in which African Americans occupy the lowest position in the ethno-racial hierarchy. Sarah's thinking here is thus in line with early-twentieth-century Jews who saw their own path to assimilation opened up by the more overt discrimination against blacks. Silverman uses her Sarah persona to critique this mode of thought. Furthermore, Silverman structures these jokes not to hide her Jewish identity but to accentuate it.

The purest manifestation of Silverman's JAP persona as well as her most fully formed exploration of black/Jewish relations occurs on her Comedy Central sitcom *The Sarah Silverman Program*. On the show, Silverman plays a fictional character also named Sarah Silverman. The fictional Sarah is very similar to Silverman's JAP stand-up persona: she is an unemployed, insensitive, unintelligent loafer who lives off of her younger sister, played by Silverman's real-life sister Laura Silverman. In terms of structure, the series follows—and mocks—the conventions of the standard sitcom; in every episode, Sarah has some sort of adventure that challenges her life of stagnancy and ignorance, but by the end, she returns to her usual state. *The Sarah Silverman Program* differs from the traditional sitcom, however, in its obsession with body humor, usually manifested in fart and poop jokes, and its commitment to dealing with potentially offensive or sensitive material.

There are many episodes in which Silverman explores Jewish identity, but one of the most compelling is the season 2 episode "Face Wars," which has Sarah literally donning blackface makeup. In the episode's opening scene, Sarah is not allowed into a stereotypical WASP country club, and she assumes that she is being discriminated against because she is Jewish. An African American waiter overhears her complaining to her friends that being Jewish is harder than anything else, and he asserts that being black is actually more difficult. Sarah and the African American man agree to change places for a day in order to decide which group suffers more. Sarah then engages a makeup artist to transform her into an

African American. The black makeup, however, is simply a layer of dark brown grease smeared over her face, and it is clear from her white neck and arms that Sarah is white. To top off the costume, Sarah ties a bandana around her head, and she becomes the offensive image of a minstrel "darky." When Sarah goes out into the world to try on her new black identity, she is berated by the public for her offensive appearance. Ignorant as always, Sarah assumes that people are yelling at her for being black, not for wearing blackface, and she concludes that it is indeed harder to be black than Jewish. The African American man with whom Sarah had made the bet undergoes a similar transformation, for his Jewish costume consists of a plastic strap-on nose, a kippah, side locks taped to his face, and a t-shirt that reads "I Love Money." When he meets Sarah again, he concedes that it is more difficult to be Jewish than black. Sarah and the black man agree to disagree.

Behind the patent absurdity of this storyline, there lurks a fascinating critique of the received logic of Jewish/black relations. Sarah's blackface mask not only invokes the long history of discrimination against African Americans, but it makes no attempt to hide the Jewish complicity in that discrimination. At the same time, however, Sarah also invokes the history of prejudice against Jews. This begins with the scene in the WASP country club (clubs of this sort were notorious throughout much of the twentieth century for both their exclusionary practices and their blatant anti-Semitism),[28] and it continues with the collection of offensive images that make up the African American man's Jewish disguise. Sarah's contest with the black man over which group suffers more is both ridiculous and potentially offensive to both groups, but it also mocks the tendency to define ethnic identity solely through the lens of oppression or victimization. Furthermore, in contrast to early-twentieth-century Jewish entertainers, Silverman uses the blackface mask as a means to highlight Jewish identity and distance that identity from an undifferentiated (read: WASP) whiteness.

As the episode moves forward, Jewish identity is seemingly eclipsed by an extended treatment of black/white relations. The black man—and his Jewish costume—are never heard from again, but Sarah's blackface getup starts a trend: white people all over town begin donning blackface as well, and Sarah is seen as a heroic race crusader. In one scene, a crowd of Sarah's devoted blackfaced followers demands the right, through a repetitive chant, to explore racial issues in America "through the use of postmodern irony." This turn of events moves the episode into the realm of highly self-aware metacomedy. While Sarah remains ignorant and insensitive, Silverman demonstrates her knowledge of not only the racist history of the blackface mask but also contemporary debates about the possible uses of that mask in contemporary culture. Spike Lee, for example, explores the very issue of "ironic blackface" in his 2000 film *Bamboozled.* While Silverman never posits a precise racial commentary, the moment in which Sarah's ignorance makes her a race crusader anticipates the politically correct backlash that the episode was likely to receive and provides a knowing wink—or, depending how we look at it, a satirical jab—to audience members who are attuned to contemporary discussions about race and its representations in popular culture.[29]

Beneath these layers of knowing irony and tongue-in-cheek humor, "Face Wars" reflects a genuine anxiety about the role that Jews play in multicultural America. For after the episode's exploration of the uses of blackface for racial commentary, it reverts to its original preoccupation with Jews and Jewish persecution. At a blackface rally, Sarah is accidentally shot in the arm by an inept police officer. The moment ironically alludes to the assassination of civil rights leaders and further highlights the ridiculousness of Sarah's position as a cultural hero. In the hospital, Sarah's sister begins to wipe away the black makeup. She is interrupted, however, by the WASP woman who had denied Sarah entrance to the country club in the opening scene. The only makeup left on Sarah's face when she greets the woman is a small patch just above her lip: a Hitler mustache. Sarah, from behind her Hitler mustache, asks the woman from the country club if she "had hated any Jews lately." The woman admits that she had not let Sarah into the club because she was Jewish but explains that when she saw Sarah on TV in blackface, she realized that "it could have been a lot worse." She tells Sarah that she is welcome to play tennis in the club any time outside of "during peak hours."

Like the rest of the episode, this final scene is joyfully absurd. Beyond the silliness, however, an ambiguity about Jewish persecution in America emerges. The implication behind the WASP woman's comment is that the American Jew stands in a midway point in the black/white racial binary. As a Jew, Sarah is not as "bad" as an African American, but she is still not fully white. It is thus presumed that while Sarah is allowed to go to the country club in the off hours, an African American would not be allowed to go there at all. The statement undermines Sarah's original position that Jews in America suffer more than blacks. But the elephant in the room during this conversation is Sarah's Hitler mustache. Even while the episode mocks the idea that contemporary American Jews suffer more than blacks, it also reminds viewers of the very real and serious persecution of Jews in recent history. While the blackface mask signifies centuries of racism directed at African Americans, the image of the Hitler mustache similarly connotes the Holocaust and centuries of European anti-Semitism. Silverman thus transforms the blackface mask into a Jewish one and, for a moment, reasserts the American Jew as an ethnic minority.

While "Face Wars" is the most explicit example, there are numerous episodes on *The Sarah Silverman Program* in which Silverman either places Jewishness in conversation with a more visible cultural minority or has her persona assume a position of otherness or abjection. In "Positively Negative," for instance, Sarah concludes that she has AIDS—before she actually gets her test results back—and spends the entire episode garnering sympathy; in "Muffin' Man," she decides that she is a lesbian but ultimately realizes, in an extreme representation of the JAP's sexual passivity, that she is actually asexual; and in "A Fairly Attractive Mind," she suspects that she is mentally disabled. In each episode, Sarah ultimately returns to her position of privilege and ignorance. She repeatedly claims the plight of various cultural others, but she is never one of them. While she may attempt to use her Jewishness to claim separation from mainstream white culture, the series (as we saw in "Face Wars") presents this possibility as tenuous at best. Consider the episode "There's No Place Like Homeless": here, Sarah loses her keys and becomes a beggar. At one point, she sits on the sidewalk with her homeless African American friend Mike, and they each hold up signs to explain their plight. Mike's sign reads "Vietnam Veteran," and Sarah's reads "Lost My Keys." Mike suggests that she will have better success with a new sign, so Sarah flips her sign over, and the other side reads "Jewish." Mike frowns and says, "maybe the other one is better." The point of the joke is clear: in contemporary American culture, Jewishness is not an effective signifier for victimization. This fact generates both anxiety and humor, and it highlights the tenuous ethnic position of Jewish people in multiethnic America. Silverman asserts Jewishness as a distinct ethnic position, but she also undermines the tendency to define that position solely through the lens of victimization.

LARRY DAVID: THE SCHLEMIEL HERO

Larry David, the star and creator of the HBO series *Curb Your Enthusiasm* (2000–), provides a more subtle version of Jewish blackface than Sarah Silverman, but it is one that reflects a similar anxiety about Jewish identity. Like Silverman, David portrays a fictional, crass, insensitive version of himself while also relying on a traditionally Jewish conception of humor. As in real life, the fictional Larry David is a wealthy Jewish TV mogul, famous for being the co-creator of the hit TV series *Seinfeld* and the basis for the nebbish character George Costanza. On *Curb Your Enthusiasm*, in nearly every episode Larry becomes a social pariah. Throughout the show's history Larry has been accused—sometimes on multiple occasions—of racism, homophobia, pedophilia, and bestiality. While Larry is innocent of these major transgressions, it is usually his own actions that lead to the misunderstanding. In this sense, Larry can be considered a schlemiel. Unlike Silverman's JAP persona, which is the product of a recent American Jewish stereotype, David's schlemiel persona harkens back much further to Yiddish folklore and literature. The simplest definition of "schlemiel" is "one whose own actions inevitably cause his or her laughable setbacks." As Sanford Pinsker explains, "the more he attempts, the greater seem his chances for comic failure."[30] As a character seemingly predestined for trouble, the schlemiel served as a stand-in for the Jewish people as a whole, especially those in the eastern European shtetls, or small villages, where chances for economic or political gain were seemingly impossible. Pinsker asserts that the shtetl Jews "saw the *schlemiel's* ineptitude as an extended metaphor for their socioeconomic plight."[31]

In *The Schlemiel as Modern Hero,* Ruth Wisse expands on this concept, arguing that the Jew-as-schlemiel is more than a simple buffoon but is rather a heroic figure of resistance whose failure serves as a viable alternative to the values of the dominant cultural framework. Wisse thus redefines the schlemiel in terms that highlight his transgressive features: "Outrageous and absurd as his innocence may be by the normal guidelines of political reality, the Jew is simply rational within the context of ideal humanism. He is a fool, seriously—maybe even fatally—out of step with the actual march of events. Yet the impulse . . . of schlemiel literature in general, is to use this comical stance as a stage from which to challenge the political and philosophic status quo."[32] In eastern Europe, where anti-Semitic pogroms regularly threatened the Jews' safety, the schlemiel's ability to challenge the status quo was immediately clear: his failure and weakness provided a direct commentary on the violence around him. In the contemporary United States, however, Jewish suffering is largely diminished, and the schlemiel's transgressive potential is not so apparent. In order to survive as a relevant countercultural figure in America, the schlemiel must adapt to the contemporary environment. Larry David constructs just such a schlemiel; he keeps the most essential aspects of the schlemiel intact, but he adapts them to twenty-first-century American culture.

While Silverman's crude JAP persona is a reflection and critique of the dominant images of Jewish American women, David's schlemiel persona fills a similar role for Jewish men. Stereotypes of the Jewish man, both in Europe and in the United States, often paint him as effeminate, physically insecure, and otherwise emasculated. The schlemiel persona, however, embraces these traits and uses them to challenge the strong, violent masculinity that is frequently celebrated in Western culture.[33] In this sense, David's schlemiel character follows in the footsteps of Isaac Bashevis Singer's willing cuckold Gimpel in the short story "Gimpel the Fool," and, more explicitly, in the footsteps of Woody Allen's protagonist in just about any of his films. More recent watered-down examples can be found in the character of Ross Geller on the sitcom *Friends* (1994–2004) or Gaylord Focker in the *Meet the Parents* films (2000, 2004, and 2010). Larry is different from these contemporary schlemiels, though, both in the extent of his Jewish affiliation and in his tendency to align himself with other marginalized individuals. Larry's schlemiel persona ultimately reflects the ethnic anxiety felt by many successful American Jews who wish to claim ethnic difference.

Larry is clearly uncomfortable with his perceived position as a wealthy white male in the United States. In the pilot episode, for example, he admits to his manager that he has "a tendency to nod to black people" to let them know that he is not "one of the bad ones." At the same time, however, Larry fully enjoys the advantages that go along with his position as a rich white man. His favorite activity is golf, after all. By frequently asserting his Jewish identity, Larry attempts to remain a distinct cultural other without giving up his privileged social status. On *Curb*, this struggle plays itself out in two distinct but overlapping ways. First, Larry uses his Jewishness to strategically distance himself from mainstream white culture, which for Larry translates into white Christian culture. And second, he forges unexpected connections with marginalized groups and other alienated individuals, thereby reaffirming his own outsider status. But since Larry is a schlemiel, both attempts typically end in Larry's failure and/or public humiliation. This failure suggests the impossibility for contemporary Jews to simultaneously maintain their privileged status in American culture and claim ethnic difference from that culture.

A large part of Larry's schlemiel predicament stems from the ambivalence that he displays toward both Jewishness and mainstream white Christian culture. Strictly speaking, Larry is not what one would call a "good Jew." He does not keep kosher, he rarely attends synagogue, and he is married to a gentile woman.[34] Around other Jews, he has little patience for discussions of ethnic solidarity or allusions to Jewish suffering. For instance, in the season 2 episode "Trick or Treat," Larry is accosted on the street by a Jewish man who overhears him whistling a refrain from Richard Wagner. Explaining that Wagner was "Hitler's favorite composer," the man goes on to accuse Larry of being a "self-hating Jew." Larry dismisses the man's claim, responding that while he might indeed hate himself, it is not because he is Jewish.[35] At the end of the episode, in one of Larry's rare moments of triumph, he appears on the man's lawn, leading a full orchestra in a performance of the same Wagner tune he had whistled earlier. As the man wakes up and looks out his window in horror, Larry gives him a mock tip-of-the-hat gesture as the orchestra plays on. The gesture sends a message similar to the oft-cited declaration in Philip Roth's *Portnoy's Complaint* (1969) when the adolescent Alex Portnoy screams to his Jewish parents to "stick your suffering heritage up your suffering ass—*I happen also to be a human being!*"[36] Like Portnoy, Larry here adamantly refuses to have his identity circumscribed by religious or ethnic categories. In a seeming reversal of Werner Sollors's assertion that ethnic humor "is a form of boundary construction,"[37] Larry here adamantly refuses to be defined by traditional ethnic categories.

But when Larry is not confronted with politically zealous Jews, his attitude toward Jewishness is drastically different. In fact, around Christians or even other lax Jews like himself, Larry may assert his Jewish identity just as vehemently as he denies it in "Trick or Treat." He posits his Jewishness most forcefully in his interactions with his Christian wife Cheryl and her family. Larry's impulse to enact Jewishness around his in-laws highlights his struggle to maintain his otherness even while he is an active member of a Christian family. In the season 4 episode "The Christ Nail," for example, symbols of Christianity and Judaism are used to represent Larry's competing familial allegiances. In the beginning of the episode, Larry tells his handyman, a Mexican American ironically named Jesus, to hang a mezuzah on the doorpost, because his father will be visiting. Cheryl's father, who is also visiting, happens to be proudly wearing around his neck a small "Christ nail" that he bought from the website for Mel Gibson's *The Passion of the Christ* (2004). When Jesus neglects to hang the mezuzah, and as his father's car pulls up in front of the house, Larry, in a moment of panic, rips the "Christ nail" from around the neck of his sleeping father-in-law and uses it to affix the mezuzah to the doorpost. The moment clearly favors Jewish symbols over Christian ones. David drains the "Christ nail" of any symbolic import by actually using it as a nail, while keeping the religious aspect of the mezuzah intact, which is emphasized by Larry's father touching it and kissing his hand as he enters the house. In this scenario, however, the cards were already stacked against the Christian symbol. The mezuzah has been affixed to Jewish doorposts for centuries, but the "Christ nail" is a commercial tie-in to a recent Hollywood movie. Furthermore, the alleged anti-Semitism of both *The Passion of the Christ* and Mel Gibson adds another layer of irony—and defiance—to Larry's appropriation of the nail for his own ends. Here Larry succeeds in being the dutiful Jewish son in the eyes of his father, but he remains a schlemiel, because to do so he must alienate himself from his wife and her family. It is clear that Larry cannot make *both* families happy. Larry attempts, but typically fails, to redraw his ethnic allegiances on a situational basis.

"The Christ Nail" hints that Larry's struggle with Christian culture stems in large part from his decision to marry a gentile. He tries to keep his marriage separate from his ethnic identity, but the season 2 episode "The Baptism" suggests that such compartmentalization is impossible and that a mixed marriage has repercussions felt by both families. Here Larry's dismissal of Christian culture ultimately wrecks his sister-in-law's engagement. Cheryl's sister plans to marry a Jewish man who will convert to Christianity—through a baptism ritual—the day before the wedding. Larry is puzzled by the conversion, telling Cheryl, "You guys come to our side; we don't go to your side. Jews don't convert." Later he is even more antagonistic, asking Cheryl, "Why do Christians take everything so personally with Christ? . . . Not only do you have to worship him; you want everybody to." Larry's aggression toward Christianity early in the episode "accidentally" manifests itself later on. Larry and Cheryl arrive at the baptism late, and from the top of a hill overlooking a lake, Larry sees one man dunking another, who really *does* appear to be struggling. Larry runs down the hill yelling for them to stop, and the baptism is interrupted. The potential groom rethinks his decision to convert, and the wedding is called off. Cheryl's family accuses

Larry of deliberately sabotaging the baptism because he "didn't want to lose a Jew," but Larry maintains that he thought the baptism was actually a man being drowned. When a Jewish member of the groom's family privately pulls Larry aside and applauds him for preventing the conversion, however, Larry cannot resist being seen as a hero and says that he "felt something needed to be done." It is clear, though, that Larry's reaction stems more from his flattered ego than from any genuine sense of Jewish solidarity.

Larry's moment of heroism is short-lived, for soon the Jews and Christians begin insulting each other, and the room erupts into conflict: the Jews (including the groom-to-be) stand on one side saying that they "resent the [Christians'] recruitment" and the Christians are on the other side arguing that "being a Christian is a wonderful thing." Only Larry stands in the middle, unsuccessfully attempting to alleviate the religious hostility. The episode thus emerges as an extremely cynical commentary on intermarriage. Rather than mixed marriages bridging two cultures and religions, "The Baptism" suggests that (unless one side is willing to convert), it only deepens the rift. Within the rift itself, we find Larry: the image of him standing between the fighting Jews and Christians, claiming neither group as his own even though he is the direct cause of the conflict, illustrates his schlemiel predicament. In his desire to maintain the privileges of a wealthy white man (not the least of which is being married to a shiksa) and also to remain an ethnically distinct Jew, he fully succeeds at neither. In a room where people are actively and openly drawing ethnic and religious boundaries, Larry is seemingly paralyzed.

One way that Larry may become unstuck is through his interactions with other cultural and ethnic groups. We see this in the opening scene of the season 3 episode "Krazee-Eyez Killa." The episode begins at an outdoor barbecue, and Larry, as usual, neglects socializing. Eventually, though, he finds himself in conversation with an African American hip-hop artist named Krazee-Eyez Killa who, on the show, is dating African American comic Wanda Sykes, who plays herself. Krazee-Eyez asks Larry for advice on a song he has written and proceeds to rap the lyrics for him. Larry, skeptical at first, smiles appreciatively and gives Krazee-Eyez feedback. The two men clearly like each other, and this is driven home when Krazee-Eyez says, "You my dog. You my nigger." Larry replies, "I am your nigger, absolutely." The moment, in which Larry rhetorically claims black identity, epitomizes *Curb*'s method of suggesting Larry's outsider status through his identification with minority groups, alienated individuals, and various cultural outcasts. By aligning himself with marginalized figures—in particular with African Americans—Larry performs a subtle form of Jewish blackface that highlights his desire to remain separate from mainstream white culture.[38]

Of course, in the case of Krazee-Eyez Killa, Larry's alignment with otherness is tempered somewhat by the fact that Krazee-Eyez, like Larry, is actually a wealthy celebrity and that his stereotypical "gangsta" persona is part of his marketability. In the season 4 episode "The Car Pool Lane," however, Larry hires a more marginal (yet equally stereotypical) African American prostitute, named Monena, to ride with him to a baseball game so that he can use the HOV lane. Monena demands that she attend the game too, and what begins as an exploitative economic situation develops into an unexpected friendship. Larry and Monena end up at Larry's father's house smoking marijuana together to help the elder David's glaucoma. This scene reaches its climax when Monena attempts to teach Larry's father how to use African American slang. He proclaims that that he is now speaking "Yiddish Ebonics," thus drawing a direct connection between Jews and blacks. This connection is driven home when Larry uses his relationship with Monena to distance himself from white Christians. At the baseball game, Larry runs into two white men who are in charge of admissions at an elite, right-wing, WASP country club that Larry and Cheryl had been trying to get into after Larry got kicked out of their own Jewish-friendly club. In the previous episode, Larry attempted to pass as a WASP himself to impress the two men. But when Larry sees them at the baseball game, he abandons all attempts to assimilate, aligning himself with outsider Monena instead. Larry looks up at the stereotypically stuffy WASPs and says, "You ever looking for a good blow job at a reasonable rate, she's your gal." Monena, sitting beside Larry, smiles enthusiastically.

The scene is significant not only because Larry openly chooses the company of an African American instead of white Christians, but also because these men are the gatekeepers at an exclusionary country club. As we saw in the Sarah Silverman discussion, resorts of this sort are notorious for their bigotry and anti-Semitism. The episode invokes this history of prejudice, and in his turning toward Monena, Larry (after some deliberation) aligns himself with the oppressed. It is important to remember, however, that the only reason Larry had even applied to this WASP country club is because he was expelled from the one for Jews (for not cleaning his locker). That Larry is banned from *both* clubs suggests that in contemporary Hollywood, wealthy Jews are not all that different from wealthy white Christians. Both groups are elitist and exclusionary; thus Larry turns to an African American prostitute to maintain a semblance of his outsider status. Of course, even this situation is layered with irony, for Monena is with Larry only because he is paying her, and despite their brief friendship, it is clear that Larry does not fit in her world any more—and probably less—than he does with the bigoted country club Christians.

"Krazee-Eyez Killa" and "The Car Pool Lane" both prefigure the more sustained treatment of Jewish/black relations that occurs throughout the ten episodes of season 6, in which Larry literally becomes a member of an African American family allegorically named the Blacks. In the opening episode of the season, Cheryl and Larry take in the Blacks, who have been displaced by a Katrina-esque hurricane. Larry is not happy about the idea of bringing a family of strangers into his house, but Cheryl—whose activism is mocked in various episodes—insists. The family consists of Loretta Black, her two children, and Loretta's aunt, called "Auntie Ray." In a later episode, Loretta's brother Leon also moves in. When Larry first meets the family, in the first episode of season 6, he is immediately fascinated by their last name: "Now let me get this straight; your last name is Black? . . . That's like if my last name was Jew, like Larry Jew." After an awkward pause, in which the Blacks look both puzzled and offended, Larry goes on to explain: "'Cause I'm Jewish. . . . Don't you see? You're black; I'm Jewish!" Larry's statements might be politically incorrect, especially considering that he has just met this family, but it is important that Larry does not hypothesize the name "Larry White." By drawing a parallel between his own Jewishness and the Blacks' blackness, Larry not only rhetorically connects Jewish and African American identity, but he sidesteps the easy white/black dichotomy through which race in America is so often constructed. Larry does not construct Jewishness here as a closed category but rather as one that is defined *in relation* to other ethnic identifications.

Throughout the rest of the season, Larry repeatedly offends the family with his outlandish behavior. He gets an erection while hugging Auntie Ray, and he even uses the "N word" in their presence—although he is only telling a story in which someone else had used it. The Blacks are appalled by Larry's antics, but unlike his own community, they ultimately look past each transgression. It is unclear whether the Blacks accept Larry back into the fold only because it suits their financial needs, but Larry himself seems to genuinely enjoy the Blacks' company and begins to play a large role in their family. He drives the children to school, sets aside space in the yard for Auntie Ray to make a garden, and even conspires behind Cheryl's back with the Blacks to use a more comfortable, non-recycled toilet paper. These moments all reinforce the concept, suggested by Gilroy and Appiah, that ethnic categories are most elastic on the microlevel, where individuals learn from interactions with each other. In particular, Larry forms a very strong bond with Loretta's brother Leon, and there are multiple episodes that suggest a symbolic kinship between the two. They carry identical cell phones, for instance, and in "The Rat Dog" they unknowingly answer each other's phones for most of the episode, ruining important calls for each other. In "The Anonymous Donor," Larry loses a baseball jersey at the dry cleaners, and Leon steals two of the same jerseys off of men walking down the street. We later see Larry and Leon sitting on the couch, wearing the identical shirts, happily playing a game of cards. Larry and Leon's identities seem to bleed into each other, suggesting that the simple categories of black/white or black/Jewish are insufficient signifiers for both men.

A little over halfway through the season, Cheryl leaves Larry (paralleling Larry David's real-life divorce from wife Laurie David), and Larry's relationship with the Blacks becomes even stronger. When Cheryl leaves, she takes Larry's entire social network with her: there is even a running gag in the episode "The Tivo Guy" where various people tell Larry that they cannot see him because they are "going with Cheryl." Friends will not talk to him; restaurants will not seat him, and he is not on the guest list at parties and fundraisers. All Larry has left is his manager Jeff and the Blacks. In the last episode of the season, Larry must attend the bat mitzvah for Jeff's daughter. Cheryl will be there, as will the entire social network that abandoned him. To make matters worse, an obscene, false rumor is circulating about Larry and a gerbil. Larry brings Loretta Black with him so as to not face such hostility alone.

At the lavish bat mitzvah, which highlights Jewish assimilation through its resemblance to the notorious "sweet sixteen" parties that rich whites throw for their daughters, Larry is ostracized by the guests, and Loretta is simply ignored. In a room full of assimilated Jews and white Christians, both Larry and Loretta are clearly outsiders. Throughout the series, we have seen Larry unsuccessfully attempt to balance his Jewish identity and his marriage to a white Christian. Now both sides of this struggle have abandoned him. For in siding with Cheryl and dismissing Loretta, the Jewish guests affirm their own claim to assimilated white identity. Larry has no community of his own left, so he turns to the Blacks. In the final scene, Larry fully embraces his outsider status and asks Loretta to dance. The song, "You Don't Know Me" is sung by R&B artist John Legend and provides an ironic juxtaposition as Larry and Loretta forge a connection on the dance floor. As they dance, both viewers and guests at the bat mitzvah become aware of a romantic connection. From here the camera cuts to Larry and Loretta waking up in bed together as Loretta's children run into the room and jump on the bed. What follows is a hilarious montage of Larry and the Blacks living as a family in Los Angeles: going to the movies, attending soccer games, and arguing with the neighbors. The final image of the episode, and the season, is a card with a photograph of Larry and the family that reads, "Happy Holidays from Larry and the Blacks."

In joining his life with the Blacks, Larry seems to take an active and personal role in African American culture. The Blacks, victims of both a natural disaster and the government's neglect, represent the legacy of racism against African Americans, especially when we take into account the allegorical nature of their name. By becoming a "Black" himself, Larry claims this legacy as his own. But since this union between Larry and the Blacks takes place at a bat mitzvah, it is clear that Larry's rhetorical "blackness" is inextricably entwined with his Jewishness. Larry does not fall for Loretta until he brings her to a Jewish ceremony at which he is ostracized. In his relationship with Cheryl, Larry continuously felt the need to assert his Jewish identity as a means of avoiding cultural assimilation. His relationship with Loretta and the Blacks, however, only reaffirms his outsider status. Larry asserts his Jewish identity by symbolically becoming black.[39]

Despite the apparent victory, this ending underscores Larry's position as a contemporary American schlemiel. Larry is unable to adhere to the values of his own community of wealthy whites and assimilated Jews, to the extent that that community literally expels him. But as in Wisse's definition of the schlemiel, this failure provides a stance from which the show can "challenge the political and philosophic status quo."[40] *Curb* challenges the worldview of wealthy white liberals (Jew and gentile alike) by suggesting their inability to forge human connections with the oppressed groups to whom they are so happy to give money. This is emphasized by the fact that when Cheryl leaves Larry, she also leaves the Blacks. At the same time, Larry's schlemiel persona highlights the predicament of contemporary American Jews who wish to maintain all of the privileges of white identity even while they attempt to claim difference from that identity. That Larry finds a home—however briefly—with the Blacks seems to suggest that the only way contemporary American Jews can remain a distinct cultural minority is to disown themselves from white identity all together.

THE CONUNDRUM: SACHA BARON COHEN

In some ways, Baron Cohen may seem an odd fit for this chapter. Not only is he British, but none of his characters are either American, black, or Jewish. Nonetheless, Baron Cohen himself is *very* Jewish: while Sarah Silverman admits an ignorance of Jewish culture and Larry David displays ambivalence toward it, Baron Cohen is devout. He keeps kosher, observes the Sabbath, speaks Hebrew, and even spent time working on a kibbutz in Israel. Also, despite his British identity, Baron Cohen exhibits a fascination with American race relations, particularly in regard to Jewish and African Americans. At Cambridge, he wrote his undergraduate thesis—titled "The 'Black-Jewish Alliance': A Case of Mistaking Identities"—on Jewish and African American relations during the American civil rights movement.[41] Like Silverman and David, Baron Cohen's humor is based on a series of fictional personas. But whereas Silverman and David create personas that share a name and some key biographical details with their creators, Baron Cohen, in contrast, creates outlandish characters—wannabe British gangster Ali G, Kazakhstani reporter Borat, and Austrian fashionista Brüno—that are drastically different from the man himself. Baron Cohen originally created these characters for his television series *Da Ali G Show* (2003–2004), and each character later went on to figure in a feature-length film. Much of his work is improvisational; in character, he interacts with unsuspecting victims, who are led to believe that they are being interviewed by an actual news agency or for a real documentary. Baron Cohen often causes his victims to embarrass themselves on camera by exposing their prejudices.

Like Silverman and David, Baron Cohen's fascination with Jewish and African American identity is readily apparent in his humor, particularly in his performances as Borat and Ali G. Discerning a precise reading of Jewish or African American culture from this humor, however, proves problematic. For even more so than Silverman and David, Baron Cohen often wraps his humor in layers of irony, and at times his personas seem constructed as deliberate ethnic conundrums. While the laughter comes easily from a Baron Cohen performance, it is often difficult for audience members to discern exactly what they are laughing about. Ultimately, though, Baron Cohen's construction of Jewish identity is not very different from Silverman's or David's, even though his representation of it is significantly more convoluted. Like Silverman and David, Baron Cohen asserts the Jew as an ethnic minority and uses various rhetorical devices to align Jewish and African American culture. In order to fully grasp his ethnic commentary, however, we must place his personas—especially Borat and Ali G—in conversation with each other and with Baron Cohen himself. His Borat character, arguably his most famous in the United States, greatly informs our understanding of Baron Cohen's "black" character, Ali G.

Borat is a Kazakhstani reporter who travels the United States in order to learn about American culture. The character is a hyperbolic stereotype of an uneducated, superstitious, eastern European peasant. In an interview by Neil Strauss, Baron Cohen explains that the reason he chose Kazakhstan as Borat's country of origin is because average Americans know virtually nothing about it: "The joke is not on Kazakhstan. I think the joke is on people who believe that the Kazakhstan I describe can exist."[42] This lack of concern with reflecting a "real" Kazakhstani culture is reinforced by the fact that when Borat is supposedly speaking Kazakh, he really uses Hebrew and Aramaic. Borat serves, in Steven Lee's words, as a "real Other."[43] His outrageous behavior, which is ostensibly based on cultural difference, tests the limits of American tolerance. He is homophobic, misogynistic, and extremely anti-Semitic. Somewhat paradoxically, given his prejudices, he also exudes an aura of innocence and charm. Both in his segments on *Da Ali G Show* and in his feature-length film, *Borat: Cultural Learnings of America for Make Benefit Glorious Nation of Kazakhstan* (2006), Borat interviews or interacts with real Americans who are, supposedly, unaware that he is a fictional character. Using his guileless veneer, Baron Cohen–as–Borat often leads his subjects into revealing their own bigoted attitudes. That Borat is himself an ethnic stereotype aids this cause.

While Baron Cohen uses Borat to explore American attitudes about a variety of issues, his most overt concern is with racism and, in particular, anti-Semitism. Through Borat's aggressive Jew-hating, Baron Cohen asserts the Jew as an ethnic minority and explores anti-Semitism in its myriad forms. Borat's own anti-Semitism is an exaggerated example of that found in eastern Europe during the late nineteenth century. For Borat, Jews embody more than the contemporary American stereotypes of the money-hungry banker or the elite controller of the media; they are inhuman, mythical shape-shifters with demonic powers, and in Borat's fictional Kazakhstan, hating Jews is a national pastime. Early in the *Borat* film, Borat relates that an annual event in his home village is known as "The Running of the Jew," in which locals wear giant masks with hyperbolically large Jewish noses and chase Kazakh children through the streets. At one point, a citizen wearing the mask of a Jewish woman squats and begins to lay an egg. Borat encourages the children to "smash the Jew chick before he hatches!" Borat's vision of demonic Jews recurs later in the film when Borat and his producer Azamat find themselves staying at a bed and breakfast. When they realize that the couple running the inn is Jewish, they hide in their room terrified. During the night, Borat sees two cockroaches walking across the carpet and assumes that the insects are the Jewish couple themselves, transformed. After they try to appease the cockroaches by throwing money at them, Borat and Azamat flee out the window.

These examples achieve their humor primarily through exaggeration; even genuine anti-Semites may recognize the ridiculous quality of Borat's hatred and fear of Jews. Nevertheless, they also contribute to Baron Cohen's method of asserting the Jew as a racial and ethnic other. In constructing Borat's Jewish hatred, he draws from a long history of anti-Semitism, in which Jews were seen as devious sorcerers, child murderers, and cloven-footed demons.[44] Borat's assumption that the Jewish innkeepers have transformed into insects alludes not only to Kafka's *Metamorphosis* but to an anti-Semitic rhetoric that maintained that Jews were vermin in need of extermination (Zyklon B, the poison used in the gas chambers during the Holocaust, was originally a pesticide). By drawing on this history of anti-Semitism, Baron Cohen provides a context for contemporary anti-Semitic attitudes. Moreover, he uses Borat's extreme hatred of Jews to suggest the roots of the more casual anti-Semitism that he finds in America. In his travels through the United States, Baron Cohen–as–Borat finds many Americans who respond with nonchalance to Borat's hatred of Jews. At a gun shop, for example, Borat asks for a weapon that will be ideal for defense against Jews, and the clerk politely chooses a handgun for him.[45] The most famous example, though, is in an episode of *Da Ali G Show* when Borat gets the patrons of a Tucson country-western bar to sing along to his song "In My Country There Is Problem" with lyrics such as: "Throw the Jew down the well / So my country can be free / You must grab him by the horns / Then we have a big party." In his interview by Strauss, Baron Cohen recalls one of his former history professors remarking that "the path to Auschwitz was paved with indifference."[46] He suggests that this anecdote may be useful in understanding the relevance of the apparent indifference toward anti-Semitism that Borat finds in the United States. Such a concern suggests that Baron Cohen deliberately uses his humor to explore Jewish ethnicity and to assert the ethnic particularity of American Jews.

Although *Borat* offers no explicit black-Jewish friendships of the sort found in *Curb Your Enthusiasm* or *The Sarah Silverman Program,* there are numerous instances throughout the *Borat* film that demonstrate Baron Cohen's preoccupation with African American issues. His primary concern in *Borat* (other than generating humor) seems to be with anti-Semitism, but he is keenly aware, as the topic of his undergraduate thesis will attest, that it is impossible to discuss Jewish ethnicity in the United States without also taking into account the role that African Americans play in Jewish self-definition. While in *Borat*'s Kazakhstan Jews are the primary ethnic other, in the United States, it is African Americans. *Borat* thus invites viewers to juxtapose Kazakhstan's hyperbolic Jew-hating with white America's ambivalence toward black people. Curiously, despite his anti-Semitism, misogyny, and homophobia, Borat displays no prejudice against African Americas. In fact, quite the opposite is true. In an early scene in the film, Borat befriends a group of young African Americans, and they give him a brief lesson in black American style and speech. A few moments later, Borat imitates this attitude and tries to get a room in a hotel. Borat acting as a black person (which can be seen as a brief nod to Baron Cohen's Ali G character) oddly generates more hostility than Borat acting as Borat.

The most explicit exploration of African American issues occurs in a scene when Borat attends an upper-class dinner party in Alabama. The guests at the party are generally tolerant of Borat's behavior, as he makes a series of obscene remarks and even comes down from the bathroom with his feces in a plastic bag and hands it to the hostess. The party falls apart, however, when an African American woman named Luenell arrives as Borat's date. Luenell is scantily clad and, in general, adheres to the stereotype of a black prostitute.[47] The guests at the party are openly offended and aggravated that Borat brought Luenell into the house. The moment is similar to the previously discussed *Curb Your Enthusiasm* scene when Larry deliberately offends the WASP country club owners by introducing them to the black prostitute Monena. It seems that for both David and Baron Cohen, a female black prostitute is the best way to offend uptight WASP sensibilities.[48] Baron Cohen makes the point even more explicitly, however, when we remember to take into account Borat's earlier outlandish behavior at the party. While the rich, white southerners displayed condescending amusement at most of Borat's antics, including his bringing a bag of feces to the dinner table, they draw the line with Luenell. Lee sums up the scene beautifully: "Despite [Borat's] 'real otherness,' he has the potential to be molded into a well-behaved multicultural Other. Luenell, by contrast, lacks this malleability: in the hosts' eyes, she is but a poor, black prostitute, rendering her more offensive than shit in a bag."[49]

In *Borat*, then, Luenell emerges as America's most unassimilable other; her race, her class, her gender, and her profession all place her on the margins of society. In other words, Luenell in Borat's America occupies a similar position to the Jew in Borat's Kazakhstan. It is interesting, then, that at the end of the film Borat brings Luenell home with him to Kazakhstan and marries her. In Kazakhstan, she lives in a nice house and is treated almost like royalty by the citizens. This ending serves as a companion to the film's opening and provides one of the most explicit instances of Baron Cohen's juxtaposition of African Americans and Jews. While the film begins by showing Kazakhstan's rabid, albeit comical, anti-Semitism, it ends with a similarly comical acceptance of an African American woman who was ostracized in the United States. This framing forces American audiences to reconsider their politically correct notions of tolerance and diversity. If Luenell is able to find acceptance in a country as backward as Baron Cohen's imagined Kazakhstan, then why can she not also find it in America? Furthermore, his method of bookending the film with Jews and blacks encourages viewers to see African Americans and Jews in relation to each other, for in different cultural contexts, either group can serve as the target of a culture's hatred and fear.

An even more complex yet puzzling treatment of African American issues is presented in Baron Cohen's Ali G character. Like Borat, Ali G is a fictional reporter who dupes interviewees into making a fool of themselves on camera. Ali G comes from Staines, a predominantly white, working-class suburb of London, but his clothing and language suggest an affinity with African American culture. Ali G is extremely ignorant of the world around him and seems to understand little beyond hip-hop music, fast food, and designer clothes. A salient example of Ali G's ignorance occurs in his discussion of books in the season 2 episode "Peace." Ali G explains that "people has been reading books for millions of years, but thanks to new technology, now they is able to write them as well." The statement demonstrates his inability to grasp logical concepts, his deviations from standard English (he mostly adheres to Ebonics), and his lack of even the most rudimentary knowledge of history. And he makes statements like this while dressed in loose-fitting track suits and draped in gold chains. Ali G's appearance, language, and personality therefore embody some of the most malicious stereotypes about African American men. It should be noted, however, that Baron Cohen does not actually black up to play Ali G, and his skin tone is thus consistent with whiteness. Despite his light skin, Ali G claims to be black, and whenever he feels he is being mistreated, he wonders, "is it because I is black?" To make matters more confusing, *Da Ali G* show's producer, Harry Thompson, explains that the name Ali G was chosen to give the character a "whiff of Islam."[50] In the feature-length film *Ali G Indahouse* (2002), however, Ali G—whose name also alludes to African American "gangsta" culture—is given a more explicitly British pedigree when it is revealed that his "real" name is Alistair Leslie Graham.

Taking all of this into account, Ali G seems to be constructed as a deliberate racial conundrum. Critics have speculated that he is from Asian, Turkish, or Jewish descent, but most consider him a white, wannabe "gangsta," or "wigger," enamored with African American culture even though he has but a superficial understanding of it.[51] However, with Ali G's sunglasses, hat, and most of his body covered with loose-fitting clothing, it is too difficult to see enough of him to make out any discernible ethnic features. This lack of ethnic specificity often drives the character's humor, especially when Ali G is interviewing unwitting celebrities. For example, in an interview with the *60 Minutes* commentator Andy Rooney on the season 2 episode "Realness," Ali G repeatedly exasperates the curmudgeonly Rooney with mistakes in verb conjugation that are consistent with Ebonics. When Rooney claims he has had enough and gets up to leave the interview, Ali G asks, "Is it 'cause I is black?" He then goes on to accuse Rooney of being "racialist." Rooney, visibly confused, looks at Ali G and asks, "You're black?" In a manner similar to Dave Chappelle's humor, Ali G's indeterminate ethnicity forces his interviewees (and viewers) to reevaluate their understanding of racial categories.

Despite his self-proclaimed blackness, Ali G is as ignorant of black cultures as he is of everything else. In the season 2 episode "Jah," for example, he claims that movies about American slavery are "racialist" because they always have black actors portraying the slaves. When it is explained to him that, historically, all of the slaves *were* black, Ali G looks puzzled for a moment and then responds, "Well then, don't you think slavery is a bit racialist?" It is as if it just occurred to him that slavery was a racist enterprise. A moment like this highlights the fact that Ali G is most certainly *not* black. He is infatuated with African American culture but only on the surface level; he has no understanding of actual black struggles, and for him, racism is not historically rooted or systematically enforced; it is simply some white people who do not like black people. In this aspect, Baron Cohen's performance is similar to (although less didactic than) Paul Mooney's, discussed in chapter 1. His performance of Ali G serves as an exaggerated manifestation of Mooney's claim that African American males "are the most imitated people on earth," and Ali G's total ignorance of the African American struggle similarly enacts Mooney's assertion that "everybody wants to be a nigger, but nobody wants to be a nigger."[52]

In Ali G then, Baron Cohen presents a peculiar sort of blackface. Like early minstrel shows, Ali G represents a recognizable cultural stereotype, but since Baron Cohen does not actually wear black makeup, the stereotype is deflated. Baron Cohen plays at playing black. Early minstrel shows, according to Eric Lott, represented the mixed emotions that whites felt toward black culture: a

As the wannabe "gangsta" Ali G, Sacha Baron Cohen acts black, but his actual ethnicity remains ambiguous. (Credit: ©HBO. Courtesy of Photofest.)

"dialectical flickering of racial insult and racial envy."[53] While whites found the dance, style, and music of African Americans fascinating, they also feared coming into close contact with real African Americans. Thus, the minstrel show provided an outlet for whites to express their fascination with black culture in a safe, all-white environment. By acting black, Baron Cohen mocks this sort of white fascination with and fear of black culture. Given that on *Da Ali G* show, segments featuring Ali G are shown alongside the more overtly Jewish Borat and Brüno sketches, viewers are never allowed to forget that behind the Ali G persona, there is a Jewish man. These confounding layers of ethnic identity are part of what drive Baron Cohen's humor. Sarah Silverman and Larry David seem to suggest that contemporary Jews must choose either to assimilate into mainstream white society or to reject it by identifying with the black minority. The Ali G persona, however, both collapses and rejects this binary, for through it Baron Cohen is simultaneously white and black, all the while maintaining his Jewishness. He thus superimposes different ethnic identities (Jewish, white, black). This superimposition assumes that racial and ethnic categories are defined not by rigid categorizations but rather in relation to each other. The result is not so much an anxiety over the Jews' place in a contemporary multiethnic landscape but an assertion that Jewishness is an integral part of it—not to be subsumed by or removed from the surrounding cultures.

In this chapter, I hope to have pointed out a fascinating trend in contemporary Jewish humor that highlights how many Jews in the early twenty-first century are realigning themselves with black culture in order to reassert their own minority status. Rather than looking for ways to hide Jewishness and blend into mainstream white society, many Jews are using the symbol of blackness to do just the opposite. On the one hand, it could be argued that this trend suggests that Jews want to have their cake and eat it too: enjoy the privileges of the dominant ethnic group and simultaneously claim separation from that group. On the other hand, it could be argued that despite the different contexts and intentions, what I have called "the new Jewish blackface" is not so new but is just another example in a long line of whites appropriating black culture for their own ends. It is clear, though, that Jewish comedians today are well aware of the myriad changes occurring both within the Jewish community and in American culture as a whole. Moreover, these comedians are finding ways to adapt the long tradition of Jewish humor to these changes and provide a humor that more fully reflects the complexity of America's contemporary, multiethnic landscape.

3 • "CRACKER, PLEASE!"

Toward a White Ethnic Humor

Midway through his 2008 comedy special, *Chewed Up*, stand-up comic Louis C.K. provides a surprisingly frank discussion about the benefits of being white:

> Oh God, I love being white. I really do. Seriously, if you're not white, you're missing out 'cause this shit is thoroughly good. Let me be clear by the way; I'm not saying that white people are better. I'm saying that being white is clearly better. Who could even argue? . . . Here's how great it is to be white. I could get in a time machine and go to any time, and it would be fucking awesome when I get there. That is exclusively a white privilege. Black people can't fuck with time machines. . . . I could go to any time—in the past. I don't want to go to the future and find out what happens to white people because we're gonna pay hard for this shit. You gotta know that. We're not just gonna fall from number one to two. They're gonna hold us down and fuck us in the ass forever, and we totally deserve it. But for now, weeeeee!

C.K.'s discussion is initially surprising simply because he is a white person talking openly and explicitly about being white. Even more important, C.K. acknowledges the existence of white privilege and admits his own complicity with and benefits from that privilege. Finally, and perhaps most significantly, he expresses an anxiety about that white privilege eventually coming to an end. This routine is reflective of contemporary attitudes about whiteness, and C.K. is not the only white comic who is openly discussing being white. In light of the increasing diversity of the American population and the knowledge that soon whites will no longer hold a majority position in the United States, many white humorists (like the white Jews discussed in the previous chapter) are wondering exactly what role whiteness plays in the multiethnic spectrum.[1]

White people, of course, have always been a primary component of American ethnic humor. As we have seen in the previous two chapters, many Jewish American humorists and nearly all African American humorists depend on mainstream white culture in their self-definition, and the same is true with the majority of humorists from other ethnic groups. Therefore, undifferentiated and generic whites work somewhat indirectly as a third important group in the construction of America's ethnic humor. Whites (and more specifically, white Protestants) serve as a foil with which ethnic humorists can compare the features of their own ethnic positions. While many ethnic humorists depend on stereotypes of their own groups to drive their humor, these stereotypes are usually placed in conversation with another set of stereotypes about white people. Whites, according to most nonwhite humorists, are uptight, bland, nervous, and sexually repressed. These features can change, however, if the comedy focuses on a particular sort of white people. For example, whites in the U.S. South are more often characterized as ignorant, bigoted, drunk, violent, or incestuous. This chapter explores the ways in which contemporary white comedians react to, reinforce, or complicate these stereotypes. The results suggest a similarity between many white comedians today and the traditional ethnic humor created by marginalized groups.

The standard reading of the origins of an ethnic humor created by oppressed or underrepresented communities is that before their own humor fully emerges, they internalize the stereotypes placed on them by the dominant ethnic group (i.e., whites). Over time, ethnic humorists reclaim the negative stereotypes, turn them into positives, and create a humor that (at least for a moment) liberates the marginalized subject from being defined by the dominant group and also critiques the dominant group for lacking the same qualities that they once ridiculed. Often such a humor is referred to as "self-deprecating," especially for American Jews, but more often than not, the critique is aimed more forcefully at the dominant group who is responsible for creating or perpetuating the stereotype in the first place. In contemporary American humor, though, the mockery of whites has become widespread enough that white comedians themselves have become familiar with the humor leveled at them by so many ethnic humorists. While some whites may feel uneasy at being the butt of so much humor, many have come to enjoy seeing whiteness lampooned by ethnic comics. One can safely assume that many whites feel that their ability to laugh at themselves (or at whiteness in general) signifies their own progressiveness and acceptance of other cultures. After all, the more his audiences became integrated, the more Richard Pryor mocked stereotypical whiteness in his act. This ability of some whites to laugh at themselves contributes to the formation of a genuine white ethnic humor. Today, many white humorists have so thoroughly absorbed the stereotypes of whiteness that they have begun to work them into their own comic productions and create a sort of self-deprecating white humor. However, given that the historical circumstances of whites are drastically different from most other ethnic groups, and that whites are still by and large the dominant group in America, this self-deprecating humor does not usually have the same potential for transgression as that created by marginalized humorists. It does, however, reflect the complexity and contradictory nature of whiteness and provide insight into the cultural anxiety felt by many white people in response to multiculturalism, the institutional push for diversity, and the increasing complexity of the U.S. population.

This chapter considers a wide range of contemporary white humorists who either directly or indirectly make whiteness an important aspect of their humor. I should note, however, that the humor I discuss in this chapter is the exception to the rule and is not widespread enough to really suggest a trend. Most contemporary white humorists still assume a position of racelessness, and those who do discuss their own whiteness, usually do so (like Louis C.K.) in isolated routines. The fact that white humorists are discussing whiteness at all, though, is a phenomenon worthy of exploration. I begin by discussing the influence of African American humor on white humor through an analysis of comedian Mike Birbiglia and the Showtime stand-up series *White Boyz in the Hood* (2006). I then examine the diversity of social positions within white culture and the ways that class and regional affiliation influence a particular subject's relationship with whiteness. To this end, I compare the "redneck" humor of the popular *Blue Collar Comedy* films with the blog *Stuff White People Like*, which mocks educated and affluent white liberals. Finally, I consider a handful of episodes of the animated Comedy Central series *South Park*. *South Park*, I argue, provides a satire of white culture that is acutely aware of the contradictory nature of whiteness as well as the myriad cultural positions covered by the too-large umbrella of whiteness. This awareness allows *South Park*'s creators, Trey Parker and Matt Stone, to construct a vision of contemporary whiteness that is both transgressive and progressive.

MAKING WHITENESS STRANGE

Over the past two decades, writers such as Richard Dyer, Eric Lott, Toni Morrison, David Roediger, and Michael Rogin have investigated whiteness in relation to a variety of disciplines, ranging from sociology to film and literature. Most critics agree that although the boundaries of whiteness are continually in flux, whiteness generally operates—and has operated in the past—by working as a signifier for universality. Other ethnic positions, in contrast, are marked by their particularity. As Ruth Frankenberg points out, viewing whiteness as an unmarked norm is essential to racist thought: "whiteness is a construct of identity almost impossible to separate from racial dominance."[2] The perceived "normalcy" of whiteness also forces marginalized groups to struggle to find a foothold in larger cultural conversations. Toni Morrison, for example, argues that "American means white, and Africanist people struggle to make the term applicable to themselves with ethnicity and hyphen after hyphen after hyphen."[3] The goal of whiteness studies is thus to dislodge whiteness from its apparently universal position and begin to see it as a particular set of cultural beliefs and practices. As Richard Dyer asserts, "whiteness needs to be made strange."[4]

While the critics cited above have done much to influence the ways in which we discuss whiteness in academic discourse, little has changed in the broader culture. Marginalized groups have certainly reached higher levels of representation in film and television, but whiteness is still the norm, and it still remains essentially unmarked. While there are a handful of black actors, such as Will Smith or Denzel Washington, who can play roles in which race is unspecified, the cultural "everyman" is still, by and large, a white man. A film or television series with a predominantly nonwhite cast will inevitably be called "ethnic," whereas works with predominantly white casts are just "regular." The same principle holds true in American humor. The American humorists who have provided the broadest critique of American culture or American politics—Mark Twain, Lenny Bruce, George Carlin, Bill Hicks—have been either "generic" whites or, like Bruce, white ethnics. A quick survey of the most prominent contemporary political humorists—such as Jon Stewart, Bill Maher, Steven Colbert, Tina Fey, and Dennis Miller—also reveals an overwhelming majority of white people.[5] In contrast, nearly all humorists who are marked by ethnicity inevitably find it necessary to make their ethnic affiliation a large part of their humor.[6] It seems that whiteness, by remaining essentially unseen, works as a license to discuss virtually any cultural issue.

This is not to say that considerations of whiteness have been wholly absent from the history of white American humor—although whiteness is rarely articulated specifically *as* whiteness. In retrospect, the early stand-up of Bob Newhart—in which Newhart performed characters overwhelmed by modern society—provided a gentle, self-deprecating mockery of white, middle-class, middle-American values. And one of Lenny Bruce's famous routines, titled "How to Relax Your Colored Friends at Parties," ridicules white anxiety about interacting with African Americans. We can see by the very title of this bit, however, that whiteness remains both unmarked and assumed, whereas blackness is clearly presented as something other. In his later career, George Carlin has been more direct in discussions of whiteness, although, interestingly, he rhetorically distances himself from it. His most explicit iteration of whiteness occurs in his

1999 stand-up show, *You Are All Diseased.* Here, Carlin provides a nice rant about the theme restaurant and bar The House of Blues:

> They ought to call it The House of Lame White Motherfuckers . . . especially these male movie stars who think they're blues artists. You ever see these guys? . . . It's a fucking sacrilege! In the first place, white people got no business playing the blues, ever. . . . What the fuck do white people have to be blue about? Banana Republic ran out of khakis? The espresso machine is jammed? Hootie and the Blowfish are breaking up? Shit, white people ought to understand their job is to *give* people the blues not to get them and certainly not to sing or play them. Tell you a little secret about the blues: it's not enough to know which notes you need to play, you gotta know *why they need to played.*

The bit is fascinating. Despite his own obvious whiteness, Carlin represents white people as something other than himself, using forms of the pronoun "they" rather than "we." In doing so, he puts himself in a position of racelessness. It is also worthwhile to note that the stereotypical traits that he assigns to white people (a fondness for Banana Republic, espresso, and Hootie and the Blowfish) are in keeping with the constructions of bland privilege that African American comics have been assigning to whites for decades. By the end of the bit, Carlin himself begins to speak as an authority on the blues, offering to tell the audience a "secret" about them. It appears that, despite his critique of the white tendency to appropriate black culture, Carlin, albeit more subtly, is doing it himself.

This is not meant to criticize Carlin, for I find his discussion here to be a successful critique of white culture that accomplishes, to a certain degree, Dyer's charge to "make whiteness strange." Furthermore, Carlin can get away with this sort of thing more easily than other white comics owing in part to his craftsmanship and in part to his long-standing status as a countercultural figure. But Carlin's rant also highlights the odd way in which whiteness operates as a universality even when it is being discussed as a particularity. Carlin's whiteness enables him to take on the persona of a misanthropic everyman and to make claims about anything that annoys him in the culture. In this instance, he is annoyed by white people who play the blues. Since his whiteness has already allowed him to speak from a position of universality, he is able to discuss whiteness even while he remains separate from it. This is the peculiar power of whiteness: it can remain unseen even while it is being dissected.

Oddly enough, when whiteness is most visible in wider cultural conversations, it is articulated not as a position of raceless privilege but rather as marker of victimization. This is particularly true for white males. Beginning in the 1970s, the country began to see a "white male backlash" against the small victories achieved by various civil rights movements. David Savran describes "the ascendancy of a new and powerful figure in U.S. culture: the white male as victim."[7] Michael Kimmel explains that these white male victims "felt besieged by frenzied 'feminazis' and a culture of entitlements, affirmative action, and special interests."[8] While this "white male backlash" achieved it apex in the 1980s, it is still very much with us today. In *Time* magazine, for example, journalist George Rodriguez lists "The White Anxiety Crisis" as one of the most important trends for the next ten years in American culture. Rodriguez argues that the recent wave of immigration from Asia and Mexico, affirmative action policies, the election of Barack Obama, and a score of other factors have caused whites, and particularly white males, to feel increasingly uneasy about their place in the culture.[9] It is thus not surprising that it is white male humorists who most overtly explore whiteness. The white male humorists whom I discuss in the remainder of this chapter approach whiteness from a variety of positions. At times, they continue the work of the numerous critics who have written about whiteness as a cultural construction and are involved in an effort to unfix whiteness from its position of power and universality. At other times, though, white humor is not so benevolent, and it reflects—like the white male backlash—an anxiety about the loss of white male power as a result of an increasingly diverse American ethnic demographic.

DOUBLE CONSCIOUSNESS REVISITED

As we saw in chapter 1, African American humor is typically driven by a *double consciousness* mode of thought. African American humorists construct a world that is split by the black/white divide and use comic comparisons of the two to critique whiteness and privilege blackness. Because African Americans are a major force in mainstream American humor, the white stereotypes perpetuated by black comics have become commonplace, especially the nervous white male stereotype as it is performed by black male comedians. It is only natural, then, that some white male comedians would eventually work these stereotypes in to their own humor. The result is a sort of white formulation of double consciousness, in which white comedians view, or attempt to view, their own cultural positions from an African American perspective. Stand-up comedian Mike Birbiglia performs stereotypical whiteness in a manner that is particularly illustrative of the ways that African American humor can influence how whites construct their identity.

Given his last name, Birbiglia may have been able to accentuate his Italian heritage as a means to claim a more specific ethnicity than generic whiteness. But early in his stand-up special *What I Should Have Said Was Nothing* (2008), he rejects this notion of Italian ethnicity, explaining that his family is an "amorphous kind of white, Olive Garden Italian." In his second appearance on the series *Comedy Central Presents*, Birbiglia explores this amorphous white identity more explicitly. He begins by overtly acknowledging the influence of African

American humorists by explaining why he likes to use the word "cracker" to refer to whites: "a lot of black comics like using the n-word. I like using the c-word." Then, assuming a stereotypically white voice, Birbiglia tells a stereotypically white story: "Me and my cracker friends were driving down the street in my Volvo station wagon, and I said, 'Hey, cracker, pass the Sun Chips.' And he says, 'Not till we get to the picnic, cracker.' And I say, 'Cracker, please' [long pause for audience laughter]. He's like, 'Cracker, what?'"[10] The humor in this performance works on multiple levels. The first is the simplest level of ethnic self-deprecation. Birbiglia exaggerates his own whiteness and puts it on display for the audience's amusement; he peppers his story with well-chosen details (especially the Sun Chips), which are in keeping with a stereotypical view of privileged white culture. The next level on which this routine works is the way in which the entire bit is in conversation with the ubiquitous performance of whiteness found in the acts of African American comedians. Birbiglia's voice and mannerisms are recognizable to any audience member who has seen a film like *The Original Kings of Comedy* or an episode of *Def Comedy Jam*. And finally, Birbiglia also derives humor by transplanting the stereotypical patterns of black speech into a stereotypically white setting. Birbiglia has to pause for a considerable amount of time after he delivers the "cracker, please" line—a revision of the infamous "nigger, please"—because it gets such a big laugh from the crowd. The juxtaposition of the white voice and black speech patterns generates an unexpected humor.

Birbiglia then continues the routine but also provides an anatomy of it—explaining some of the humor even as he adds new jokes. He explains that the audience just witnessed his "white guy doing a black guy doing a white guy voice" and then comments that "a lot of black comics have that one white guy voice . . . like we all talk like British detectives. I feel bad for the one guy on earth who does talk like that." Birbiglia then resumes his "black guy doing a white guy voice" and exclaims, "This is preposterous! That doesn't sound anything like me. Wait till I get my hands on that black fellow. But first let me dance." He then begins an awkward, off-beat, white man's dance. The dance is, again, reminiscent of the ways in which African American humorists mock white people's supposed lack of rhythm. This second part of the routine is interesting for the ways that Birbiglia shifts the emphasis of his humor. While the initial story about a group of white guys eating Sun Chips on their way to a picnic was primarily a self-deprecating critique of whiteness, the second half functions as a critique of the often static ways in which black comics represent white people. By highlighting the exaggerated and two-dimensional impersonations of whites that many black comics rely on, Birbiglia is in fact suggesting that whiteness is much more fluid. Just as black, Jewish, and other ethnic humorists have been doing for years, Birbiglia is reclaiming a stereotype, exaggerating it, and ultimately deflating it.

Birbiglia's routine, as brief as it is, is a successful example of the ways that a white humorist can build a white ethnic humor by drawing from black sources. A less successful yet more sustained example of this sort of humor occurs in the short-lived Showtime stand-up series *White Boyz in the Hood* (2006). The series features a variety of white comedians performing for a predominantly black, urban audience. The premise, as the African American emcee Talent Harris states at the opening of every episode, is intended to "flip the crossover." For decades, black comics have been forced to cross over to white audiences; on *White Boyz in the Hood*, Harris explains, white people "gotta cross over to us." The most noticeable aspect of this series is its similar format to the HBO series *Def Comedy Jam*. Both shows use a hip-hop soundtrack, a black emcee, and an urban, primarily African American audience in order to establish themselves as a predominantly black space. *White Boyz in the Hood* simply uses the black environment to highlight white comedians, and as its title suggests, these comedians are mostly male. In its premise, the series is an admirable attempt to make whiteness strange by placing white comedians in a setting where their whiteness cannot be easily used as a signifier for universality. Unfortunately, the comedians themselves are not of a high enough quality, in terms of both their ability to generate humor and their ability to interrogate ethnic issues, to significantly further the development of a white ethnic humor. The series, however, does warrant a brief discussion for the ways in which it makes explicit the influence of black comedians on white self-image and also for the manner in which it reflects white anxiety about interactions with nonwhites.

The actual humor of *White Boyz in the Hood* is fairly conventional, and much of it falls flat. The most interesting aspect of the show is the various rhetorical strategies that the featured comedians use to deal with being a white person performing for a large group of African Americans. Whiteness, as we have seen, is typically viewed as raceless or normal, but *White Boyz in the Hood* puts whiteness on display in order to view it as raced and particular. The comedians are thus in the uncommon position of being a racial other for a few minutes. There are a number of ways that the comedians present themselves in order to either alleviate this othering or to use it to generate humor. The first, and simplest, is through identification. A number of the comics attempt to displace their own whiteness by demonstrating various ways in which they could or should be included in black culture. Comic Jason Andors, for example, attempts to assert his black credentials by performing a lengthy breakdancing routine. And the fortuitously named AG White speaks in a stereotypically urban or black accent and tells the audience that "I've been around you all my life. You can tell by the ways that I say 'motherfucker.'" The late Mike DeStefano makes similar avowals of identification in a slightly more contentious manner. DeStefano describes African Americans who claim they are tired "of the white man holding [them down]." After providing some details from his own life (for instance, he has been both a drug addict and a drug counselor), DeStefano exclaims that he is also held down by the white man: "Let's get him. Let's kill whitey!" In all of these examples, the comedians attempt to diminish their difference by suggesting various ways in which they are "down" with black culture.

A similar strategy used by the *White Boyz in the Hood* comedians is to employ comic comparisons between black and white cultures, at the expense of whiteness. The southern comedian Redbone opens his act with stereotypical comparisons between black and white people, and AG White switches from his "urban" accent to a stereotypical white voice when he explains that the only time he acts white is when he gets pulled over. Furthermore, jokes about the superior size of the black penis abound throughout the entire series. While these black/white juxtapositions are occasionally amusing, they are virtually identical to what Bambi Haggins has called the "white people be like" jokes that are frequently found on shows like *Def Comedy Jam*. Lacking the sort of metacommentary that Birbiglia provides, these jokes simply reinforce black/white stereotypes without providing any real insight into them. In using this humor, it seems that the comedians are more interested in placating their African American audiences than they are in interrogating black/white interactions. These white/black comparisons, however, do demonstrate the extent to which African American humor has influenced the ways that whites may define themselves.

The most interesting—and puzzling—trend to be found on *White Boyz in the Hood* is the tendency of the white comedians to create jokes at the expense of nonblack minority groups. The longest bit in AG White's act is an extended impersonation of a Latino man (whom he refers to as Hector) attempting to give directions. DC Benny impersonates—in a horribly exaggerated voice—Chinese men who try to coerce him into getting a massage at the mall. And Doug Saulnier has an extended bit about Latinos (whom he refers to throughout as "Spanish") who loiter at Target all day. Speaking of a particular child that he saw at Target, Saulnier explains that he knew the child "was Spanish because he was five and he had a mustache." In most televised comedy venues, routines such as these are rare. White comedians tend, in the service of political correctness, to shy away from humor that involves marginalized groups, especially in such a stereotypical manner. The fact that the comedians here focus so much on other groups may, again, be indicative of their mediocrity, but it also reveals their anxiety. By focusing on Asians and Latinos, these comics attempt to divert attention away from their whiteness and from white/black antagonisms in general. By laughing at a third, unrepresented group, the "white boys" and the black audience can form their own community. Werner Sollors asserts that ethnic humor is a "form of boundary construction,"[11] and the comedians on *White Boyz in the Hood* attempt to redraw the traditional boundaries between whites and blacks in order to displace their own temporary minority status.

Not surprisingly, the African American audience usually provides a lukewarm response to these acts. Most of the comedians receive polite applause but little enthusiasm, and some receive little more than puzzled looks. The comedians who are the most successful in winning over the audience are the ones who focus on issues other than race. A comedian who goes by The Greg Wilson, for example, received a standing ovation after he performed an extremely bawdy set that culminates in his impersonation of Arnold Schwarzenegger performing fellatio. And Jay Black got massive applause after a routine in which he criticizes women for not being able to give adequate "hand jobs." The enthusiastic response to these raunchy and masculinist performances may suggest that sex trumps race and may thus serve as an ingredient for a "universal" humor. Of course, focusing on sex rather than race often displaces racial antagonisms with misogynistic or homophobic humor.[12] I suspect, though, that the explanation for these responses is that the audience at *White Boyz in the Hood* is more sophisticated than the comics give them credit for. They recognize attempts to pander to them and feel freer to laugh when the obvious issue of racial difference is off the table.

DIVERSIFYING WHITENESS

The most common stereotype of whiteness, as we have seen, is the privileged, nervous, and uptight white male impersonated by a nearly endless array of black comics. This uptight white stereotype is rarely fleshed out, and it is not easily associated with a particular region or even with a particular political preference. The tight, nasally white voice that black comics (and white comics like Mike Birbiglia) love to perform is an exaggerated version of the bland, accentless voices of news anchors, game show hosts, and 1950s sitcom dads, all highly constructed white identities that are intended to appeal to the broadest possible audience. Nevertheless, it may be assumed that this white stereotype is directed most pointedly at the white, suburban, middle to upper-middle class. We know, however, that this is only one particular sort of whiteness, and that the term "white," like other ethnic signifiers, can never fully account for the complex and contradictory subject positions that it supposedly covers. As we saw in chapter 2, American Jews are largely considered white, even though they often have their own particular ethnic associations, and the same point can be made about Irish Americans or Italian Americans. Once we take into account social class and regional affiliation, there is no end to the diverse array of subject positions that fall under the umbrella of whiteness. Humor based on regional or class affiliations of course have a long history in the United States, including nineteenth-century folk-humorists such as Artemus Ward and Mark Twain and class-conscious early film comics like Charlie Chaplin and the Marx Brothers. There is also a long tradition of class-based situation comedies, ranging from *The Honeymooners* (1955–1956) and *All in the Family*

(1968–1979) to *Married with Children* (1987–1997) and *Roseanne* (1988–1997). In the early twenty-first century, class-based humor continues, but it is more explicitly attached to ideas circulating about whiteness. This section considers two class- and region-based visions of whiteness that hold currency in contemporary American humor. The first is a fairly new set of stereotypes associated with affluent, educated, liberal whites; and the second is a very old set of stereotypes associated with working-class white southerners. Viewed together, it becomes clear how the generic term "white" can never successfully signify the full range of whiteness in American culture.

Humorous articulations of liberal, affluent whites can be found most prominently in the blog *Stuff White People Like*, found at www.stuffwhitepeoplelike.com, written by white, Canadian-born Christian Lander (with some occasional entries written by Lander's Filipino collaborator Myles Valentin).[13] While the blog's title may suggest that it relies on broad generalizations about generic whiteness, a quick glance over the list makes it clear that *Stuff White People Like* is concerned with a very particular sort of white people and that the items on the list are extremely specific to a narrow white demographic. In an interview with CNN, Lander explains that he wanted to avoid overused white stereotypes like "mayonnaise or dancing poorly" and that he avoids stereotypes attached to "the wrong kind of white people," such as "guns, NASCAR, [or] trailer parks."[14] Lander's observation about "the wrong kind of white people" indicates not only his awareness that the term "white" has many contradictory connotations, but also his focus on one specific subsection of whiteness. Lander also argues that the items on his list are not stereotypes because "they're true."[15] In a sense, Lander may be right; many educated white liberals follow Lander's blog not only to read funny descriptions of white people but also to read about their favorite films, television shows, and hobbies. Nevertheless, Lander achieves his humor through exaggerated descriptions—which do border on stereotype—of white privilege, liberal guilt, and pretentious intellectual posturing. In a manner similar to the humor created by other ethnic groups, these exaggerations form a self-deprecating humor for liberal whites. The difference is that these stereotypes are still in the process of being fleshed out, and they are not rooted in oppression, as are the stereotypes attached to most marginalized groups. Other than generating humor, then, the most useful result of Lander's blog is its attention to one particular whiteness as a specific set of cultural beliefs and practices rather than as a generic category.

While Lander's target audience is white people like himself, the blog is written as a mock anthropological tract designed to teach nonwhites how to interact with white people and navigate the white world. For example, in the entry titled "Free Health Care," Lander explains, "if you need to impress a white person, merely mention how you got hurt on a recent trip [to] Canada/England/Sweden and though you were a foreigner you received excellent and free health care. They will be very impressed and likely tell you about how powerful drug and health care lobbies are destroying everything." Lander's method of guiding a nonwhite person through the intricacies of the white world creates a rhetorical distance between the reader and the subject matter. This contributes to *Stuff White People Like*'s ability to make whiteness strange. White people on Lander's blog are represented not as an unmarked norm but rather as a peculiar ethnic curiosity whose customs and beliefs warrant exploration and study. The juxtaposition of the pseudo-anthropological language and the mundane subject matter also drives much of the blog's humor.

One of the most prominent aspects of *Stuff White People Like* is its attention to the details of American liberal consumerism. Lander explains that "it's an update of the idea of the yuppie."[16] Like the "yuppies" of the 1980s, Lander's white people are extremely materialistic. This materialism, however, is complicated by a concern for the environment, the health food boom, and a heightened awareness about the means of material production and distribution. Lander thus constructs a white hypocrisy, where material goods are used as status symbols even though materialism itself is officially looked down upon. Buying the right products is a sign of ethical awareness rather than wealth. Of course, the goods that have the most ethical prestige are often the most expensive. Lander's list includes trendy but not necessarily expensive items like coffee, tea, wine, bottles of water, and sea salt, but there are also a number of other products or activities that require a significant amount of wealth or leisure time, such as yoga, graduate school, traveling, organic foods, the Toyota Prius, taking a year off, Apple products, and writers' workshops. Lander's list thus gets to the heart of a particular sort of white anxiety, which is often characterized as "liberal guilt." The blog explores the ways that white people attempt to use their privilege in productive ways. For Lander, however, these attempts achieve little more than white self-congratulation.

This point is most apparent in the entries that deal explicitly with ethnicity and class. Lander asserts, for example, that white people like diversity, having black friends, having gay friends, being the only white person around, and knowing what's best for poor people. In addition, the blog lists a number of products or artists that similarly suggest an affiliation with marginalized culture, such as sushi, Asian fusion food, Bob Marley, Mos Def, Barack Obama, and the inner-city HBO drama *The Wire*. All of these touch on issues of white appropriation that have been discussed in the previous chapters, but Lander suggests that such affiliation is not only a signifier for hipness but also for progressive thinking and morality. Lander drives this point home nicely in his entry titled "Awareness." He explains that "what makes [awareness] . . . appealing for white people is that you can raise [it] through expensive dinners, parties, marathons, selling t-shirts, fashion shows, concerts, eating at restaurants and bracelets. In other words, white people just have to keep doing stuff they like, EXCEPT now they can feel better about making a difference." Lander goes on to explain that popular issues that white people like to raise awareness about include AIDS, homophobia, Africa, and political prisoners. Lander connects white political activism with white consumerism, suggesting the two are inextricably linked. The blog suggests that affluent white liberals, in their efforts to align themselves with various marginalized groups, actually end up reinforcing the boundaries constructed around white identity. Their ability to organize fundraisers and concerts only further highlights their privileged status.

In its commitment to highlighting the hypocrisies of affluent white liberals, *Stuff White People Like* is similar to the pointed critique of subsections of African American culture offered by Chris Rock or *The Boondocks*. The difference, of course, is that there is no history of oppression and systemic inequality tied to rich white people, so Lander's critique is less risky but perhaps more piercing. While Lander's prose is light and glib, beneath the ironic surface (and irony *is* on the list) Lander offers a scathing jeremiad for so-called progressive whites. In spite of their wealth, education, good intentions, and seemingly inexhaustible leisure time, white people, according to Lander, fail to actually *do* anything. Ultimately, *Stuff White People Like* is a significant addition to white ethnic humor. In its attention to a specific subsection of white America, it complicates the ability to construct whiteness as a monolithic category, and in its anthropological approach, it defamiliarizes the category of whiteness, which is so often viewed as an unmarked norm. In its critique of white people, it follows the tradition of an American ethnic humor based on self-deprecation, but it adapts this model to account for the privileged position of white wealth.

Standing in diametric opposition to the wealthy, hipster liberals lampooned by *Stuff White People Like*, we find the popular southern, working-class humor of Jeff Foxworthy—most known for his "You might be a redneck" joke cycle—and the "Blue Collar Comedy" offered by Foxworthy and fellow humorists Bill Engvall, Ron White, and Daniel Whitney (better known as Larry the Cable Guy). In some aspects, redneck/blue collar humor can be situated within a tradition of southern humor that can be traced back (at least) to Mark Twain and was carried into popular media by artists like Andy Griffith and Jerry Clower.[17] Like these fellow southern humorists, redneck/blue collar comedy mocks pretension and celebrates simplicity. It favors common sense over formal education and the country/small town over the city. Unlike the tradition of southern humor, however, popular redneck/blue collar comedy relies more on one-liners than the humorous tall tales that Twain, Griffith, and Clower are known for. Foxworthy, for example, builds many of his routines by stringing together a series of "You might be a redneck" jokes. Larry the Cable Guy, likewise, relies on familiar catchphrases like "Git-R-Done" and "Lord, I apologize." In this manner, redneck/blue collar comedy is driven more by the contemporary conventions of mainstream stand-up than it is by the tradition of southern humor.

Like *Stuff White People Like*, redneck and blue collar humor focuses on a specific subsection of the white community and complicates our ability to view whiteness as a homogenous category. Unlike Lander's blog, however, redneck/blue collar humor is both less satirical and less overtly about whiteness. In fact, the colored terms "redneck" and "blue collar" call attention away from whiteness and place it instead on economic and regional affiliation.

Nonetheless, the humor is clearly directed toward southern working-class whites, a point made clear in the concert film *Blue Collar Comedy Tour: The Movie* (2003), which follows the model of the African American stand-up film *The Original Kings of Comedy*, discussed in chapter 1. Like *The Original Kings* and *Def Comedy Jam*, the *Blue Collar* films are a space for cultural celebration. In a manner very similar to *The Original Kings*, the *Blue Collar Comedy Tour* film and its two sequels use framing devices and extended shots of the audience to establish itself as a community event. While much of the humor is about the stereotypes of rural white southerners, it offers no real criticism of its demographic.

In his closing speech as host of the CMT (Country Music Television) Awards, Foxworthy makes it clear that his humor, while self-deprecating, is more about southern, working-class pride than ridiculing so-called rednecks. Foxworthy, making no attempt to be funny, asserts that country music is "real music sung by real people for real people, the people that make up the backbone of this country. You can call us rednecks if you want. We're not offended, 'cause we know what we're all about. We get up and go to work, we get up and go to church, and we get up and go to war when necessary."[18] While Foxworthy ties country music and his own humor to traditional American values such as hard work, religion, and patriotism, the line "you can call us rednecks if you want" also calls attention to the fact that "rednecks" are an often maligned group in the cultural imagination. Foxworthy's thinking here is in line with Anne Shelby, who argues that rural whites are the last group in American culture that it is okay for others to stereotype: "even people . . . who would never make bad jokes about Polish people and lightbulbs . . . feel perfectly free to stereotype rural southerners."[19] Shelby goes on to explore the socioeconomic implications of such joking: "It is not a coincidence that redneck jokes, like hillbilly stereotypes, take as their subject some of the poorest people in America. These jokes effectively dismiss poverty as a function of politics and economics. Redneck jokes define poverty as a matter of inferior taste. If these people are poor, they probably deserve it, and it's probably their own fault."[20] If we read Foxworthy's redneck pride through the lens of Shelby's argument, then redneck and blue collar humor seems to bear a very close resemblance to a more traditional ethnic humor, which typically emerges from a history of victimization. Like many African American and Jewish American humorists, for example, Foxworthy and company reclaim a harmful stereotype and turn it into fodder for cultural/ethnic self-assertion. The only problem with this reading is that the blue collar humorists are by no means representative of "the poorest people in America" nor are the fans who attend their concerts, purchase their DVDs, or watch their stand-up specials on cable. Rather, their humor (as suggested by the term "blue collar") is most appreciated by the southern working class. Also, as implied by the Foxworthy speech above, the humor usually aligns itself with conservative values.

The actual performances in *The Blue Collar Comedy* films, however, are not openly political, and discussions of race are never overt. Rather, the political orientation of the Blue Collar comics manifests itself through the humorists' adherence to traditional family values and gender roles. Bill Engvall, for example, sticks mostly to standard marriage and children humor, discussing stereotypical differences between men and women. And when Foxworthy is not running through his redneck cycle, most of his humor revolves around marriage and family life as well. Ron White's boozy persona (he always has a cigar and a glass of whiskey nearby) is probably the most overtly political of the group; for example, in *Blue Collar Comedy Tour: The Movie*, White receives massive applause when he announces that "we've got the death penalty in Texas, and we use it!" Larry the Cable Guy's act, full of malapropisms and catchphrases, is the most ethnically charged: he performs a redneck caricature that is so over the top that it borders on white minstrelsy; maybe we could call it "white trash–face." For example, he jokes about knowing a woman whose breasts were different sizes and who therefore won both first and third place in a wet t-shirt contest. The punch line of the joke, though, is that the woman is his sister. The sexist and incestuous connotations of the joke adhere to the most demeaning stereotypes of white southerners. This sort of content, especially in conjunction with his sleeveless flannel shirts, establishes Larry the Cable Guy as a comic foil, serving to normalize the rest of the cast and the audience. No matter how much of a "redneck" a viewer may be, he or she will not reach Larry the Cable Guy's redneck status.

Despite the tendency to provide simple or seemingly apolitical humor, the *Blue Collar Comedy* films reveal ethnic anxiety in a number of ways. One of the most interesting is the manner in which *Blue Collar Comedy Tour: The Movie* is framed. In the opening sequence, the film establishes itself not only as a white, southern space, but it deliberately distances itself from blackness. The film opens with the four comedians in a lake, sitting in a small fishing boat. The scene is deliberately idyllic. As they float on the calm waters, the comics quietly banter with each other. A moment later, the camera pans to the edge of the lake where we see a highway, and a limousine pulls up to the edge of the water; the window

Jeff Foxworthy celebrates southern working-class culture through his "You might be a redneck" joke cycle. (Credit: ©WB Television. Photographer: Kwaku Alston. Courtesy of Photofest.)

rolls down, and oddly enough, African American comedian David Alan Grier (most famous as a cast member on the sketch comedy series *In Living Color*) is sitting in the back of the limo. "Come on guys," he yells, "we've got a show to do!" This strange opening is revelatory of the film's ethnic anxiety. The *Blue Collar* comics, drifting in a placid lake, are associated, as we might expect, with nature and simplicity. Grier, the only African American to appear in the film, is associated with wealth and style, as suggested by his limousine. Furthermore, Grier is also presented as a sort of authority figure for the comedians. If Grier did not arrive to pick them up, the opening suggests, the *Blue Collar* comics may still be out there fishing and joking, oblivious to their show-business obligations. By aligning blackness with wealth and power, the film may subvert black stereotypes. At the same time, however, it betrays an anxiety about a perceived lack of power for white people.

During the rest of the film's opening sequence, this peculiar binary suggested by Grier and the *Blue Collar* comics continues. In the dressing room, Grier comments that he wants to "give some color" and brings the comedians a collection of brightly colored suits of the sort stereotypically associated with African American pimps. Shots of the comedians getting dressed are intercut with shots of audience members (all of whom are white) telling their favorite redneck jokes. After the comedians put on the suits, Grier (now dressed like a cowboy) comments that "they look like his relatives." Foxworthy exclaims, "There's a lot of white people in here this evening," and Larry the Cable Guy asks, "Where's my whores? Where's my whores?" This whole dressing room scene is ultimately moot, for when the *Blue Collar* comics finally take the stage, they are dressed in their regular clothes.

This odd little montage is the most overt exploration of race offered by the film. The intention, I think, is to generate humor by juxtaposing the *Blue Collar* comics' rustic simplicity with the "urban" sophistication of Grier. This is driven home when the *Blue Collar* comics' brightly colored suits are complemented by the equally silly appearance of Grier dressed like a cowboy. On the surface, the fact that Foxworthy and company appear to get along so well with Grier suggests an intercultural dialogue and a certain level of racial harmony. At the same time, however, the opening highlights racial difference and reinforces strict cultural codes. Grier and the *Blue Collar* comics may get along, but they clearly do not dress the same way or go fishing together. Perhaps most disturbingly, the sequence suggests a rigid racial essentialism. You can dress the comedians like African Americans, but they will always be white because that is what they are. At best, then, the film adheres to a separate but equal conception or ethnic relations, suggesting that African Americans and working-class whites each have their own culture, but that they do not need to mix. At worst, the film betrays a startling level of white anxiety and imagines a world in which African Americans have both more power and more resources than southern whites.

The third *Blue Collar* film, *Blue Collar Comedy Tour: One for the Road* (2006), has another interesting moment that betrays a similar ethnic anxiety. In his act, Foxworthy performs a variation on his "you might be a redneck" jokes by making comic observations about "redneck" fashion. For example, Foxworthy explains that "if your stomach blocks your view of your feet, cover it up! The only people who should be wearing belly shirts are people who don't have bellies." There are at least a dozen of these jokes, and the audience laughs appreciatively after each one. In the midst of this cycle, however, Foxworthy includes a joke that does not really apply to so-called redneck fashion: "If your mother still drives you to school, you ain't no 'gangsta.' Pull your pants up! Your back pockets should not be behind your knees!" The joke receives massive applause, and a number of audience members actually stand up to clap. The description of what is clearly an African American fashion style, Foxworthy's derisive pronouncement of the word "gangsta," and the audience's reaction (which is disproportionate to the quality of the joke itself) all combine to betray a white anxiety about the influence that African American culture has on white youth. As in the framing device discussed above, Foxworthy's joke also adheres to a rigidly pluralist view of American culture. Actual "gangstas," that is, black people, can where their pants however they want; Foxworthy and the audience clearly don't care, but when such fashion choices bleed into their own culture, there is indignation. The moment highlights, more than any other in the *Blue Collar* oeuvre, the exclusive "we-ness" of the event.

Viewed together, *Blue Collar Comedy* and Lander's blog *Stuff White People Like* reveal how slippery and confusing the term "white" really is. The differences in class and culture between Lander's affluent, overeducated liberals and *Blue Collar Comedy*'s working-class southerners seem to be as big as any differences between other American ethnic groups. So what, other than skin tone, makes them a single ethnicity in our cultural imagination? Unlike other ethnic groups, there is no shared diasporic history to hold them together, nor are there present inequalities over which they can join in a common cause. Trey Parker and Matt Stone, the creators of the Comedy Central series *South Park* (1997–), explore this question by presenting a vision of white America that attempts to account for the contradictory and confusing nature of whiteness.

THE SPECTRUM OF WHITENESS IN *SOUTH PARK*

American ethnic humor, as we have seen, tends to construct whiteness in very specific ways. Most often, whiteness is presented as a homogenous, nonspecific category; these generic representations can be found most often in the works of African American humorists but also in the work of white humorists who have been influenced by black humor. In contrast, there are also a number of comic works that present whiteness in much narrower, more specific categories, such as the wealthy liberals of *Stuff White People Like* or the working-class southerners of *Blue Collar* humor. There is very little humor, however, that attempts to represent whiteness in its full spectrum. In contrast, the animated series *South Park* presents whiteness in all of its diversity, focusing at different moments on liberals and conservatives; Catholics, Protestants, and Jews; and a number of social-class positions. In doing so, it makes no attempt to present whiteness as wholly homogenous. Nonetheless, it does suggest that in spite of the numerous distinctions that can be drawn within the broad category of whiteness, there are still a number of overlaps between the various subsections of whiteness. These overlaps reflect cultural anxieties and habits of perception that may apply to white people regardless of a more specific ethnic position or regional/class affiliation.

South Park is about the comic misadventures of a group of foul-mouthed fourth graders growing up in South Park, Colorado. The series is well known for its subversive satire, which mocks numerous political and social positions, including those of marginalized groups. This has caused many critics and fans alike to view *South Park* as an "equal opportunity offender," in which all social groups and ethnicities are equally lampooned. The logic of this, for some, suggests that because the show makes fun of mainstream white Americans, it is okay for it also, equally, to make fun of homosexuals, African Americans, Asians, Muslims, Jews, and so forth. Stephen Groening, among others, does not accept this viewpoint, asserting that the show's so-called equal opportunity racism "falsely renders horizontal the real histories of domination and oppression in the United States."[21] While Groening's point is important, I think that he and others are too quick in accepting the view of *South Park* as an "equal opportunity offender." I contend that rather than making fun of all groups equally, *South Park* is primarily and explicitly about white culture and that the main target of its satire is white America in all of its manifestations.

Perhaps because of the peculiar power of whiteness to remain unseen, most critics have ignored or quickly passed over the show's representation of white identity. Lindsay Coleman, however, points out that "Parker and Stone carefully satirize white assumptions about ethnic minorities."[22] More specifically, the series presents whiteness as a specific cultural category—made up of smaller subsections—with its own particular beliefs and practices. While they acknowledge differences within white culture, Parker and Stone also suggest that whites, regardless of station, are bound together by a shared sense of privilege, belonging, and a fundamental inability to see whiteness as anything but an unmarked norm.

Parker and Stone make it clear in numerous ways that the town of South Park is a microcosm of white America. Even though most episodes focus on the children of South Park, it is apparent throughout its first fifteen seasons that the entire town (as suggested by the title) is the show's real subject. Following the tradition of Mark Twain's Hadleyburg, Sherwood Anderson's Winesburg, Ohio, and Springfield of the FOX series *The Simpsons* (*South Park*'s less subversive animated forebear), *South Park* uses the happenings of its town to critique dominant cultural attitudes in American society. On *South Park*, these dominant cultural attitudes explicitly belong to white people. Most television series with a cast of predominantly white characters seem blissfully unaware that they are representing a specifically white culture rather than just a generic American culture. Many shows make feeble gestures toward diversity by having one or two "token" ethnics in the cast—for example, the characters Deacon Palmer on *The King of Queens* (1998–2007), Gary Thorpe on *What I Like About You* (2002–2006), or Brad Williams on *Happy Endings* (2011–) are singular African Americans in an otherwise homogenous white cast. *South Park* openly mocks this tendency toward ethnic tokenism by naming South Park's one African American child Token Black. Other than Token and his family, the only other recurring African American character is the school cook, simply named Chef. To drive the joke home, Token is most often seen wearing a purple shirt with a capital T on it. As Toni Johnson-Woods notes, Token's "heavily ironic name . . . counters political correctness; he is both the show's token black kid and a reminder of tokenism on television."[23] In addition, by calling attention to the singularity of Token's blackness, Parker and Stone also highlight the rest of the town's whiteness. Token's presence does not allow viewers to see South Park's white residents as normal or raceless. With the exception of Token and Chef, all of the other regularly recurring characters on *South Park* are white. Despite this overwhelming white population, the show goes to great pains to complicate our ability to view whiteness as wholly homogenous. For example, out of the four main children (Stan Marsh, Kyle Broflovski, Eric Cartman, and Kenny McCormick), two of them are often singled out for their difference: Kyle's family is Jewish, and Kenny's family lives in poverty. For their difference, both Kyle and Kenny are continuously ridiculed by Eric Cartman, an obese sociopath who embodies the culture's most detestable traits.

The series also splits South Park's white people along political lines. In this manner, the series is able to satirize the current "culture wars" between liberals and conservatives that the twenty-four-hour news networks make so much out of. Parker and Stone suggest that both groups reap the benefits of white privilege without fully understanding it. The season 10 episode "Smug Alert," for example, focuses its satire on liberal, white environmentalists. When the citizens of South Park take up driving hybrids, they become so self-congratulatory that their egos

South Park, Colorado, is a very white town. (Credit: ©Comedy Central. Courtesy of Photofest.)

create a dense cloud of "smug" that threatens the entire country. The episode has an extended sequence in San Francisco, "the leading cause of smug," and depicts its residents as being so "full of themselves" that they enjoy the smell of their own flatulence. In its critique of privileged white liberalism, the episode is remarkably similar to the blog *Stuff White People Like.* The white liberals in this episode actively judge those who are less environmentally concerned than themselves, but they never consider that it is their material wealth that allows them to purchase hybrids and live in an expensive city such as San Francisco.

While much has been made out of the series' tendency to satirize classically liberal positions, *South Park* critiques conservative values as well.[24] Numerous episodes attack religious groups (particularly Catholics and Mormons), and Jesus himself is a recurring character who hosts a local talk show and cannot really perform miracles. Conservative politics are also a target. In the season 8 episode "Goo Backs," for example, a group of time travelers from the future arrive in South Park looking for work. At first the "Goo Backs" (traveling through time causes their bodies to be covered with a slick goo) are welcomed, but when the townspeople start losing their own jobs to the time travelers, who will work almost for nothing, riots ensue. The episode is a clear attack on the common fear of illegal Mexican immigrants taking American jobs, and most of the citizens who lose work to the "Goo Backs" fit the white redneck stereotype. Much of the episode's humor is produced from the hyperbolic repetition of "They took our jobs" in a gravelly southern drawl. Occasionally, the townspeople yell this phrase with such inarticulate passion that it comes out sounding like incoherent grunts rather than actual words. Like most *South Park* episodes, "Goo Backs" endorses moderation and suggests that while they should have compassion for the time-traveling immigrants, they can't "let everyone in." Despite this "moral" at the end of the story, most of the episode actively ridicules its "redneck" characters.

Even as it separates its white characters along political lines, *South Park* also suggests that whiteness—and more specifically, white privilege—holds its white characters together in various ways. This is most apparent in the season 7 episode "I'm a Little Bit Country." This episode aired in April 2003, shortly after the U.S. invasion of Iraq. The town (like the country) is split in their support for or protest of the invasion, and the citizens' allegiance generally follows the current stereotypes for liberal and conservative political positions. For example, supporters of the war include the hunting and gun enthusiast Uncle Jimbo and Kenny McCormick's working-class parents. The protesters, on the other hand, are generally more educated and more affluent—although not necessarily smarter—including Kyle's father Gerald Broflovski, who is a lawyer, and Stan's father Randy Marsh, who is a geologist. Throughout the episode, then, familiar stereotypes of weak, self-righteous, white liberals and ignorant, violent, working-class whites are reinforced as the two sides hurl insults at each other and break out into hyperbolic violence. The stereotypes and the political positions are simplified to comic proportions when both groups must share the same stage for a rally: the war supporters enjoy country music, whereas the protesters prefer rock and roll.

The majority of the episode thus satirizes two different and seemingly contradictory representations of whiteness. In the end, though, Parker and Stone suggest that the groups have more in common than they initially suspect. Amid their bickering, the liberals and conservatives have assigned the children the task of researching America's "founding fathers" in order to see what they would say about the war. Both groups share a reverence for America's founders, and they both agree that whatever these supposed American sages would have to say about the matter would be the last word. The liberals and conservatives both view themselves as the rightful descendants of the official white, patriarchal version of American history. As white people, both groups are able to claim the country (and its origins) as their own. The similarities are driven home again when, after Cartman travels through time to get the opinion of Benjamin Franklin, the two groups decide that they should support the war and protest it at the same time. The liberals agree that if it were not for the war-supporting conservatives, then

America would look weak to her enemies, and the conservative side admits that the protesters are needed so that America does not look like a war-mongering nation. The episode ends with the two groups singing a revised version of the Donny and Marie Osmond song "I'm a Little Bit Country, I'm a Little Bit Rock and Roll." The singing seems to signal that neither group cares that much anyway. The compromise suggests that, for both liberals and conservatives, appearances are more important than the actual realities of the war. Both groups betray their privileged position in the culture: as white, middle-class Americans, they have the luxury to debate, compromise, and sell out.

This oblivious white privilege is even more apparent in the episodes when South Park's residents are confronted with racially charged issues. *South Park*'s whites, regardless of their political or economic affiliations, all want, at least on the surface, to be progressive and open-minded toward other ethnic groups, but they continuously display ignorance, confusion, and anxiety about how to go about doing so. And very often, *South Park* suggests that white people, even if they mean no ill will and have good intentions, are wholly incapable of seeing the point of view of another ethnic group. In the season 4 episode "Chef Goes Nanners," for example, the African American Chef argues that South Park's town flag is racist and should be changed. There is no question that Chef is correct, for the flag depicts, with crude stick figures, four white people joyously hanging one black person on a gallows. While Chef receives opposition from Uncle Jimbo, who argues that the flag should remain unchanged because it is a symbol of the town's history, most of the white citizens of South Park express apathy about the status of the flag.

Much humor, however, is driven by the white townspeople's inability to see the flag's racist content. In the episode's ironic resolution, it is revealed that the white children of South Park are unable to see the flag as racist because they don't see it as four white people hanging a black person; they simply see it as four *people* hanging another *person*. For the children, race does not enter into the equation. Chef is ultimately touched by the children's color-blind attitude, and he and Jimbo agree to compromise on the flag. The new South Park flag still features a black man hanging from a gallows, but this time, the four people hanging him are white, black, red, and yellow. All of the figures, including the one hanging from the gallows, are holding hands. The flag hilariously mocks the institutionalized multiculturalism that is often signified with the clichéd image of people of all colors holding hands underneath a rainbow. The revised flag brilliantly suggests that even if some sort of idyllic ethnic harmony were to emerge in American culture, it would always be tainted by the country's legacy of violence. The townspeople are willing to accept this legacy as their own, but they are unwilling to admit that this violent history was racially motivated. They are even more unwilling to consider that the country's history of racial violence has any bearing on the present day.

The townspeople's, including Chef's, happiness with the new flag, despite its contradictory images of racial antagonism and harmony, also underscores the irony of the episode's easy resolution. While Chef might be touched by the simple innocence of children who fail to see the racial implications of the original flag, it is abundantly clear that anyone with even the most rudimentary understanding of American history should be troubled by such a flag. Herein lies the episode's primary critique of whiteness. Only white people, who typically view themselves as an unmarked universality, would be able to *not* see the racial implications of a picture of a lynching. Parker and Stone use the extreme example of the racist flag to suggest white America's ignorance of, and apathy toward, the historical conditions of nonwhite groups. The color-blind attitude of the children may at first seem admirable, but it is ultimately problematic in its attempt to wipe the slate clean and forget the country's history of racism. While the flag itself serves as a reminder of the fact that real white people actually did lynch and hang African Americans, the failure of South Park's citizens to recognize this fact is a denial of the ways in which history informs, both materially and psychologically, present circumstances.

The season 6 episode "The Death Camp of Tolerance" tackles white attitudes toward politically correct behavior even more scathingly. In this episode, the children's homosexual teacher, Mr. Garrison, decides that if he were to get fired for being homosexual that he could sue the school system and collect millions of dollars. Mr. Garrison then sets out to act "really gay" in class so that his students will complain and he will get fired. He brings in a teacher's assistant who is dressed in S&M gear and named Mr. Slave. In class, Mr. Garrison spanks Mr. Slave with a paddle, inserts a gerbil named Lemiwinks into his anus, and engages in other nonnormative sexual activities. At first, the episode seems to reinforce some of the most demeaning stereotypes of homosexual males. Mr. Garrison and Mr. Slave's antics, however, are so over the top that it is hard to take them seriously. Furthermore, it is clear that Mr. Garrison is engaging in this stereotypical behavior in an attempt to play on the culture's worst fears about homosexuality.

His plan, however, backfires: when the students complain to their parents about Mr. Garrison's "really gay" behavior in class, the parents, who are unaware of Mr. Garrison's actual antics, react with appalled disgust that their children would dare to be so "intolerant." In order to teach their children to be more politically correct, the parents take them to the Museum of Tolerance. Here, Parker and Stone begin their extended critique of white liberal guilt. At the Museum of Tolerance, there are various displays—such as "The Hall of Stereotypes" and the "Tunnel of Prejudice"—intended to educate patrons about the harmfulness of bigotry. The "Tunnel of Prejudice" is simply a dark tunnel in which disembodied voices yell various slurs at the people who pass by. The tunnel's ineffectiveness is made clear when Cartman describes it as "awesome." After the children emerge on the other side of the tunnel, the white female tour guide for the museum says, "Now you know how it feels." The supposition that a white person can understand what discrimination "feels" like simply by being called a "beaner" or a "slope" is of course ridiculous. The museum thus emerges not as a space for cultural dialogue or education, but rather as a manifestation of white anxiety and guilt and an excuse for white self-congratulation. The museum gives its white patrons the ability to feel as if they are tolerant of diverse peoples without actually having to engage with any real marginalized subjects. The moment recalls Christian Lander's critique on *Stuff White People Like:* the museum allows white people to feel good about themselves without actually having to do anything.

This point is made clear in the "Hall of Stereotypes." The hall features wax statues of various ethnic stereotypes, such as an Arab terrorist, an Asian man with a calculator, and a "covetous Jew." The patrons are all proud of their ability to recognize and dismiss each stereotype, but their self-congratulation is complicated when the wax statue of the stereotypical "sleepy Mexican" comes to life. It turns out that what the visitors thought was a statue is actually the janitor for the museum who had fallen asleep on the job. The janitor wanders off with his bucket and mop, mumbling about how sleepy he is while the museum's patrons stand uncomfortably by. The moment raises interesting questions about the relationship between representations of marginalized groups and actual marginalized subjects. On one level, the presence of an actual Mexican janitor asserts that stereotypes, no matter how much we would like to dismiss them, often have a basis in reality. But more important, it suggests that simply denying the existence of stereotypes will do little to combat the systemic and institutional conditions that force disproportionate numbers from certain groups into low-earning, menial jobs. The Museum of Tolerance itself is a great example of this: while its official rhetoric is about equality for all, it still depends on cheap labor. Later, the episode moves into even more exaggerated territory, as the Museum of Tolerance is supplanted with the Death Camp of Tolerance, a concentration camp where intolerant children are forced to create endless arts and crafts projects that display their respect for other cultures, lifestyles, and belief systems. Like the Museum of Tolerance, the Death Camp offers no education about actual alternative lifestyles; it simply asserts a blind rhetoric that ultimately reinforces ignorance rather than combating it.

White attitudes toward other cultures are treated in a similarly derisive manner in the episode "With Apologies to Jesse Jackson." As in "The Death Camp of Tolerance," politically correct behavior is represented in this episode as borderline fascist. Here, Stan's father, Randy Marsh, gets himself into trouble when he guesses "niggers" as the answer to the clue "People Who Annoy You" on the game show *Wheel of Fortune.* The actual answer was "naggers." Most of the episode is about Randy Marsh being socially ostracized after saying the word "nigger" on national television. In an ironic turn of events, everywhere Randy goes, he is taunted by people, both black and white, calling him a "nigger guy," and Randy cannot readjust back into society after the incident on television. Despite this mockery of politically correct policing, the butt of the humor, as in "Chef Goes Nanners," is still white people who are unable to comprehend the emotional and historical resonance of racist images and language. Randy eventually meets up with a group of white celebrities, such as Michael Richards and Mark Fuhrman, who have experienced similar fallout after using the N-word in public. Together, Marsh and the other "nigger guys" petition Congress to have the phrase "nigger guy" made illegal. While the moment is in conversation with various activist groups who have sought to abolish the word *nigger*, the humor is clearly directed at whites who fail to see the harm in using it—or who don't understand why black people are allowed to use it while they are not. In his explanation for why the phrase "nigger guy" should be made illegal, Randy Marsh explains that "separately the words mean nothing, but once combined, these words can form a missile of hate." In a manner similar to the townspeople's inability to see the inherent racism of the South Park flag in "Chef Goes Nanners," Randy's comment evinces a hyperbolic ignorance of and apathy toward African Americans.

Working in dialogue with Randy's story, is another plot arc featuring Randy's son Stan. Unlike Randy's storyline, which is full of irony and hyperbolic humor, Stan's is fairly straightforward. After his father becomes infamous for saying "nigger" on television, Stan attempts to placate Token, the only black child in the school, by telling him that his father's gaffe was a simple mistake. Token, however, refuses to tell Stan that everything is okay. Throughout the episode, Stan tries in various ways to convince Token that his father's use of the word was "no big deal," but Token rebuffs every attempt. In the episode's conclusion, Stan admits that there is nothing he can say because, as a white person, he will never be able to understand what it is like for an African American to hear the word. Token accepts Stan's explanation and tells him that he "finally understands." The moment of Stan's realization that white people can never really know what it is like to be another subject position is as close to irony-free as Parker and Stone ever get. Not only does this moment undermine the ridiculous antics of Stan's father in the same episode, but it also works in conversation with an episode like "The Death Camp of Tolerance," where white people believe that they can know "how it feels" simply by attending a museum. The moment between Stan and Token is important because Stan reaches his realization not through abstract means or bureaucratic nonsense, but rather—taking the route suggested by scholars like Kwame Anthony Appiah and Paul Gilroy—through a series of conversations with Token himself.

The episode that most explicitly critiques whiteness—and its attitudes toward difference—is the season 7 episode "Red Man's Greed." This episode details the attempt of a Native American tribe to buy South Park so that they can build a highway in place of the town. The new highway will give greater access to a Native American casino. Throughout the episode, Parker and Stone mock white attitudes toward the Native Americans and suggest that whites' understanding of them is a confusing mixture of racism, guilt, and anxiety. This is most apparent in the ways that the white citizens of South Park describe the Natives who are trying to displace them. In their descriptions of the Natives, the white characters continuously correct themselves and each other whenever they use the term "Indian" rather than "Native American." For example, one character refers to them as "greedy ass Indians" but then corrects himself by saying "Native Americans." This joke occurs again and again throughout the episode; the humor lies in the fact that the white people feel the need to be politically correct even while they are expressing racist ideas. This is similar to the muddled understanding of politically correct behavior that Parker and Stone mock in episodes like "The Death Camp of Tolerance" and "With Apologies to Jesse Jackson." Racist attitudes are completely acceptable as long as those attitudes are expressed using the appropriate rhetoric.

The storyline of Native Americans' taking away white people's land is of course an inversion of the story of white settlers stealing the land from natives. Throughout the episode, Parker and Stone play on this familiar narrative, generating humor by replacing the well-known tropes of Native American culture with stereotypes of white American culture. For example, when Stan explains why he and his family cannot leave South Park, he argues that "we take fish from the stream and bread them to make fish sticks, . . . [I]t is our way of life." By discussing cheap processed foods with a romantic rhetoric that is typically used to describe the "simple" lives of Native Americans, Parker and Stone defamiliarize white culture. This defamiliarization reaches its climax later in the episode. In order to drive the citizens of South Park out of town, the Natives give them all blankets that have been infected with the SARS virus, again a comic inversion of white imperialists giving smallpox-infected blankets to Native Americans. Stan is one of the only people in town who does not get sick, and his father tells him that it is up to him to find a cure. Stan's father explains, "The spirit of middle-class white people runs strong in you, Stan." In a parody of Native American initiation rituals, Stan then goes to see a wise man and breathes from a "bag of visions." This is simply an old white man who lives in a trailer park and a bag of paint thinner. Stan inhales the paint thinner fumes and successfully has a vision in which he learns the secret medicine of white culture that can help his people recover from SARS: DayQuil, Campbell's Chicken Noodle Soup, and Sprite. The moment is an excellent example of Parker and Stone's ability to make whiteness strange. From an undifferentiated white perspective, Stan's remedies are just "normal," but the episode views them through the lens of cultural customs and traditions, thus forcing viewers to understand whiteness not as an unmarked universal but—in the manner in which we typically understand native cultures—as a collection of particular habits, customs, and beliefs.

South Park and a number of other humorists discussed in this chapter succeed in representing whiteness as a distinct ethnic position rather than a universal signifier. This is an important phenomenon that illustrates the ways that multiculturalism, America's increasing diversity, and the humor of other ethnic groups have enabled some whites to see their whiteness in more complex ways. It is important to remember, though, that whiteness is still viewed, by and large, as raceless. The humorists who discuss their whiteness overtly *choose* to do so; they are not compelled to by audience expectations (as are most nonwhite humorists). Furthermore, white humorists who discuss whiteness do not necessarily make it central to their humorous productions. White stand-up comedians can develop one or two routines about whiteness and feel free to discuss whatever else they want throughout their acts. Even *South Park*, which provides the most consistent and explicit representation of whiteness in contemporary American humor, is not defined as a "white" show, and most critics pass right over its white critique. Returning to Werner Sollors's assertion that ethnic humor is a "form of boundary construction," it becomes clear that white humorists have the most elastic boundaries. Within a single work, white humorists can draw rigid lines around whiteness, and then, a moment later, collapse all boundaries and speak for everyone. As ethnic humor continues to be reshaped, we can hope that more nonwhite humorists will come to enjoy this freedom as well.

4 • IMAGINING DIVERSITY

Corporate Multiculturalism in the Children's Film and the Situation Comedy

IN THE *SOUTH PARK* episode "The Death Camp of Tolerance," discussed at length in the previous chapter, one of South Park's children, in an attempt to appease the Nazi-like enforcer of tolerance, finger paints a picture of "people of all creeds and colors holding hands underneath a rainbow." The moment—like the town flag in the earlier episode "Chef Goes Nanners"—satirizes the most simplistic notions of multiculturalism, which are often enforced in public education or in mainstream mass entertainment. This sort of facile, easily digestible multiculturalism at which Parker and Stone direct their humor reached its apex in the mid-1980s with public relations campaigns such as "Hands across America" or group fundraising songs like "We Are the World," which conflated African famine, American homelessness, and multicultural ideals. While these media-driven events succeeded in raising money for various causes, they also ignored the real struggles involved with living in a multicultural society by suggesting that cultural difference and economic disparity could be overlooked if people would simply hold hands and/or sing a song together. While contemporary works of popular culture often deal with multicultural issues in much more complex ways than this, the easy hand-holding notions of diversity still circulate in mainstream media.

The remainder of this project—rather than considering one ethnic group at a time—will explore the ways that contemporary ethnic humor deals with the broader issues of diversity and multiculturalism. This will also entail, for the most part, a turn away from works that are the creative product of one or two *auteur* humorists and toward comic productions that require prolonged collaboration from a large group of writers and performers. While the next chapter will focus on innovative and challenging representations of diversity, this chapter considers ethnic humor that, like the multicultural museum ridiculed in "Death Camp of Tolerance," grossly oversimplifies the challenges facing a multiethnic society and that often, in its representations of various ethnic groups, reverts to—and reinforces—broad, traditional ethnic stereotypes. In comparison to many of the comic performances I have considered, the ethnic humor discussed in this chapter is much less overt in its boundary construction. Rather than drawing clear lines around certain identifications, these works (like the image of people of all backgrounds holding hands beneath a rainbow) suggest that ethnic and cultural boundaries are either nonexistent or easily overcome. Despite this open, boundary-free surface, however, this humor ultimately privileges a white, middle-class, usually male perspective and draws rigid boundaries around traditional, middle-American values.

The works considered in this chapter embody, to varying degrees, Paul Gilroy's conception of a "corporate multiculturalism in which some degree of visible difference from an implicit white norm may be highly prized as a sign of timeliness, vitality, inclusivity, and global reach."[1] These works package and market the idea of diversity without really engaging with issues of ethnic conflict, inequality, or racism. In my discussion of "corporate multiculturalism" in American ethnic humor, I focus on two distinct and well-known media genres: the animated children's film and the network situation comedy. In their use of ethnic humor, I argue that both genres demonstrate Gilroy's claim that in contemporary culture, "racial alterity has acquired an important commercial value."[2] This is equally true, of course, for other works of humor discussed in this project. Any artist, regardless of ethnicity, who manages to make it in mainstream television or film has done so only with the approval of some sort of corporate entity who feels that the artist may be profitable. As Jennifer Fuller points out in her discussion of black images on cable television, "it is the exigencies of the television industry, not the inherent goodwill or good taste of cable executives and subscribers, that shape what blacks are on the TV screen."[3] Works like *Chappelle's Show* or *Curb Your Enthusiasm*, though, are both less restricted by the demands of sponsors and designed to appeal to a specific and relatively small demographic; the artists are accordingly given a certain amount of freedom. Furthermore, cable networks have figured out that if marketed well, so-called edgy material can be extremely profitable. In contrast, children's films and network sitcoms are meant to appeal to the broadest possible audience. Network sitcoms not only adhere to FCC regulations, but they must also appease large corporate sponsors who generally wish to avoid controversy. Children's films, likewise, must earn a G or PG rating and provide content that reflects traditional "family" values. The dominant messages in these works, then, are typically less subversive and are often outright regressive.[4] It follows that in their treatment of race and ethnicity, these genres typically simplify and gloss over ethnic difference in order to project a nonthreatening worldview. An analysis of these works is essential to a full understanding of ethnic humor in multiethnic America, because they represent the most conventional, widespread, and inoffensive forms that ethnic humor can take. Furthermore, these works illustrate what representations of diversity are most palatable for mass audiences; this can, in turn, tell us something of the impact of the multiculturalist project on the popular imagination.

While my emphasis here is on mainstream and "family" comedy, it should be noted that the drive to embrace multiculturalism (at least superficially) can be found in other popular formats as well. The success of recent dramatic "race" films such as *Crash* (2004) and *Gran Torino* (2008), for example, point to an increasing acceptance of diversity in American film, but the television drama, in particular, has been transformed by corporate multiculturalism. Vincent Brook brands a recent wave of network dramas such as *Lost* (2004–2010), *Heroes* (2006–2010), and *Grey's Anatomy* (2005–) as "neo-platoon" shows, a label that recalls multiethnic World War II platoon films like *Wake Island* (1942) and *Bataan* (1943).[5] According to Brook, these shows, which feature large multiethnic casts, were brought about by the "increased pervasiveness and acceptance of multiculturalism in U.S. society"[6] as well as by the 1999 "lily-white controversy," in which various media watchdog groups criticized television networks for failing to represent nonwhite characters in their programming. The formats considered in this chapter, particularly the sitcom, were influenced by similar factors. The neo-platoon shows discussed by Brook, however, represent diversity in slightly different ways than the works under discussion here. In particular, Brook explains that neo-platoon shows depend on "*egalitarian positioning* of the main characters," in which "people of color are placed on a par with or even a notch above their white cohorts, both in screen time and in social or occupational standing."[7] In contrast, the corporate multiculturalist sitcoms and children's films privilege their white characters much more explicitly. The comic works discussed here, because they depend on the devices of ethnic humor—primarily the ethnic stereotype—also tend to highlight difference more overtly. In both the neo-platoon drama and the corporate multiculturalist sitcoms and children's films, however, "ethno-racial inequalities are ignored . . . if not denied altogether."[8]

Separate contexts for each format are provided below, but the children's film and the sitcom were chosen primarily for their long, problematic history of ethnic representation and for their mainstream appeal. Both genres, which can be traced back to the 1920s and 1930s, are firmly entrenched in the American popular imagination and designed to be suitable for viewers of all ages. In their attempts to market themselves to the largest possible audience, children's films and network sitcoms are well known for ignoring or glossing over problematic social issues. While there are notable exceptions (especially in sitcoms), both genres tend to imagine a homogenous, middle-class, white audience and to adhere to traditional gender roles. And it should be noted that white males overwhelmingly hold the creative power in both network sitcoms and children's films. While both genres utilize large multiethnic casts, the performers have little creative input on the works themselves. The "diversity" of these works is therefore fairly superficial. Ethnic characters can be seen and heard, but they are still largely controlled by white people. In some ways, then, this discussion can be considered an extension of the previous chapter, but the works discussed here do not dismantle or interrogate whiteness; rather, they make overtures to an idealized multiculturalism but ultimately reinforce the idea of whiteness as an unmarked norm. While contemporary children's films and sitcoms have indeed changed drastically since the days of *Song of the South* (1946) or *Amos 'n' Andy* (1951–1953)—which both depend on broad, minstrel show stereotypes—both formats often remain tied to their generic conventions and thus serve as, at best, problematic vehicles for exploring issues of ethnic relations.

ANIMATING ETHNICITY

In recent decades, numerous critics have discussed representations of gender and ethnicity in children's films, particularly those produced by Disney. While all pop-cultural productions are thought to be purveyors of ideology, children's films—because they rely on broad moralizing and are often used as teaching tools—have long been a particular target of academic discussion. Because of the tendency of children's films to reinforce conservative and even regressive gender roles, feminist scholars have provided the most thorough critique of the genre.[9]

Considerations of ethnicity, however, also encompass a broad range of positions. Henry Giroux, for example, argues that Disney, as a corporate and cultural powerhouse, creates narratives that privilege middle-class whiteness and conservative values at the expense of all other subject positions.[10] In contrast, Douglas Brode provides a passionate defense of Disney's ethnic representations and even goes so far as to assert that Disney "is actually the most subversive among Hollywood entertainers" and "ought to be lauded for providing in the form of easily accessible popular culture the most iconoclastically envisioned alternatives to supposed social norms."[11] Most critics, including myself, lean heavily toward Giroux's side of the argument.

While it will come as no surprise to most readers that animated children's films tend to reinforce stereotypes and reproduce the dominant ideology, it is worthwhile to examine the specific ways that many recent films, produced primarily by Disney's cultural heirs DreamWorks and Pixar, are doing so. In particular, I want to focus on two phenomena that are prevalent in many recent children's films: the ethnicizing of animated nonhumans and the use of well-known celebrity voices (often comedians) to underscore the ethnic identity of animated characters. For the first phenomenon, Carmen Lugo-Lugo and Mary Bloodsworth-Lugo provide us with the useful term "racialized anthropomorphism." According to the authors, "Even though animals (and other nonhuman characters) are anthropomorphized in children's animated films, these films also, unfailingly, racialize nonhuman characters in the process. That is to say, these characters are not simply transformed into some generic 'human' (for there are no generic humans); rather, they are inscribed, for example, as White 'humans,' Black 'humans,' Asian 'humans,' or Latino 'humans.'"[12] Since nonhuman characters do not usually have the physical signifiers that mark racial difference, animators typically rely on speech patterns and well-known stereotypes to make clear a character's ethnicity. This process of racialized anthropomorphism is not a new occurrence in children's films. An infamous example is the black crows in *Dumbo* (1941) who teach the title character how to fly. The crows, the leader of whom is named Jim Crow, speak in an exaggerated African American dialect and seem to spend most of their time hanging around on tree branches (i.e., they are unemployed). Furthermore, the crows' role in the narrative—to help the unracialized and thus presumably white Dumbo—conforms to a long history of fictional African Americans helping white characters with their problems. Similar examples of racialized anthropomorphism can be found in the characters of King Louis in *The Jungle Book* (1967) or Sebastian in *The Little Mermaid* (1989).

Racialized anthropomorphism is the most fascinating when the ethnic characters are voiced by familiar celebrities, especially the voices of well-known ethnic humorists. In the past, animators have occasionally used celebrity voices for animated characters, but more often, professional voice actors were employed. After the popularity of Robin Williams's performance as the Genie in Disney's *Aladdin* (1992), however, animators began to consider the commercial potential of using celebrity voices. Three years after *Aladdin*, Tom Hanks and Tim Allen voiced the lead characters in Pixar's *Toy Story* (1995), and since then, nearly every theatrically released animated film has used celebrity voices. These voices often work intertextually with the performer's previous work, and the performer will bring to the role not only his or her voice but also a recognizable persona. Williams's wisecracking, fast-talking Genie is a perfect example, as is the voice of Woody Allen to portray a nervous and insecure ant in the film *Antz* (1998). Of course, many children who watch these films might be unaware that certain celebrity voices are being used in this way; presumably, then, the use of celebrity voices is intended to make children's films more appealing for adults.

The issues of intertextuality associated with celebrity voice-overs become even more complex when the actors, as is often the case, are well-known ethnic humorists. Surprisingly, this phenomenon in children's film has been neglected by critics. Bambi Haggins, however, provides a useful discussion of black stand-up comedians who also perform in film and television. According to Haggins, the "stand-up iteration of the comedian's voice is the articulation of the core of his or her comic persona. One must discern, however, the ways in which that voice is mobilized within a variety of media in order to understand the place of the black comic persona in American popular culture."[13] Although she does not mention children's films explicitly, Haggins's point—as well as her use of the word "voice"—is pertinent to our discussion. A large number of the African American comedians discussed by Haggins, including Eddie Murphy, Chris Rock, Whoopi Goldberg, and Wanda Sykes, have used their voices in animated films. This practice raises two important questions: How do the voices of ethnic humorists—who may, in other contexts, be quite subversive—impact the ethnic representations in children's films? And, how do children's films affect our understanding of the comic personas of their performers? The answers vary from film to film and from comedian to comedian, but more often than not, the cheery animation and sloppy moralizing of children's films serve to contain and neutralize the voices of its comic performers. The voices of the ethnic comedians are used in the simplest possible manner and thus help to reinforce stereotypes while maintaining little of their transgressive potential.

An early example of this phenomenon is the Disney blockbuster *The Lion King* (1994). Scar, the primary villain in the film, is a devious lion voiced by the English actor Jeremy Irons. Scar's villainous minions, however, are a pack of hyenas, the leaders of whom are voiced by Whoopi Goldberg and Cheech Marin. Both performers have distinctive and easily recognizable voices, and in other contexts, they have aligned themselves with progressive and/or countercultural attitudes. Here, though, they are simple thugs, and while the film takes place in the jungle, their voices, as Giroux points out, embody the accents of a "decidedly urban black or Hispanic youth."[14] The racial hierarchy is reinforced further because these urban hyenas take their orders from a lion who is coded, through his British accent and royal aspirations, as white and aristocratic. Of course, just because a stereotype is represented does not mean that it is always being reinforced. As we have seen in previous chapters, comedians like Dave Chappelle or Sacha Baron Cohen present stereotypes in a manner that ultimately challenges or deflates them. Children's films like *The Lion King*, however, transplant ethnic stereotypes into imaginary settings and thus strip them of any relevant historical or social context. This makes it difficult for viewers, especially children, to view a stereotype as a cultural construction or as a result of particular historical circumstances. The result, then, is simply to reinforce the stereotype as an essentialist trait.

More recent examples of racialized anthropomorphism are usually not as derogatory in their racial coding, and it seems that contemporary animators are more cautious about overtly ethnicizing their villains. More often, ethnicity is signified in a playful way, as the animators use familiar ethnic stereotypes in an ironic, tongue-in-cheek manner or as a knowing wink to adult viewers. This is especially true in animated features produced by DreamWorks, which follow fairly conventional storylines but also actively market themselves to older viewers by employing contemporary soundtracks, numerous pop-cultural references, and of course, familiar celebrity voice-overs. DreamWorks is most famous for the *Shrek* franchise (2001–2010), which parodies well-known children's fairy tales. *Shrek* does not rely very heavily on ethnic humor, although it does feature Eddie Murphy as the voice of a clingy, obnoxious donkey, and its sequels feature Antonio Banderas as the cat Puss in Boots, a stereotypical Latin lover. Murphy's Donkey character does not necessarily reinforce specific black stereotypes, but it does follow the tradition of representing African Americans as the comic sidekicks to white (or in this case, green) heroes. Ethnicity is more interesting in the DreamWorks productions *Bee Movie* (2007) and *Shark Tale* (2004), as well as the first two *Madagascar* films (2005 and 2008) discussed in the next section.

Bee Movie, written by and starring Jerry Seinfeld, tells the story of Barry B. Benson, a disenchanted bee who leaves his hive to seek adventures. Out in the world, he learns that humans have been stealing bees' honey for years, and he files a class-action lawsuit against humanity. The film codes the bees as Jewish in numerous ways, not the least of which is Seinfeld's ironic persona, which he brings to his portrayal of Barry. As in the sitcom *Seinfeld*, though, this Jewishness is rarely overt, but it is certainly there for anyone who is looking. Barry's parents, for example, are the overbearing, nervous sort that can be found in numerous Jewish American texts. The most explicit Jewish reference occurs when Barry confesses to his friend Adam that he has met a girl. Adam asks him first if the girl is "bee-ish" and then says, "[N]ot a wasp? Your parents will kill you!" This is probably the funniest line in the film, and it works because the wasp/WASP pun is clever and unexpected, especially in the context of an animated children's film. Nonetheless, this joke does not interrogate or explore the sociocultural phenomenon of Jewish men seeking out WASP women as a pathway to assimilation; it simply points out the stereotype in passing. This two-dimensional treatment of ethnicity is enough for most children's films, which ethnicize characters but then present that ethnicity in isolation, absent from its cultural context.

Later in the film, Barry—in keeping with the trend, discussed in chapter 2, of Jewish characters identifying with African Americans—befriends a mosquito named Mooseblood, who is voiced by African American comedian Chris Rock. As discussed in chapter 1, Rock has been one of the most successful black comedians in the mainstream media, and his persona is steeped in African American signifiers. His voice, in particular, calls upon the rhythm and cadences of African American preachers.[15] This is most true in his stand-up performances, but these patterns are evident in Rock's film performances as well. When we take into account Rock's distinctive voice and his performance history, Mooseblood is certainly coded as an African American mosquito. The characterization of

Mooseblood himself not only continues this coding, but it relies on tired black stereotypes. For example, in contrast to the beehive, which Barry explains is a "close community," Mooseblood asserts that "every mosquito is on his own." If you're a mosquito, Mooseblood exclaims, "you're in trouble! Nobody likes us." The Jewish (and thus white) bees are therefore presented as industrious community members who manufacture a useful product, whereas the black mosquitoes are homeless drifters, literally living off of the blood of other species. The film uses simple ethnic humor to reinforce a reductive racial hierarchy even as it strips that ethnic hierarchy of any historical or social context.

The DreamWorks film *Shark Tale* is much more explicit in its ethnic representations, and it is the main film discussed by Lugo-Lugo and Bloodsworth-Lugo in their discussion of racialized anthropomorphism. The film stars Will Smith as the voice of Oscar, a fish who lives on the "South Side of the reef." Oscar has dreams of making it big, but he is in debt to Sykes, a puffer fish voiced by Martin Scorsese. Sykes works for a shark named Don Lino, voiced by Robert DeNiro, and Don Lino's son Lenny (voiced by Jack Black) is a vegetarian pacifist and thus is a misfit among the other sharks. The stock character types are immediately clear: the voices of DeNiro and Scorsese (as well as two actors from *The Sopranos*) rely on the gangster stereotype of Italian American men, and Will Smith embodies the black urban smart aleck that he played on the sitcom *The Fresh Prince of Bel-Air* (1990–1996). The ethnic stereotypes are not used subtly, and *Shark Tale* seems to rub the viewer's face in them, as if transplanting ethnic caricatures onto aquatic life is the only point of the film. For example, at one point Oscar attempts to teach some dance moves to Sykes but then comments that most "white fish" cannot dance. *Shark Tale* further emphasizes this stereotypically urban black perspective by using a hip-hop soundtrack throughout and by peppering the South Side of the reef with urban motifs. The South Side, for example, is clearly in a lower socioeconomic position than the rest of the ocean. Oscar additionally works at a "whale wash," which openly refers to the African American comedy film *Car Wash* (1976).

The most surprising ethnic representations in *Shark Tale*, however, are not those presented by Oscar or the Italian-shark-gangsters but rather in Sykes's henchmen Ernie and Bernie, voiced by Doug E. Doug and Ziggy Marley. Ernie and Bernie are electric jellyfish anthropomorphized into Jamaican Rastafarians.[16] The jellyfish tentacles become dreadlocks, but they are also used as electric torture devices when Ernie and Bernie need to make debtors pay what they owe. As in *The Lion King*, the film thus uses ethnic characters to portray subservient hoodlums. The fact that they are two nearly identical jellyfish with rhyming names further strips the characters of any individuality and reinforces their representation as a two-dimensional type. What is most surprising to me is not that this stereotype is used and reinforced but the actual appearance of Ernie and Bernie. In addition to

In the DreamWorks film *Shark Tale*, two jellyfish (voiced by Doug E. Doug and Ziggy Marley) are anthropomorphized into stereotypical ethnic thugs. (Credit: © & ™DreamWorks LLC. Courtesy of Photofest.)

the dreadlocks, both characters have prominent white teeth, large round eyes, and large red mouths, which are often wide open in either a grin or a scream. While their skin coloring is blue, the rest of their representation bears an uncomfortable resemblance to the image of the happy minstrel show darky. When *Shark Tale* premiered, it initially received protests from Italian American organizations that objected to the film's use of violent gangster stereotypes. It is odd that there have not been similar protests about Ernie and Bernie.

ANIMATING DIVERSITY

The examples discussed above do not account for the entire spectrum of children's films that mix racialized anthropomorphism with celebrity voices. While films likes *Bee Movie* and *Shark Tale* represent ethnic stereotypes in the simplest possible manner, there are other films that are more complex, both in their representations of various ethnic groups and in the stories that they tell. Several contemporary children's films not only use ethnic characters but engage more explicitly with diversity or multiculturalism by working ideas of cultural and ethnic difference into the narratives themselves. The Pixar film *Cars* (2006) and the DreamWorks films *Madagascar* (2005) and *Madagascar: Escape 2 Africa* (2008) both represent more multiethnic communities than those found in most children's films. However, these multiethnic communities are represented in a confusing or stereotypical manner. Following Paul Gilroy's description of "corporate multiculturalism," *Cars* and the *Madagascar* films promote a muddled idea of intercultural dialogue without truly engaging with the struggles involved in this exchange.

Unlike DreamWorks, which depends on pop-culture references and hip soundtracks to garner audience attention, Pixar films are typically driven by pathos and often have more complex storylines. The films themselves are typically of higher quality, and nearly every Pixar film to date has received positive reviews and been profitable.[17] Pixar also is the most obvious heir to the Disney mantle of creating films that are designed to pull on the heartstrings of white, middle-class America, and nonwhite characters (anthropomorphized or not) are typically absent. The studio's flagship, for example, is the *Toy Story* franchise, which features the adventures of a group of toys who come to life whenever Andy, the child to whom they belong, is absent. Andy and his family seem to fit the white suburban ideal with the exception that a father is never seen or alluded to. The image of the strong patriarch, however, is represented through Andy's two primary toys, the cowboy Woody (voiced by Tom Hanks) and the space ranger Buzz Lightyear (voiced by Tim Allen). Both toys, as adventurers and explorers, represent the ideal of a strong white masculinity. Most Pixar films similarly ennoble masculinity and privilege white, middle-American values.[18]

Cars is no exception in this regard, but it does attempt to place its white male hero in a more multicultural environment. Rather than animals, which are the norm for most anthropomorphism, all of the characters in *Cars* are vehicles of some sort. The main character is a cocky race car named Lightning McQueen (voiced by Owen Wilson) who, on his way to an important race in California, gets sidetracked in the small, run-down town of Radiator Springs. After McQueen inadvertently ruins the main road running through Radiator Springs, the town's judge, Doc Hudson (voiced by Paul Newman), sentences McQueen to fix the road before he can leave to attend his race. Predictably, McQueen learns to love Radiator Springs, as well as a pretty female Porsche there named Sally (voiced by Bonnie Hunt), and he eventually becomes part of the community. In his future car races, the inhabitants of Radiator Springs become McQueen's pit crew. The film clearly places mainstream white characters at the center of its narrative, as McQueen (whose name alludes to movie star and amateur race car driver Steve McQueen), Doc Hudson, and Sally are all coded as white. Many of the minor characters in Radiator Springs, however, are ethnicized, and it is suggested that this ethnic diversity is part of what makes the town so idyllic.

One key difference between animated vehicles and animals is that the makes and models of cars, unlike most types of animals, often carry with them cultural signifiers. Thus when animators ethnicize a car character, they can, in addition to voice and the choice of actor, choose a particular type of vehicle that will further underscore the ethnic identity. It therefore makes sense that the main character of *Cars*, presented as white, is also a shiny, high-performance race car; this is in keeping with the film's privileging of a white perspective. The most prominent example of an ethnicized vehicle can be found in the character of Mater, a stereotypical southern "redneck." Mater eventually becomes McQueen's best friend in the film, and he is the first other car with whom McQueen makes a connection. Mater's redneck status is highlighted by the fact that he is a rusty old tow truck with two prominent buck teeth. Furthermore, he is voiced by redneck extraordinaire Larry the Cable Guy (discussed in more detail in the previous chapter), who manages to work in some of his familiar catchphrases, such as "Git-R-Done" and "That's funny right there." In addition to his voice and appearance, Mater's redneck status is driven home by his personality: he is naive, uneducated, and one of his favorite hobbies is "tractor tipping," with the tractors characterized as cows.

Other characters in Radiator Springs are depicted in a similarly stereotypical way. For example, Mexican American comic Cheech Marin provides the voice of Ramone, a purple low-rider. As with Mater, the type of car, as well as the voice, helps to highlight the ethnic identity, for low-riders are stereotypically associated with urban Latinos. Ramone is married to Flo, a classic Motorama show car who is coded as African American. Flo is voiced by the African American actress and singer Jenifer Lewis, who has long been a staple in films and television series with black casts.[19] Flo's African American identity is not quite as overt as that of the other ethnic characters, but it is still apparent through her speech patterns and the choice of Lewis to voice her. It is worth noting that the two nonwhite characters in *Cars* are thus married to each other. While this represents an interracial marriage, it also forms a couple out of the film's only two nonwhite characters, a move that could be seen to reinforce a reductive white/other binary. Other characters that are ethnically based include the Italians Luigi and Guido, voiced by Tony Shalhoub and Guido Quaroni. Luigi is an Italian-made Ferrari, and Guido is his assistant, a forklift who helps him change tires. As their names would suggest, Luigi and Guido are heavily accented Italian caricatures. The next example is not, strictly speaking, an *ethnic* type, but it should be noted that George Carlin provides the voice for Fillmore, a pastel-painted Volkswagen bus with a large peace sign on the hood. Carlin's voice and countercultural connections underscore Fillmore's identity as a stereotypical hippie/stoner.

Radiator Springs thus represents a multicultural community, and it is these "colorful" characters that eventually seduce McQueen into loving the town. We learn that, years earlier, McQueen's love interest Sally was similarly taken in by the town's charms. The ethnic diversity of Radiator Springs, however, is only surface-level. In most ways it adheres to the traditional "small-town values" that are seen in fictional and homogenous towns like Bedford Falls in *It's a Wonderful Life* (1946) or Mayberry in *The Andy Griffith Show* (1960–1968). Furthermore, the film offers no real explanation for how all of these diverse characters came to live together in the same town, and there is no evidence that their different cultural positions had ever created conflict of any kind. Rather, the hippie, the redneck, the African American, the Latino, and the Italian immigrants all live together in peaceful harmony, their only concern being how to attract more tourists to the town's businesses. I am not suggesting that such a vision, in and of itself, is inherently bad or would be damaging to children viewers. All of the ethnic characters in the film are presented as likable and productive community members, and this is surely a step above the thuggish Jamaican jellyfish of *Shark Tale*. It should be stressed, though, that this vision is a fantasy that can only be achieved by presenting these cultural types in isolation, removed from the cultural or historical circumstances that fostered them. Fillmore is a hippie because that is what he is, not because he dodged the draft, protested the Vietnam War, or has any genuine countercultural ideals.

This raises another important point about ethnic representation in *Cars*. The use of particular car types to underscore ethnic identity reinforces an essentialist and biological vision of race. The film offers little explanation as to how cars are reproduced in this society of cars, but it does seem to suggest that one's make and model will determine his or her personality traits (I'm not even trying to figure out how gender is determined). McQueen is cocky *because* he is a fast race car; Ramone speaks with a Mexican American accent *because* he is a low-rider. Mater speaks with a southern accent and likes to tip tractors *because* he is a rusty old tow truck, and so forth. In other words, each car represents an essential ethnic or cultural position. While the film may project a fantasy vision of a multicultural community, it also suggests that individual cars are at the mercy of their make and model, predetermined to act a certain way based on how they were made. It is not a far leap from here to the racist belief that genetic background will determine one's interests and aptitudes. The film's idealistic portrait of diversity is undercut by its implicit biological racism. This racism, however, remains hidden beneath the film's seemingly quaint ethnic humor.

A less essentialized but more bizarre vision of ethnicity is presented in the DreamWorks productions *Madagascar* and its first sequel *Madagascar: Escape 2 Africa*.[20] These films offer a more complex representation of diversity than *Cars*, but their multiethnic vision is ultimately muddled and downright odd. The story is about a group of New York City zoo animals (mainly a lion, a zebra, a giraffe, and a hippo) who, after a series of errors, find themselves in the African wild. In the first film, they end up on the island of Madagascar, and in the sequel, they are on a wildlife preserve on the African mainland. Both films are essentially fish-out-of-water comedies, as the pampered and urbanized zoo animals must learn how to live in the wild. This proves particularly difficult for Alex the Lion (voiced by Ben Stiller), who, in the first film, must fight against his innate urge to eat his best friend, Marty the Zebra (voiced by Chris Rock), and in the second film must find a way to prove himself to his parents and the other lions, who actually grew up in the wild. This storyline has immediate ethnic implications, raising questions about whether identity is innate or culturally constructed. The fact that these questions are raised through the return to an African homeland makes the issue particularly thorny, especially if we are reading the characters in relation to an American ethnic paradigm, which the film invites us to do in various ways. It is unclear, however, how ethnicity works in the film: for example, all of the characters, as animals indigenous to Africa, could logically be constructed as black, but the film also suggests in various ways that every species of animal is its own distinct race, although this is truer for some species than others.

One of the primary ways in which the film ethnically marks its characters is through the use of ethnic humorists to voice the various animals. The cast of the *Madagascar* films has a wide list of actors whose personas have an ethnic dimension; these include primarily the Jewish performers Ben Stiller, David Schwimmer, and Sacha Baron Cohen and African American performers Chris Rock, Cedric the Entertainer, Bernie Mac, Jada Pinkett Smith, Sherri Shepherd, and will.i.am. Not all of these performers explicitly play on their ethnic identities, however. For example, Sacha Baron Cohen voices King Julien XIII, the raucous leader of the lemurs on the island of Madagascar. There is nothing recognizably Jewish about King Julien, who speaks in a thick yet mysterious accent, which marks him as ambiguously foreign. While Ben Stiller is widely recognized as a Jewish performer, his character does not adhere to any Jewish stereotypes, and African American actors play his parents in the wild. David Schwimmer, on the other hand, capitalizes on the nervous, Jewish American persona that he is well-known for after playing Ross on the sitcom *Friends* (1994–2004). Schwimmer voices Melman, a hypochondriac giraffe who, in the New York zoo, is in constant need of medical attention for a series of psychosomatic symptoms. In the sequel, when he meets many other giraffes on the African mainland, Melman becomes the giraffes' doctor. At one point, Melman directly refers to the Jewish doctor and Jewish mother stereotypes, by exclaiming, "My mother will be so happy."

The African American performances also vary in terms of ethnic representation. The film features Bernie Mac and Cedric the Entertainer, two of the four "Original Kings of Comedy" discussed in chapter 1. Both characters voice wild animals native to Africa—a lion and an aye-aye, respectively—but their characterization does not particularly depend on African American codes. Also, neither performer has an overly distinct or familiar voice that would cause most viewers to characterize them as black. The same could be said of Jada Pinkett Smith's character, a female hippo named Gloria. In the first film, there is nothing in particular that would code Gloria as black. In the sequel, however, Gloria meets a score of other hippos in the wild, most of whom *are* characterized as black. In particular, Gloria has a brief flirtation with a male hippo named Moto-Moto, voiced by the singer will.i.am. Moto-Moto's voice is more stereotypically African American, and he makes much out of Gloria's large body, repeatedly telling her that she is "chunky." The moment depends on the often-celebrated ideal of curvaceous black women, and the African American themes are driven home by an R&B soundtrack that plays during Gloria and Moto-Moto's brief romantic scene.

Chris Rock's zebra is the most interesting in relation to ethnicity, not only because of Marty's ethnic characterization but also because of the way he drives the storyline of the two films. As I explained in the above discussion of *Bee Movie*, Chris Rock's voice (both in terms of the voice itself and the persona that is attached to it) is clearly coded as black. As a character, Marty the zebra does not really reinforce black stereotypes, although he does occasionally speak in an urban vernacular. For example, in the first film, after they arrive on the island of Madagascar, Marty explains that the place is "off the chiz-ain." And in the sequel, in which Rock voices not only Marty but *all* of the zebras, Marty and the other zebras agree that running is "crack-a-lackin." Granted, these examples are phrases that mainstream white culture has largely appropriated and commodified, but it should be pointed out that the other main characters in the *Madagascar* films do not talk like this; the language choice thus underscores Marty's black identity and helps to further connect the character to Rock's persona.

More important, though, is the role that Marty plays in the films' narrative. Even though Alex the Lion is the official protagonist, Marty is the catalyst for the plot and for the group's return to Africa. In the first film, Marty is discontented with his life as a zoo animal, and he dreams of being free. This dream is tied up with confusion over his identity, for Marty laments that he does not even know if he is "black with white stripes" or "white with black stripes." This might, on the surface, be a simple kids' joke about a zebra, but it has an undeniable ethnic dimension when that zebra has dreams of moving to Africa and is voiced by Chris Rock. Later in the film, after they are somewhat at home in the wild, Marty counts his stripes and finds that he has thirty black and twenty-nine white. He is thus black with white stripes after all. Therefore, while all four of the main characters are indigenous to Africa (rather than New York City), it is only Marty, the animal coded the most explicitly as black, who has the innate urge to return to the wild. In case this point is not apparent enough, in the sequel, when the animals finally arrive on the African mainland and find animals of their own kind, Marty exclaims that "it's like *Roots*!"

The sequel, however, also provides Marty with a new identity crisis. For when he meets the other zebras, he finds that they all have the exact same voice and the same opinions that he does. Marty's friends initially cannot even distinguish him from the other zebras. If we were to view zebras as a distinct "race," which I think is a viable reading of the film, then this aspect reinforces, as in *Cars*, the racist idea of biology determining our lives and personalities. In *Madagascar*, though, this is really only true of the character who is represented the most overtly as African American. Marty has a dilemma as to how he can remain a part of the collective zebra community and still maintain his individuality. This dilemma, of course, is one that is widely discussed by ethnic theorists, but in the film, it is couched within a biological vision of ethnic determinism.

In the sequel, the other animals experience similar struggles, although less overtly than Marty. Gloria is at first enamored with, but eventually distances herself from, the other hippos. Melman finds that all of the giraffes are hypochondriacs (albeit less knowledgeable about specific ailments), and the main plot of the film is built around Alex's attempt to prove himself to the other lions, especially his parents. It becomes clear, throughout the film, that while each animal has undeniable ties to his or her species, he or she must also remain part of their makeshift zoo community. Marty is an individual because his time in the zoo and his friendship with the other animals has made him different from the other zebras (even though he still looks and sounds exactly like the rest of them). While identity is defined in racist terms, the zoo animals emerge as an odd sort of multiethnic community formed by individual experience. This community is significantly more complex than the one presented in *Cars*, for it has a clearer history and there is a concrete reason for why the animals are all together. Furthermore, it suggests that personal experience and intercultural (or interspecies) dialogue can reshape the boundaries of identity.

The film's haphazard ethnic jokes and anthropomorphized animals, however, make this multiethnic community more confusing than idyllic. A case in point is the ending of the second film, in which Melman the giraffe and Gloria the hippo become romantically involved. Melman's love for Gloria is apparent to viewers from early in the first film, but Gloria does not reciprocate until after her failed romance with Moto-Moto. Viewed through the ethnic coding that the film provides, we can see this romance as one between a Jewish man and an African American woman—a relationship that has particular resonance with the reading of Jewish American identity that I discuss in chapter 2. The ethnic dimension is reinforced when the king of the lions asserts, while Melman and Gloria are onscreen, that "love transcends all differences." It turns out, oddly enough, that the king is actually speaking of the love between one of the penguins and a doll, but the shot is set up in such a way that it applies equally to Melman and Gloria. In a way, this hippo/giraffe romance could be seen as a positive representation of intercultural dialogue. Logic, however, intrudes on this reading. How, for example, will this relationship be consummated? For it seems very problematic to equate interracial romance with interspecies romance. Perhaps I am asking too much of a children's film, but even a child knows that giraffes and hippos do not have romantic relationships. So if this inter-animal romance is strictly imaginary, then why should we take the interracial romance that it symbolizes as anything but a fantasy as well? These questions illustrate one of the many problems inherent in the process of racialized anthropomorphism: rather than creating a vehicle through which ethnic relations can be explored, it muddies the waters and creates considerable confusion. Rather than constructing or destabilizing ethnic boundaries, animated films build a confusing maze of ethnic representation and then tell us that ethnic identity has no meaning as long as we agree to get along. The contemporary network sitcom works in much the same way.

DIVERSITY AND THE SITUATION COMEDY

Not very long ago, the thirty-minute network situation comedy was *the* most mainstream American art form. In the early years of television, there were only a handful of channels to choose from, and every major network aired sitcoms, which were intended to appeal to the broadest possible audience. The popularity of cable television beginning in the 1980s only added to this fact, as many cable stations aired reruns of sitcoms at all hours of the day. In a 1985 essay on the sitcom, Lawrence Mintz asserts that "television is the most powerful communication medium of our popular culture, and over the years situation comedy has consistently been the dominant genre."[21] Since Mintz's writing, the cultural power of the sitcom has undoubtedly slipped, and some critics have even gone so far as to announce that the sitcom is either dead or dying.[22] Indeed, cable networks almost all air original programming and thus depend less and less on reruns, and the rise of reality television and the increasing popularity of *CSI / Law & Order*–style police procedurals have left less time in the network schedule for sitcoms. Nevertheless, while sitcoms are not as ubiquitous as they once were, one could not channel-surf for very long without finding one, and all four major networks still regularly air sitcoms.[23] More specifically, the situation comedy still remains a dominant (if not *the* dominant) vehicle for mainstream humor. And in terms of ethnic representation, the sitcom (like the children's film) typically sidesteps or ignores issues of ethnic conflict or inequality.

This section focuses specifically on the network sitcom, those airing on one of the "Big Four" networks: ABC, CBS, Fox, or NBC. Sitcoms on these channels reach the largest audience share and thus represent the most mainstream iteration of the sitcom genre. It should be noted, however, that many much more progressive and controversial works are often considered sitcoms. For example, a handful of the works discussed in previous chapters—*The Sarah Silverman Program, Curb Your Enthusiasm,* and *South Park*—are considered sitcoms. These works, however, overtly parody or work against the conventions of the genre, and they all appear on cable networks and thus are designed to appeal to a narrower and more specific demographic. Cable series also do not have to placate sponsors to the same degree. Other recent cable series that subvert sitcom conventions include *It's Always Sunny in Philadelphia* (2005–), *Louie* (2010–), and *Weeds* (2005–), discussed in the following chapter. Occasionally, network sitcoms challenge the genre, such as the critically acclaimed but ratings-impaired *Arrested Development* (2003–2006) and the long-running animated sitcoms *The Simpsons* (1989–) and *Family Guy* (1999–), all of which air or aired on Fox.[24] Most network sitcoms, however, remain, in David Marc's words, an "art of the middle."[25]

The history of the sitcom displays the genre's uneasy relationship with race and ethnicity. Marc argues that the sitcom is a "representational art committed to harmony and consensus," so it therefore makes sense that issues of racism would typically be ignored or easily resolved within the thirty-minute story arc.[26] In the late 1940s and early 1950s, there were a handful of ethnic sitcoms, like the African American–focused *Amos 'n' Andy* and *Beulah* (1950–1952) or *The Goldbergs* (1949–1956), about a Jewish immigrant family.[27] These shows reinforced ethnic stereotypes, but, more important, they sidestepped issues of ethnic conflict. As Mintz asserts, early ethnic sitcoms "tend to portray minority cultures as quaint, amusing, but not essentially different from 'mainstream' America."[28] Throughout the 1970s and 1980s, there were a greater number of shows that featured ethnic, especially African American, characters. In particular, the 1970s offered popular Norman Lear sitcoms like *Sanford and Son* (1972–1977) and *Good Times* (1974–1979), and the 1980s saw the massively popular *The Cosby Show* (1984–1992). Herman Gray, in his important work, *Watching Race*, outlines three types of African American sitcoms during these decades. The first are "assimilationist" shows, which, according to Gray, "treat the social and political issues of black presence in particular and racism in general as individual problems. . . . Such programs consistently erase the histories of conquest, slavery, isolation, and power inequalities, conflicts, and struggles for justice and equality that are central features of U.S. society."[29] Examples of assimilationist programs include the integrationist fantasy *Julia* (1968–1971) and scores of other shows that have primarily white casts yet occasionally feature a "token" African American. The second model that Gray provides is the "pluralist" show, which maintains a "separate-but-equal" ideology. For Gray, shows like *Family Matters* (1989–1997), *The Jeffersons* (1975–1985), or *That's My Mama* (1974–1975) represent isolated black worlds that "depend on the logic of a cultural pluralism that requires a homogenous, totalizing blackness."[30] The final model, and the one that he sees as the most productive, Gray calls "multiculturalist." Programs such as *Frank's Place* (1987–1988), *Roc* (1991–1994), and *A Different World* (1987–1993) contain complex and contradictory representations of blackness and "position viewers . . . to participate in black experiences from multiple subject positions."[31]

Gray's distinctions still remain useful in considering contemporary television shows. We should notice, however, that the programs that Gray labels as "multiculturalist" are still primarily about black culture; they just represent black culture in a more complex way. Gray does not mention any shows that are genuinely multiethnic (featuring a cast of characters from a wider array of ethnic groups) because shows like this did not exist until recently. The time is ripe, though, for broadening the playing field and discussing works with casts that represent more than just one or two ethnic groups at a time. When we widen our gaze, many of the same types of shows emerge, just with different ethnicities. For example, in a number of recent series that Gray would most likely label as "assimilationist," such as *Parks and Recreation* (2009–) or *The Big Bang Theory* (2007–), the "token black" character has been replaced with or supplemented by a "token Asian" who fills a similar role. Along similar lines, *George Lopez* (2002–2007) represents a pluralist sitcom that focuses on a Latino family.

In the contemporary television landscape, we can, however, locate a slightly different type of sitcom that, like *Cars* and the *Madagascar* films, capitalizes on the idea of ethnic diversity but does so in a way that ultimately simplifies it and privileges a white, middle-class point of view. We might label this type of show "corporate multiculturalist," and the most prominent examples include *Modern Family* (2009–), *Community* (2009–), and the American version of *The Office* (2005–), although *Scrubs* (2001–2010), *30 Rock* (2006–), and *Outsourced* (2010) also fit this model to a certain extent. With the exception of *Modern Family* and the last two seasons of *Scrubs,* all of these shows air(ed) on NBC, whose slogan since 2009 has been "More Colorful." The slogan, while ostensibly referring to the network's multicolored peacock logo, demonstrates NBC's conscious attempt to diversify its programming and to brand itself as multicultural. Despite this attempt, most of these sitcoms are similar to the programs that Gray defines as "assimilationist" in that they gloss over issues of oppression and systemic inequality. They are different, however, in that they demonstrate an awareness of the increasing complexity of the American ethnic demographic, and they openly engage with issues that are raised by the multiculturalist movement, such as the institutional push for diversity and the concept of "politically correct" language and behavior.

At first, many contemporary network sitcoms may appear to be drastically different from the sitcoms of the past. The staged, multi-camera sitcoms with intrusive laugh tracks have largely been replaced by single-camera shows with higher production values.[32] Hit series of the 1990s, like *Seinfeld* (1989–1998) and *Friends,* which are still popular in syndication, look and feel dated when compared with a shinier, single-camera series like *30 Rock.*[33] Furthermore, characters in recent sitcoms rarely have corny catchphrases, and the humor is more sophisticated and ironic. Overall, I would argue that sitcoms today are better, both in their willingness to address traditionally taboo topics and in their ability to generate humor. Nonetheless, if we look closely at many contemporary sitcoms, we can see that, despite the increased sophistication of their storylines, production, and humor, they are still tied to their generic conventions and ultimately project a fantasy world in which problems are easily solved and diverse characters coexist in a rarely disrupted harmony.

A case in point is the ABC sitcom *Modern Family*, which is filmed in a single-camera mockumentary style that allows characters to talk directly to the camera. The series has earned high ratings (for a sitcom) and numerous critical accolades. As its title suggests, *Modern Family* is an attempt to represent the ways in which "family" is being redefined in contemporary American culture. In this light, the series is not really so modern; it follows a long line of sitcoms that focus on non-traditional family arrangements: *My Three Sons* (1960–1972), *The Brady Bunch* (1969–1974), *Diff'rent Strokes* (1978–1986), *Webster* (1983–1987), *Kate and Allie* (1984–1989), *My Sister Sam* (1986–1988), *My Two Dads* (1987–1990), and *Full House* (1987–1995), among others, have all focused on "different" types of families. What all of these shows have in common is that despite their surface differences from the old-fashioned nuclear family, traditional family values are still reinforced in every episode. Minor problems come up; kids and/or parents learn minor life lessons, and at the end of the day, the notion that family and the home are the most important aspects of life is reinforced again and again. Moreover, the majority of these shows, like most sitcoms in general, privilege a white, middle-class perspective and adhere to traditional gender roles. Different lifestyles are celebrated, as long as their difference is contained in a palatable white, middle-class package. While it is hipper and more stylized than the series mentioned above, *Modern Family* is no different in this respect. The series foregrounds differences in ethnicity and sexual orientation but almost always shifts the focus away from these differences in order to reinforce traditional family values.

The series focuses on three separate family units that interlock to form one larger, extended family. The first third of this extended family consists of Jay Pritchett, a wealthy older white man who, after splitting with his first wife, remarried a much younger Colombian immigrant, Gloria Pritchett. Gloria has an adolescent son, Manny Delgado, from a previous marriage. The second family consists of Jay's homosexual son, Mitchell; Mitchell's partner, Cameron Tucker; and their adopted Vietnamese daughter, Lily Tucker Pritchett. The third and most traditional family consists of Jay's daughter, Claire; her husband, Phil Dunphy, and their three children, Haley, Alex, and Luke. Most episodes give each family unit its own storyline, although they usually interlock either thematically or at key plot points. Despite the diversity of this extended family, the narrative typically privileges the more traditional Dunphy household over the other two.

This narrative focus on the Dunphy home is reinforced by the episode titles, which usually refer to the dominant storyline. Often, this principal storyline involves two or all three of the family units, but of the first forty-two episodes, twelve titles refer explicitly to a main plotline that involves only the Dunphys. Four titles refer exclusively to Mitchell and Cameron's plot, and three refer to Jay, Gloria, and Manny. This emphasis on the Dunphys reinforces the series's tendency to privilege the traditional white, middle-class point of view. Traditional gender roles are also reinforced, as Phil is the sole provider for the family, and Claire is a stay-at-home mom.

While the sitcom genre is well-known for representing nontraditional (yet traditional) families that have been formed by divorce, adoption, or the death of a parent, *Modern Family* adds interethnic marriage and homosexuality into the mix. The series provides positive representations of its homosexual parents and its interethnic/May-December marriage and has received critical acclaim for its diversity. It does rely, however, on fairly broad and familiar stereotypes. Both Mitchell and Cameron, for example, embody the contemporary stereotypes of gay men, both in their mannerisms and speech patterns and in their hobbies. They both, for instance, enjoy decorating and musical theater. Likewise, Gloria Pritchett is a sort of voluptuous female incarnation of Ricky Ricardo from *I Love Lucy* (1951–1957), and the punch lines of many jokes are made at the expense of her loud voice and thick Colombian accent. While these stereotypes should be acknowledged, they are not necessarily harmful. Mitchell, Cameron, and Gloria, I would argue, all have sufficient character depth and individuality as to ensure that these stereotypes do not define them.

There are occasional moments on *Modern Family* that use humor to explore more complex issues of interethnic dialogue. For example, the first season's Christmas episode, "Undeck the Halls," features a conflict between Jay, Manny, and Gloria over how to celebrate Christmas. Jay wants to adhere to the same American traditions that he used when his own children were young, and Manny and Gloria hope to integrate Colombian traditions (such as fireworks and practical jokes) into the Christmas celebrations. Early in the episode, Jay is dismissive of the Colombian traditions, saying, "As you can tell from the absence of goats in the street, we are not in Colombia." By the end of the episode, though, Jay comes around, buys fireworks for his family, and happily celebrates Christmas as they do in Colombia. The episode adheres to the sitcom convention of easily solving the problem within the thirty-minute story arc, and its ending is a bit sentimental. "Undeck the Halls," however, is more complex than most prime-time network comedy. The episode acknowledges the possibility of interethnic conflict and posits a fluid vision of cultural exchange, in which influence moves both ways. The nonwhite characters do not blindly assimilate into mainstream American culture but have a part in shaping the way culture is practiced.

Most episodes of *Modern Family*, however, suggest that differences in ethnicity and sexual orientation can (and should) be easily absorbed into the dominant cultural framework. For example, in the season 1 episode "Run for Your Wife," Gloria's son (and Jay's stepson) Manny wants to wear a poncho on the first day of fifth grade in order to display his Colombian heritage. Jay, who tells Manny that his poncho looks "like an old Christmas tree skirt," is sure that the poncho will only embarrass him in front of his classmates. Gloria is at first proud of Manny, but when she learns that Manny also plans on playing the pan flute for his peers, she comes around to Jay's side and laments that these displays of heritage will cause Manny to "die a virgin." Jay "accidentally" breaks the pan flute in order to save Manny from being socially ostracized. The fact that Manny wanted to wear these things at school in the first place feels fairly far-fetched, and I have a strong suspicion that even in Colombia the kids do not wear ponchos to school and rarely play the pan flute for their classmates. It is a remarkably simplistic way of dealing with cultural assimilation: the episode presents extreme and stereotypical signifiers of Colombian heritage and then systematically discards them so that Manny will be more likely to fit in. Assimilation is easy; just don't wear a poncho.

And things are even easier for the gay parents raising an adopted Vietnamese daughter. In the pilot episode, both Mitchell and Cameron are on the defensive, expecting to be judged for their alternative family structure. When a woman makes a comment about the little baby with the "cream puffs," Mitchell assumes that the term "cream puffs" is referring to Cameron and himself, and he makes an impassioned speech about her intolerance. It turns out, though, that Lily had literally been eating cream puffs. Mitchell is forced to apologize. A similar scenario occurs in the very next episode, titled "The Bicycle Thief." Here, Mitchell is concerned that he and Cameron will be judged by the other parents at their play group, and he urges Cameron to not act demonstrably gay. He is put at ease, however, when another, and more flamboyant, gay couple arrives at the play group. And throughout the series, Mitchell and Cameron point out Jay's uneasiness with their relationship, but in episode after episode, Jay surprises them by acting in an accepting and open-minded manner. There is certainly nothing wrong with representations of gay parents who are accepted by their family and community, but all of these scenarios suggest, again and again, that homophobia *only* exists in the minds of the gay characters.

The season 2 episode "Unplugged" most explicitly iterates the series's vision of multiculturalism. Here, Cameron and Mitchell are trying to get Lily enrolled in a preschool. They believe that because Lily is a nonwhite child adopted by a gay couple, that the most elite schools will want to enroll her in order to make their student body more diverse. At the interview, however, Mitchell and Cameron learn that Lily is competing for a spot with an African American child who is adopted by an interracial lesbian couple. To top it off, one of the lesbian parents is also in a wheelchair. Confronted with a family that is more diverse than his own, Cameron tries to convince the admissions director that he is a Native American in order to up the ante. Cameron's impersonation is rife with stereotypes of Native Americans and only succeeds in offending the director. There is genuine humor to be found in the competition between two families over who has the greater claim to the much-sought after mantle of "diversity." But despite this humor, the episode suggests that difference from a heterosexual, white norm is a privilege without any struggle. The lesbian woman's wheelchair is a commodity rather than a handicap. On the surface, the episode makes fun of this notion, but if we look at the series as a whole, it becomes clear that the commoditization of difference is what *Modern Family* is all about. The series never confronts the issues of racism or homophobia directly; it imagines a world without inequality and uses its difference so that it can be "modern."

The popular NBC mockumentary series *The Office*—an American remake of the critically acclaimed British sitcom—presents diversity in the workplace in a very similar way. *The Office* is one of the latest in a long line of workplace sitcoms, including *The Mary Tyler Moore Show* (1970–1977), *Taxi* (1978–1982), and *Cheers* (1982–1993), that present the workplace as a sort of pseudo or replacement family. While most workplace sitcoms of the past have had a fairly homogenous cast, *The Office* is deliberately multicultural. As Jeffrey Griffin points out, one of the key changes made in adapting the series from a British to an American context was the diversification of the office workers in order to more accurately represent the U.S. demographic.[34] The regular recurring cast of *The Office* includes two African American characters, an Indian American, and a Mexican American. Despite this multiethnic casting, however, *The Office* clearly privileges a white perspective. The storylines typically revolve around the misadventures of office boss Michael Scott, the love story between Jim and Pam, the love triangle between Dwight, Andy, and Angela, or—in later seasons—the love triangle between Andy, Gabe, and Erin. All of these characters are white, and the ethnic characters are usually relegated to the sidelines with minor plotlines and little development. There are occasional episodes that focus more explicitly on the ethnic characters' cultural backgrounds. In the season 3 episode "Diwali," for example, all of the office workers attend a Hindu Diwali celebration at the behest of Kelly Kapoor, the office's Indian American customer service representative. The episode, which was written by Mindy Kaling, the actress who plays Kelly, effectively and respectfully portrays the holiday, but even here, the celebration mainly serves as a backdrop for the plot developments of the white characters.

To its credit, though, *The Office* deliberately writes its ethnic characters against ethnic stereotypes. Kelly fits the mold of a materialistic Valley Girl much better than any of the stereotypes associated with Asian Americans. Stanley, an African American salesman, grew up in a small town, sends his daughter to a Catholic school, and is very bad at basketball. And Oscar, a Mexican American accountant, is well educated and homosexual. The show often flaunts this avoidance of ethnic stereotypes and turns it into a joke of its own. For example, in the season 7 episode "China," Oscar annoys his coworkers by correcting many of their comments. Later, Jim remarks that Oscar "really does fit that old stereotype of the smug gay Mexican." The joke forces viewers to recognize how different Oscar is from the majority of Latino representations in the media; at the same time, though, it also goes to show how stereotypes, even in their absence, are an essential building block of ethnic humor.

The main point of the ethnic cast of *The Office,* other than being a gesture toward multicultural ideals, seems to be to provide fodder for the ignorant and insensitive comments of their boss Michael. Michael sees himself as hip, progressive, and open-minded, but in nearly every episode he reveals himself to be woefully uneducated and inclined toward racist modes of thought. This is especially true in the early seasons before Michael's love life began to take center stage in the narrative. The most overt example is the second episode of season 1, titled "Diversity Day," which is the first episode not to use material adapted from the British version. In this episode, an African American corporate consultant named Mr. Brown is sent to the office to put the staff through a diversity seminar. It is revealed, though, that the real reason Mr. Brown is there is due to complaints made by employees about Michael's performance of an obscene Chris Rock routine for the staff. (The routine is "Niggas vs. Black People," discussed briefly in chapter 1.) The episode consists of an endless stream of occasions in which Michael horrifies Mr. Brown and the staff with ignorant comments. Michael cannot, for example, understand why the same routine can be funny when it is performed by Chris Rock and offensive when performed by a white man.

After Mr. Brown leaves, Michael decides to lead his own diversity seminar. This includes an attempt to create a dialogue with the office staff about their ethnic backgrounds; of course, Michael repeatedly displays his ignorance. He asks Oscar if there is a term to describe him that would be less offensive than "Mexican," which, according to Michael, has "certain connotations." Similarly, he expresses his desire to have a multiethnic meal, complete with "colored greens." When Stanley corrects him with the proper term, "collard greens," Michael expresses disbelief, saying, "They're not called collard people. That's offensive." In these moments, Michael is the sole butt of the humor; unlike, for example, the social awkwardness of Larry David on *Curb Your Enthusiasm* (discussed in chapter 2), Michael's social transgressions do not challenge the viewer to see unwritten social rules from a new perspective or to rethink our understanding of "political correctness." Rather, his ignorance presents an extreme example that would likely get a real office manager fired and would probably make most viewers feel safely up-to-date in their own ideas about ethnicity.

Michael's insensitivity reaches its climax when he compels the office staff to play a game in which everyone tapes a label to his or her head with the name of an ethnic position written on it. They are then supposed to treat each other as if they were the ethnicity on the card; eventually, staff members should figure out their own card's ethnicity based on the way others treat them. The majority of the office staff attempt to behave in the most politically correct manner possible. For example, when Pam is conversing with a white coworker whose card reads "Asian," she first says, "I like your food." When this does not work, she says, "based on stereotypes that are completely untrue, you might not be the best driver." Michael, however, does not want this sort of politically correct behavior; rather, he wants the staff to treat each other like stereotypes. He demonstrates on the Indian American Kelly (who is not aware of the game and has no card taped to her head) by speaking to her in an exaggerated Indian accent and pretending to be a convenience store worker. When Kelly inevitably slaps him, he tries to hide his embarrassment by saying, "Now *she* knows what it feels like to be a minority." The ridiculousness of this comment speaks for itself. The slap proves cathartic, though, for Michael is put in his place, and the unacceptability of his actions is made clear.

The Office in general—and "Diversity Day" in particular—actively engage with the increased rhetoric surrounding diversity and politically correct behavior in the workplace and the corporate world. Many of the show's viewers have probably had to attend similar, albeit less outrageous, diversity seminars themselves. A point that is made clear again and again throughout the episode and the series, though, is that the office would have little or no problems with its multiethnic staff if it were not for the singular insensitivity of Michael Scott (and occasionally Dwight Schrute). And even this critique of racism is ameliorated by the fact that Michael really does seem to mean well. In this manner, *The Office* adheres to the traditional sitcom: as Marc explains, "racism [in the sitcom] is shown to survive only as a pitiable character flaw of the unhip and the unhappy."[35] Issues of difference that really do affect the office workplace (affirmative action policies, equal pay, or glass ceilings for women and minorities) are not addressed. If we could only educate the Michael Scotts of the world, *The Office* suggests, then living in a diverse society will be a piece of cake.

Another idyllic representation of difference can be found in the NBC series *Community*. While the ratings for this series have been lukewarm, *Community* occupies a prominent position on American television, airing on Thursday nights at 8:00 P.M. ET, a slot once held by long-running, highly successful, yet ethnically homogenous sitcoms like *Friends* and *The Cosby Show. Community* is about a diverse collection of misfit students who form a study group (their own community) at a Denver city college. The central character, Jeff Winger, is a handsome, smooth-talking white lawyer who is attending classes because the bar association learned that his undergraduate degree was from an unaccredited institution. However, the other main characters—including two unstereotypical African Americans, a Palestinian American, and a Jewish American, as well as two other Caucasians—are given plenty of screen-time and narrative space to develop. In particular, Abed Nadir, a Palestinian American film student and pop-culture expert, drives much the show's humor. There are also prominent supporting characters who contribute to the multiethnic cast, such as Señor Chang, the students' Chinese American Spanish teacher who eventually becomes a student himself. While in many ways *Community* is a traditional sitcom, dealing with a group of friends who help each other out of their various problems, in other ways it is quite innovative, building its jokes on often obscure pop-culture references and devoting entire episodes to alternative methods of storytelling, such as the season 2 episode "Abed's Uncontrollable Christmas," which is shot entirely in stop-motion animation.

The innovative techniques, however, do not transfer to the show's treatment of ethnic relations. Rather, most episodes gloss over the drastically different backgrounds of their characters; the multiethnic community is thus very similar to the uncontextualized harmony of Radiator Spring in *Cars* (discussed above). This is reinforced by the show's seemingly muddled understanding of its characters' ethnic identity. Abed, for example, states in the first episode that he is Palestinian American, but the American-born actor who plays him is from Indian and Polish descent, and the actor who plays his father is Pakistani American. Additionally, when Abed's father speaks English, his accent sounds more Pakistani than Arab, and when Abed and his father speak to each other, they use formal Arabic rather than the actual Palestinian dialect.[36] To make matters more confusing, other characters playfully refer to Abed as "Slumdog," referencing the 2008 India-based film *Slumdog Millionaire*. Generous viewers may interpret this confusion as a satirical commentary on American culture's habit of conflating South Asian and Middle Eastern cultures, and cynical viewers may read it as simple carelessness on the part of the show's writers. Either way, ethnic specificity is clearly not a primary goal of the show's creators.

Nevertheless, *Community* does offer occasional moments of sophisticated intercultural dialogue that is rarely, if ever, seen on network television. Ultimately, however, these moments of ethnic conflict revert back to the easy fix of sitcom convention. The episode "Comparative Religion," for example, highlights the struggles of multiculturalism even as it mocks "politically correct" approaches to it. Like the *Modern Family* episode "Undeck the Halls," "Comparative Religion" explores how Christmas should be celebrated by

The diverse cast of NBC's *Community* presents an idyllic vision of multiethnic America. (Credit: ©NBC. Courtesy of Photofest.)

people with different cultural backgrounds. The episode begins when Shirley, an African American and a devout Christian, attempts to coerce the group into celebrating Christmas by wearing bracelets with *WWBJD?* (What Would Baby Jesus Do?) inscribed on them. None of the other group members, however, celebrate Christmas: the group is made up of a Jew, a Muslim, a Jehovah's Witness, an atheist, an agnostic, and a member of some sort of fictional neo-Buddhist cult. While the episode focuses on religion rather than ethnicity, the characters' religious differences clearly underscore their ethnic and cultural differences as well.

As the episode progresses, the characters struggle to maintain their group solidarity without alienating each other. Shirley plans an "all-inclusive" Christmas party, which involves bizarre holiday conflations like hanging a menorah on a Christmas tree, but the party is threatened when half of the group wants to see Jeff fight a bully in the parking lot. Eventually, the entire study group puts their differences aside and comes to Jeff's aid in fighting the bully and his friends. After a comic *West Side Story*–style rumble, the community gathers again for their multicultural Christmas party. At the episode's end, Shirley sings the group a nondenominational revision of "Silent Night":

Sensible night; appropriate night
Snow on ground, left and right
Round yon purchase of decorative things
Tolerant rewrite of carols to sing
Function with relative ease
Function with relative ease.

The song, and the episode in general, provide a gentle mockery of politically correct behavior and engages with seasonal media debates over the so-called war on Christmas. However, it also rewrites the reality of the debates over Christmas celebrations, for only one character out of seven actually celebrates Christmas. Therefore, the episode makes the debate about individuals with different belief systems rather than about a dominant cultural group using its religious celebration to control the national discourse. On the surface, the episode may appear to resemble the sort of cosmopolitan conversation between individuals encouraged by critics like Kwame Anthony Appiah. But when the conversation ignores the existence of actual inequalities, it becomes simple fantasy, and ethnic conflict appears to be a much smaller issue. The characters on *Community* get over their initial disagreement very easily; they simply decide to ignore their differences for the sake of tolerance and getting along.

The works discussed in this chapter are remarkable in that they manage to be old-fashioned in new ways. The children's film, which has long been a bastion of comfortable mainstream values, manages to appropriate the voices of familiar yet often subversive ethnic humorists in order to reinforce an idyllic vision of ethnic harmony. And the network sitcom, in contrast to edgier cable fare, is well known for avoiding any sort of in-depth exploration into significant social issues; in recent years it has merely transferred its simplistic version of difference into a hipper, more ironic and stylishly sophisticated package. The works discussed here are not necessarily bad or mean-spirited, and they often succeed in being funny and entertaining, but they are simply tied to their genres and therefore do what they have always done. Despite their inability to transcend their generic conventions, both formats display a remarkable awareness of the changes going on in the American ethnic demographic and in conversations about it. But as products intended to appeal the widest possible audience, children's films and sitcoms make issues of multiculturalism and diversity as palatable as possible. If it is handled in the right way, diversity clearly sells. These simplistic visions are worth discussing on their own, for they tell us something about the way the culture would like to see itself. Furthermore, they serve as a foil for those works of ethnic humor, discussed in the next chapter, that genuinely engage with American ethnicity in all of its complexity.

5 • COMEDY WITHOUT BORDERS?

Toward a Multiethnic Humor

As THE PREVIOUS CHAPTER demonstrates, many works of contemporary popular culture like to imagine a diverse yet fundamentally color-blind America. This vision upholds a facile understanding of racial harmony by suggesting that diverse ethnic backgrounds create only surface differences that individuals should look past. These "corporate multiculturalist" works imply that in order to create this harmony we only have to educate the handful of real racists and be nice to each other. Such a vision may be commendable on a certain level, yet it tends to gloss over systemic inequality and ignore the histories of oppression that have shaped the present circumstances. A truer and more sophisticated vision of American diversity may acknowledge racial harmony as a fundamental goal, but it must also take into account the historical circumstances that have led to racial discord in the first place. And on the individual level, this vision must also recognize that racial harmony will not be achieved either by ignoring or simply celebrating difference for its own sake but rather through a series of ongoing dialogues and intercultural conversations. Such cross-cultural dialogue may initially sound idyllic, but in reality, a genuine discussion of difference will inevitably entail an element of conflict. My conception of this sort of cross-cultural dialogue is drawn from Kwame Anthony Appiah's discussion of "cosmopolitan conversation." Appiah explains that the word *conversation* is used "not only for literal talk but also as a metaphor for engagement with the experience and the ideas of others. . . . Conversation doesn't have to lead to consensus about anything, especially not values; it's enough that it helps people get used to one another."[1] Cosmopolitan conversation, then, may lead to discomfort and anxiety, but it can also cause individuals to view their own ethnic positions from a new perspective. And, of course, such dialogue can also generate humor.

We have already seen this sort of intercultural conversation in a number of examples throughout this book, such as Dave Chappelle's chance encounter with a Native American at Walmart or the series of dialogues about racism between Stan and Token on *South Park*. The works discussed in this final chapter, however, provide a more sustained vision of multiethnic conversation, and equally important, they depict a wide range of ethnic positions without claiming to represent the point of view of any one ethnic group. These comic works also stand in sharp contrast to the "corporate multiculturalism" discussed in the previous chapter, for they interrogate diversity in a much more nuanced manner. The Showtime series *Weeds* (2005–2012), the *Harold and Kumar* films (2004, 2008, and 2011), and the work of stand-up comedian Russell Peters all contribute to what may be termed a "multiethnic humor," which focuses not on collectivity but on the ways that individuals may reexamine their own ethnicity through interactions with other cultural groups. Genuine multiethnic humor does not offer any simple images of different ethnicities holding hands under a rainbow. Multiethnic humorists understand that real intercultural dialogue will be fraught with conflict and anxiety. While multiethnic humor depends on many of the same devices of traditional ethnic humor (such as self-deprecation and exaggerated ethnic stereotypes), it is not necessarily, in Werner Sollors's words, a "form of boundary construction."[2] Instead, multiethnic humor redraws, challenges, and occasionally collapses the traditional boundaries of ethnic identification.

These works are in line with the thinking of those scholars, discussed more fully in the introduction, who seek to complicate the often reductive ways in which ethnic identity is constructed. David Hollinger and Appiah, among others, have offered various models (postethnicity and cosmopolitanism, respectively) for ways in which we may more fully understand and perform ethnic interaction. These models delineate the problems with many of the current methods of understanding difference and offer somewhat utopic visions of what we should strive for in academic discussion, political action, and even everyday life. The works of popular culture discussed in this chapter serve as useful counterparts to these theoretical models. While they share in what Hollinger calls "the cosmopolitan will to engage human diversity," they also offer concrete dramatizations of interethnic dialogue that suggest not only the ways in which individuals may benefit from speaking across cultural lines but also the conflict and humor that are often generated by such conversations.[3] Works of genuine multiethnic humor are therefore sites of some of the most complex and revealing articulations of diversity to be found in mainstream popular culture. Although these productions are by no means the norm, the fact that they have gained popularity at all suggests that audiences can be receptive to works that look beyond the fantasies of corporate multiculturalism and engage with American ethnicity in more meaningful ways.

A MULTIETHNIC EDUCATION

The Showtime series *Weeds*, which, as of this writing, recently ended its eighth and final season, is one of the most prominent examples of multiethnic humor. Created by the Jewish American writer Jenji Kohan, *Weeds* has a playful attitude toward ethnic stereotypes and constructs much of its humor through the unexpected juxtaposition of different ethnic characters. Although it has a large multiethnic cast, the core of the show focuses on the attractive white woman Nancy Botwin.[4] The series begins as a comedy about Nancy's attempt, after the death of her husband, to maintain her family's lifestyle by selling marijuana to her suburban neighbors. But by the end of the fifth season, Nancy has married the mayor of Tijuana, given birth to a half Mexican baby, and led her other two sons into a life of crime and violence. In the sixth season, Nancy herself becomes literally marginalized, as she and her family are forced to go into hiding and live "off the grid," and in season 7, she is an ex-convict stuck in a halfway house. Like many recent television series, *Weeds* has perhaps run longer than necessary, for the latest seasons are both less intriguing and also engage with ethnicity in less overt ways. In the first five seasons, however, Nancy forges important relationships with an array of ethnic characters that provide her with a multiethnic education by challenging and dismantling her highly constructed white identity. After this white identity is disassembled, it seems that the series does not know where to go. In its early years, however, *Weeds* offered a fantastic example of how a series can utilize a multiethnic cast not to project racial harmony but rather to explore a complex web of intercultural relationships. In doing so, the series allows individual characters to understand their own ethnic affiliation in a much wider multiethnic context.

In the first three seasons, *Weeds* was viewed primarily as a satire of suburban American life, in which weed represents not only an illegal drug, but also, as Kera Bolonik asserts, "every dirty little secret behind the closed doors" of the suburban upper-middle class.[5] Reviewer Alessandra Stanley agrees, describing the show as "a little bit like *American Beauty* and a little bit like *Desperate Housewives*."[6] This view of *Weeds* as a suburban satire is seemingly reinforced by the show's theme song "Little Boxes" (written and initially performed by Malvina Reynolds in 1962), which mocks a suburban neighborhood in which both the houses and the people are all alike. *Weeds*'s suburban critique, however, is more aware of ethnicity than either *American Beauty* or *Desperate Housewives*, despite the latter's token ethnic characters. While its Los Angeles suburb Agrestic (later absorbed by the larger suburb Majestic) does have

On the Showtime series *Weeds,* Nancy Botwin (portrayed by Mary Louise Parker) uses her whiteness and her sex appeal to survive in the drug business. (Credit: ©Showtime. Photographer: Mark Seliger. Courtesy of Photofest.)

nearly identical houses owned almost exclusively by whites, it is presented not as a wholly closed-off community but as one that is part of a much larger multiethnic web, even if the citizens of Agrestic choose not to notice. As might be expected in a wealthy Los Angeles suburb, the nannies, housekeepers, and gardeners are all Latino/a, and there is a nearby college from which parents can hire Asian American tutors for their children. The marijuana that so many Agrestic residents enjoy comes to them, via Nancy, through African American and Mexican American channels. The homogenous whiteness of Agrestic's residents is also complicated by the acknowledgment that at least some of the families are half Jewish. Nancy's deceased husband, Judah, was Jewish, as is Dean Hodes, the husband of Nancy's suburban friend/nemesis Celia Hodes.

Weeds's commitment to placing Agrestic within a network of multiethnic influences is indicated in seasons 2 and 3, when, in each episode, the theme song "Little Boxes" is sung by a different performer. The covers include versions in French, Spanish, and Russian and feature musicians from a variety of ethnic groups and countries. The diverse styles of music thus complicate the bourgeois conformity described in the song. The suburb's inability to exist in a completely hermetic environment is driven home when, at the end of the third season, Agrestic gets caught in the crossfire of a drug war (started partly by Nancy) and is burned down by Guillermo Gomez, the Puerto Rican head of the Los Angeles branch of a Mexican drug cartel. With Agrestic in ashes, the Botwins move to Ren Mar, a California beach town near the Mexican border. When the suburbs are left behind, *Weeds* also stops using "Little Boxes" as its theme song.

In many ways, the burning of Agrestic mirrors the destruction of Nancy's identity as a white, upper-middle-class woman. At the beginning of season 1, Nancy appears to be invested in a stereotypical bourgeois, soccer-mom identity. She deals pot primarily for the sake of her family, not as a revolt against her prescribed ethnic and gender roles. It soon becomes clear, though, that she is excited by the danger of the lifestyle and attracted to the "exotic" characters who are her business partners and competitors. These characters teach Nancy about the drug business, but they also introduce her to a new social perspective of which most Agrestic residents remain ignorant. As Nancy learns the ropes of drug trafficking, the humor is often driven by the juxtaposition of her whiteness (and her femininity) with the often stereotypical ethnic traits of the other characters. But the show avoids the reductive white/other divide of traditional ethnic humor by the sheer multiplicity of ethnic characters that Nancy encounters, by the specificity with which each group is treated, and by its process of placing different ethnic characters in dialogue with each other.

Nancy's multiethnic education began before the series even starts, when she married her first husband, Judah, and became part of a Jewish American family. Although it is unclear exactly how seriously Judah took his Jewish identity, it is apparent that, even after his death, Jewish culture and ritual continue to have an ethnicizing effect on Nancy and her sons. The most prominent Jewish character is Nancy's slacker, live-in brother-in-law Andy Botwin, who infuses the dialogue with Yiddishisms and even briefly attends a rabbinical school. And despite traditional Jewish law stating that a Jew must have a

Jewish mother, Nancy's son Shane, in the season 3 episode "He Taught Me How to Drive By," claims Jewish ethnicity as his own, proudly shouting, "I'm a blasphemous liberal Jew!" This attention to Jewish ethnicity is maintained throughout the series. When the family moves to Ren Mar, for instance, they live briefly with Andy and Judah's father, played by Jewish humorist Albert Brooks, and after Andy's grandmother dies, the whole family even sits shiva for her (mourns for seven days). *Weeds*'s preoccupation with Jewishness is suggestive of its larger multiethnic project. As we saw in chapter 2, Jewish American identity can often be seen to stand somewhere in the middle of the white/other divide, thus complicating the reductive binary. Jewishness works in a similar way for Nancy, serving as a sort of "gateway ethnicity" before she immerses herself in the cultures of America's more visible ethnic others.

The first of these major ethnic influences are Nancy's African American suppliers: Heylia James, her daughter Vaneeta, and her nephew Conrad Shepherd. While this family, in some obvious ways, enforces certain African American stereotypes, especially in regards to Heylia's sassy demeanor, they are not the sort of black drug dealers that are typically shown on film and television. Conrad, for instance, is not only nonviolent, but he is also a skilled botanist dedicated to growing his own strain of marijuana. Heylia, Vaneeta, and Conrad teach Nancy where to hide her stash, to use disposable cell phones when doing business, and how to set up a front to launder her profits. Through them, Nancy is also exposed to the harsher realities of the drug trade. In the season 1 episode "Lude Awakening," for example, there is a drive-by shooting at Heylia's home while Nancy is there. Heylia, Conrad, and Vaneeta immediately drop to the ground at the sound of gunshots, but Nancy, oblivious, stands frozen as bullets whiz by her. The scene uses dark humor and violence to highlight Nancy's inexperience. The moment, however, fundamentally changes the way she understands her environment; later in the same episode, Nancy falls to the ground at the sound of a car backfiring.

Nancy changes so much that the next time she is involved in a drive by, she is the driver, and another African American mentor, U-Turn, is doing the shooting. U-Turn is a fairly stereotypical black "gangsta," who robs other dealers at gunpoint and throws knives at his subordinates. He likes Nancy, however, and decides to groom her into a lieutenant. In season 3, episode 6, he takes to calling Nancy "grasshopper" and teaches her the drug trade with humorous aphorisms like "thug means never having to say you're sorry."[7] After U-Turn is murdered in the next episode, Nancy commemorates him with a tattoo of a U-Turn symbol on her buttocks, thus symbolically marking her white skin. At U-Turn's funeral, she earns the respect of an African American mourner when she explains that U-Turn "taught me how to drive by." These moments all suggest an ethnicizing of Nancy's identity, as her white suburban values are complicated by an urban, African American perspective.

When Nancy and her family move to the California/Mexico border, her multicultural education becomes transnational. Under the tutelage of Guillermo Gomez and her eventual new husband Esteban Reyes (a corrupt Mexican politician), she becomes a smuggler, sneaking drugs across the border. In the season 4 episode "The Whole Blah Damn Thing," Guillermo forces Nancy to expand her understanding of the drug business, telling her, "You've been thinking East/West. Start thinking North/South." Nancy later becomes the front-woman for a maternity store built over a secret tunnel connecting the United States and Mexico. Once again, Nancy confronts harsher realities than expected when she learns that the tunnel is used to transport not only drugs but also guns and female slaves. The tunnel literally posits an underground economy linking the two countries.[8] While earlier seasons highlighted the white suburb's inextricable link to multiethnic influences, seasons 4 and 5 treat the entire United States in a similar way, suggesting that seemingly fixed international borders are made fluid by a hidden black market: for instance, in a side plot, Andy becomes a "coyote," helping Mexican immigrants sneak across the border. Nancy's own white American identity is similarly destabilized by Mexican influences. After marrying and having a baby with Esteban, Nancy becomes a public figure in Mexican politics. By the end of the series, she could not be more different from the first season's suburban soccer-mom selling dime bags to her neighbors.

Along with the ethnicizing of Nancy's identity, there is also an element of masculinizing. For, as we saw in the above examples with U-Turn, her movement into the drug trade causes Nancy to participate more and more in a violent world that is largely dominated by men. This causes her to simultaneously distance herself from the roles typically associated with women: the faithful wife/girlfriend or the obedient mother. Ironically, however, even as Nancy moves further away from a white, feminine identity, it becomes clear that the combination of whiteness and femininity is Nancy's primary commodity in the drug business, enabling her to work beneath the radar of a legal system conditioned to look for nonwhite males. Therefore, the more Nancy tries to distance herself from her bourgeois soccer-mom roots, the more her ethnic associates expect her to perform a wealthy, white female stereotype. As Guillermo tells her in the first episode of season 4, "Your job is to be the pretty American lady." Nancy's whiteness and her sexuality are also why U-Turn takes her under his wing, and it is part of the reason why her marijuana sells so well. In the season 2 episode "MILF Money," African American hip-hop star Snoop Dogg appears as himself and is so impressed by Nancy that he names her marijuana—which was actually created by Conrad—"MILF Weed" and sings an impromptu song about Nancy in which he emphasizes her "white ass."[9] The name MILF Weed catches on, and the demand for her product goes up. Nancy herself is just as much a commodity as the pot that she sells. These examples all suggest that the characters, as well as the viewers, see the unexpected ethnic humor in the concept of a female white suburbanite in the illegal drug business. The series, then, treats whiteness not as an unmarked given, but rather as another ethnic construct, subject to its own reductive stereotypes and understood in relation to gender and class positions.

While Nancy's multiethnic education is the primary narrative, *Weeds* also has a number of side plots in which ethnic characters interact with each other for humorous effects. Most of these moments contribute to the show's commitment to collapsing rigid group boundaries, and many of them suggest that multiethnic relationships help individual characters to more fully articulate their own ethnicity. Andy Botwin, for example, posits his Jewishness most actively when he interacts with other ethnic characters. In the season 2 episode "Corn Snake," Andy applies for rabbinical school (as a means to avoid army service); here he dismisses his Jewish ethnicity, joking that "being a Jew means I have no foreskin, and I may be a Tay-Sachs carrier." But later, in the season 4 episode "I Am the Table," Andy, as a "coyote" smuggling Mexican immigrants into the United States, embraces his Jewish identity. He feeds his charges matzo, explaining "this is what my people ate as we wandered the desert for forty years." And as the immigrants pass into the United States, Andy raises his arms, his poncho blowing dramatically in the wind, and announces, "You shall be a free people!" The juxtaposition of contemporary Mexican issues and Old Testament imagery creates a surprising multiethnic humor, but Andy clearly takes his position as a coyote seriously and uses it as a means to rearticulate his Jewish ancestry.

Another ethnic character who resists easy categorization is Sanjay, a homosexual Indian American college student. Nancy originally hires Sanjay as a math tutor for her oldest son, but she soon has him selling marijuana on campus. The ethnic humor is apparent in the season 1 episode "Higher Education": after Nancy asks Sanjay to sell for her, she explains that she has begun "outsourcing." In many ways, though, Sanjay's story is another version of Nancy's. As a college student and math tutor, Sanjay fulfills the reductive "model minority" Asian American stereotype, but once he is introduced to Nancy's multiethnic drug ring, his situation changes drastically. He eventually ends up having a mixed-race baby with Clinique, an African American woman who U-Turn coerces Sanjay into having sex with in order to "fix" his homosexuality. It is fitting that Sanjay fathers a mixed-race child, for he is often the character to instigate cross-cultural dialogue. For instance, in season 2, episode 5, a group of Armenian drug dealers threaten Nancy and her organization; Sanjay attempts to contextualize the situation, explaining that Armenians are "a historically put-upon people." In the season 2 episode "Yeah, like Tomatoes," Sanjay comments on the deplorable conditions in the "third world." This prompts Conrad to cite statistics about violence and poverty in inner-city African American neighborhoods, saying "this is the fucking third world." As in Appiah's definition of cosmopolitan conversation,

Sanjay and Conrad do not reach an agreement at this point; however, the process of engaging in such dialogue forces them to see their own situations from a different perspective.

Such moments are a far cry from the clichéd and simplified ideals of corporate multiculturalism; rather, they suggest a genuine intercultural dialogue in which ethnic characters are given a forum to position their own ethnic predicament within a larger multiethnic context. *Weeds*, however, never allows its characters to achieve an easy resolution. As such, its depictions of ethnicity are fluid and complex. In order to keep the series going, *Weeds* continuously introduces new conflicts and new characters. While in the most recent seasons this has been less successful, at least in terms of ethnic interrogation, the first five seasons of *Weeds* present multiethnic America as a complex web in which characters, especially Nancy, can interrogate their ethnic affiliation. In doing so, it presents a genuine multiethnic humor that encourages viewers to look beyond both the classic dichotomy of white and other and the rigidly defined categories of cultural pluralism.

THE QUEST FOR WHITENESS

The films *Harold and Kumar Go to White Castle* and, to a lesser extent, its sequels *Harold and Kumar Escape from Guantanamo Bay* (2008) and *A Very Harold and Kumar 3D Christmas* (2011), use ethnic humor to present a similarly complex vision of multiethnic America. *Harold and Kumar Go to White Castle,* directed by Danny Leiner, follows in the footsteps of the Cheech and Chong movies. It is a road trip film about two stoners (Korean American Harold Lee and Indian American Kumar Patel) who spend an entire Friday night traveling through New Jersey in an attempt to fulfill their marijuana-munchies with a meal at the fast-food restaurant White Castle. Their mock-heroic quest provides a bizarre tour of the multiethnic American landscape as Harold and Kumar encounter members of multiple ethnic groups along the way. On the simplest level, the film is a gross-out, horny-young-man movie along the lines of the *American Pie* franchise. But it also demands its audience's familiarity with racial and ethnic issues, for much of the film's humor (and conflict) is driven by its complex and unexpected treatment of ethnic stereotypes. This is especially true in the development of the two protagonists, for both Harold and Kumar have an uneasy relationship with the stereotypes of intelligent-yet-effeminate Asian American men. Harold, an investment banker, continuously grapples with his perceived identity as "the nerdy Asian guy," and Kumar, despite an amazing medical aptitude, spends much of his time resisting pressure to become another Indian doctor like his father and older brother. Once they reach White Castle—an ambiguous symbol of mainstream white America—both characters find ways of negotiating their personal identity in relation to their ethnic ancestry.

Harold and Kumar's journey thus engages with the classic American struggle between individualism and group identity. Most critics, unfortunately, miss this aspect of the film, focusing instead on its place within the "stoner" genre. Dennis Lim, however, is well attuned to the symbolic weight of Harold and Kumar's quest and calls the film an "allegory of seeking and gaining entry to the Caucasian fortress that is present-day America."[10] As Lim suggests, *Harold and Kumar* explores the trials and pitfalls of assimilation—a popular topic for many ethnic humorists—but like *Weeds, Harold and Kumar* allows its protagonists to interrogate their ethnic identity in relation to other groups. Even more so than *Weeds*, though, *Harold and Kumar* challenges the simplistic ways in which ethnicity is often discussed in American culture. The film's dismissive attitude toward bureaucratic approaches to race is clear in an early scene when a bumbling white doctor, while interviewing Kumar for medical school, refers to African Americans as "colored." The doctor tries to correct himself with the labels "Negro," "black," "African American," and finally, "people of colors." Aside from mocking a middle-aged white man's failed attempt to use politically correct language, the moment critiques the history of racial labeling in America and highlights the vagueness of the term "persons of color," which is now often used to refer to all nonwhite ethnic groups. By pluralizing *color*, and suggesting that there are indeed multiple colors, the white doctor inadvertently highlights the label's lack of specificity and the tendency behind it to force all nonwhite ethnic groups into a single category.

Harold and Kumar works against such reductive thinking. For example, both Kumar and Harold fall into the broad category of "Asian American," but the film goes to great lengths to demonstrate each character's ethnic specificity. At the same time, though, it makes no claim to represent the point of view of any particular ethnicity and never spends more than a few minutes focusing on only one group. Harold and Kumar's journey, for instance, eventually leads them to Princeton, where Harold finds himself at a gathering of stereotypically nerdy, ambitious Korean American students. Harold is clearly uneasy being there, and the film also dispels the homogenous atmosphere, for it is not long before Kumar, who is treated as an outsider by the Korean American students, drags Harold away. Even though the narrative rejects the Korean American students' impulse to fraternize only with each other, the film itself challenges the reductive stereotype of Asian restraint and sobriety, for Harold and Kumar later learn that the Korean American gathering has transformed into a wild, lascivious party. The moment suggests that Harold himself is guilty of buying into stereotypes about his own ethnicity. This sort of playful attitude toward stereotypes drives much of the film's multiethnic humor. At times, it seems to reinforce stereotypical ethnic traits but will often undercut them a moment later. In this manner, the film critiques the cultural tendency to stereotype ethnic groups, but it also acknowledges the ways that these stereotypes are often internalized by their targets. Harold and Kumar themselves both reinforce the stereotypes of Asian American intelligence, with specific aptitudes in math and science, but their pot smoking, sex craving, fast-food eating habits simultaneously destabilize this generalization.[11]

The film treats other groups in a similar manner. Two well-spoken and well-dressed British women undo the idea of English modesty and decorum when, after a meal of fast-food tacos, they play a game of "battleshits" to see who can make the most noise with their bowel movements. The most interesting character in regards to ethnic stereotypes is probably Tarik, an African American with whom Harold shares his cell after being arrested for accidentally punching a white police officer. Tarik seems to subvert almost all of the most demeaning stereotypes about African American men. Even after being the victim of racial profiling, he is calm and soft-spoken and sits quietly reading a collection of essays on civil disobedience. When Harold asks how he can remain so relaxed, Tarik says, "Look at me. I'm fat, black, can't dance, and I have two gay fathers. People have been messing with me my whole life. I learned a long time ago that there's no sense getting all riled up every time a bunch of idiots give you a hard time. In the end, the universe tends to unfold as it should. Plus I have a really large penis. That keeps me happy." Tarik's words are indicative of the film's disorienting treatment of ethnicity. Just as viewers get used to a character that undermines nearly every common African American characterization, Tarik mentions his "really large penis," thus embodying the most well-known stereotype of black male sexuality. Furthermore, it is Tarik's adherence to this stereotype that "keeps [him] happy" despite his life of adversity. Rather than simply challenging or upholding ethnic stereotypes, *Harold and Kumar* allows each character to articulate his or her identity in relation to them.

Tarik's presence also contributes to the film's method of undermining an overly simplistic white/other binary. Harold, Kumar, and Tarik all fall under the broad rubric of "persons of color," but the film suggests vast differences in their placement in the American ethnic landscape. While Kumar and Harold do suffer from various acts of racism at the hands of bigots, we do not see them suffer from systemic inequality, and it is clear that they have been granted access to the American middle class and all of the privileges that it entails. Tarik, on the other hand, is the object of violent racism on a day-to-day basis, and it is suggested, to the point of humorous hyperbole, that he is the continuous target of police harassment simply for being black. The different ways in which the characters are treated suggest that while Asian Americans may remain culturally separate from the mainstream, African Americans are still the country's primary other on whom "white America" projects its fears. This depiction is in keeping with characterizations of Asian Americans as the "model minority," who, in C. N. Le's words, "parlay a strong work ethic, high levels of education, and a greater tolerance for racial inequality and structural discrimination into greater acceptance among Whites and socioeconomic attainment and mobility levels that match or in some instances surpass that of Whites."[12] This point is clear when a group of white police officers walk in to the police station while Kumar is attempting to break Harold out of his cell. When the officers see the jail cell standing open, they ignore Harold and Kumar and instead jump on Tarik, who is quietly reading and making no attempt to escape. While the officers are thus preoccupied, Kumar and Harold take the opportunity to quietly slip away. Their escape symbolically suggests that the continual oppression of African Americans enables less threatening—and lighter-skinned—ethnic groups to climb the ladder of American status. The moment even goes so far as to implicate Kumar and Harold themselves, as they continue on their quest to White Castle and show little concern for Tarik's well-being.

Even while Harold and Kumar try so hard to reach White Castle (and the promise of acceptance into white America that it seems to represent), the film undercuts the Grail-like quest by continuously portraying whites, and particularly white males, as villains. In fact, the film's funniest racial stereotypes are in its representations of white men as ignorant, racist, rude, and pompous. Although comic, most of the film's white men—like the white police officers in the above example—fulfill bell hooks's description of "whiteness as terrorizing."[13] This begins in the opening scene, when two of Harold's white coworkers coerce him into doing their work for them by threatening to complain to their presumably white boss. And a group of "extreme sports" aficionados appear at various moments to terrorize Kumar and Harold with racial slurs, homophobic speech, and the threat of physical violence. In many other mainstream movies, these white males would be the protagonists, and their aggressive brand of white masculinity would be recast as "rugged" or "heroic." Here, however, these generic white villains serve as mere roadblocks, impeding Harold and Kumar's entry into white America, a point made clear in Harold's dream sequence when the white police officer who arrested him stands as guardian before the threshold of a literal white castle.

In keeping with its multiethnic project, however, Harold and Kumar also encounter a collection of more likeable "white ethnics" (like the previously mentioned British girls) who complicate our ability to view whiteness as a homogenous entity. They get their car fixed, for example, by an unattractive southerner named Freakshow who, although white, fits more easily into the category of "white trash ," a label that, as Ruth Frankenberg points out, "actually marks the boundaries of whiteness."[14] And aside from each other, Harold and Kumar's closest friends are Rosenberg and Goldstein, two Jewish American potheads who live down the hall.[15] Every appearance they make in the film is a compendium of Jewish jokes and stereotypes: they speak with an exaggerated Yiddish accent, their apartment has a menorah filled with joints instead of candles, and at one point Goldstein asserts that Katie Holmes's breasts are "the opposite" of the Holocaust. Cleary, Rosenberg and Goldstein—who, in a side plot, go on their own journey to eat a meal at Hot Dog Heaven—are a Jewish version of Harold and Kumar themselves. As such, they present a possible model of assimilation. As we saw in chapter 2, American Jews were not always considered white, and even in contemporary America, Jewishness is often constructed as a distinct ethnic category. Rosenberg and Goldstein thus exemplify the status of many Jews who, although officially white, have a more specific ethnic heritage. The similarities with Harold and Kumar are clear, for even the most common stereotypes about Jewish men (cheap, crafty, and good with numbers) are the same as those applied to Asian American men.[16] Therefore if Tarik stands on one end of the American ethnic spectrum as the country's most visible and inassimilable other, then Rosenberg and Goldstein stand at the other end as a distinct minority that has nonetheless achieved the class, status, and privileges of whiteness.

While Harold and Kumar are clearly somewhere in the middle, the film makes no definitive statement about where exactly they fit in this ethnic spectrum. And given the ambivalence with which the narrative treats white culture, it is unclear, when they finally reach White Castle, whether it will live up to its

The heroes of *Harold and Kumar Go to White Castle* negotiate their ethnic identity through personal interactions with a diverse group of individuals. (Credit: ©New Line. Courtesy of Photofest.)

promise. Just before they arrive, Kumar makes a speech that stresses the symbolic import—and the ambiguity—of their journey: "Our parents came to this country escaping persecution, poverty, and hunger. . . . They were very, very hungry. They wanted to live in a land that treated them as equals, a land filled with hamburger stands, and not just one type of hamburger, okay, hundreds of types with different sizes, toppings, and condiments. That land was America. . . . Now this is about achieving what our parents set out for. This is about the pursuit of happiness. This night is about the American dream." The comparison between eating burgers and the American dream draws a direct connection between democracy and consumerism and is consistent with the film's irreverence, but Kumar's words also underscore the central dilemma about assimilation and ethnic identity. By citing "the pursuit of happiness" and "the American dream," Kumar invokes a traditional melting pot model of American ethnicity. But in describing America as a land with "hundreds of types with different sizes, toppings, and condiments," he also paints a picture of a pluralist America, in which each group remains ethnically distinct. As the preceding narrative demonstrates, however, neither option reflects the complexity of the actual American ethnic landscape, but no single narrative can.

This is driven home when Harold and Kumar finally eat at White Castle. Harold explains that eating the White Castle burgers made him "feel like a new man." And indeed, the food seems to have a rejuvenating effect on both characters. After the meal, they each achieve personal breakthroughs that allow them to understand their ethnicity in more productive, although different, ways. Kumar decides to stop resisting the Indian doctor stereotype, explaining that "my whole life I've just been scared of being one of those nerdy Indian guys turned doctor, but . . . there are far worse things in this life than being tapped for having a natural ability in medicine." Harold has a much different epiphany. After the meal, he runs into his white coworkers and confronts them: "You guys think you can party all weekend and leave the work to the quiet Asian guy in the office? . . . I'm not doing your work for you anymore." Kumar finally accepts his ethnic stereotype while Harold literally fights against his. Ultimately, then, the film ends on a somewhat conservative note, adhering to the classic American ideals of individualism and free choice. Viewed in the context of the rest of the film, however, it is clear that this ability to choose is restricted to those individuals who are wealthy and light-skinned enough to be given the opportunities for upward mobility. Tarik, for example, has far fewer freedoms available to him. Therefore, while Harold and Kumar achieve their respective epiphanies only after eating at White Castle, it is clear that the quest itself, as much as the destination, allows them to articulate their identities. Only after juxtaposing their own ethnic predicaments with a score of other ethnic characters are they able to be at peace with their ancestry.

The 2008 sequel, *Harold and Kumar Escape from Guantanamo Bay*, is similar to the original film but, lacking the internal identity struggle of the main characters, is ultimately less interesting. Here, Harold and Kumar are suspected of being terrorists and, as its title suggests, are imprisoned in Guantanamo Bay. They escape, hop on a boat to Miami, and go on an episodic journey to prove their innocence. As in the first film, during their quest they get into adventures with various ethnic characters, and white villains also play a prominent role. For example, they are pursued throughout the film by Ron Fox, a white, ignorant, and racist Homeland Security agent. As in *White Castle, Guantanamo Bay* has a playful and disorienting approach to ethnic stereotypes. Here, though, the method is even more overt. At one point, for example, Harold and Kumar get a flat tire in an urban, African American neighborhood. When they see a group of black man approaching them, Harold and Kumar run. It turns out, though, that the leader of the group is a well-educated dentist, and he only wanted to help them change their tire. In another scene, Harold and Kumar spend the night at a white couple's home in Alabama. At first, the couple displays a level of sophistication that goes against the "redneck" stereotype, but we later learn that they are actually brother and sister and have a mutant, inbred son living in the basement. These and other examples create a sort of game with the viewer; every time that an ethnic position is delineated, viewers must wonder whether its related stereotype will ultimately be deflated or reinforced.

This approach to ethnic stereotypes is often amusing and is certainly effective in highlighting the culture's socially constructed and often ridiculous understandings of ethnic identity. Unlike the original film, however, *Guantanamo Bay* does not use its humor to place different ethnic positions in genuine conversation with each other, and the characters do not really learn anything though their ethnic interactions. Instead, the film's most effective use of ethnic humor is the way that it satirizes the ethnic dimension of American politics and, more specifically, the War on Terror. This is done primarily through the characterization of the villain, Ron Fox. The film's plot is driven by Fox's assumption that Harold and Kumar are agents of North Korea and al-Qaeda, respectively. A key joke in the film, then, is Fox's confusion—which is a confusion that seems to be shared by many Americans—between South Asians and Arabs (see my discussion of *Community* in the previous chapter). The critique of these narrow understandings of ethnicity, though, never reaches the level of sophistication of the first film.

The second sequel, *A Very Harold and Kumar 3D Christmas*, strays even further from the ethnic explorations of the first film. *3D Christmas* takes place several years after *Guantanamo Bay*, and the two friends have drifted apart. After Kumar mistakenly sets fire to Harold's Mexican American father-in-law's prize Christmas tree, the two go on yet another picaresque adventure to locate a replacement tree. The film is most concerned with exploiting three-dimensional special effects, and much of the humor depends on outrageous and raunchy sight gags. Nonetheless, the film is still extremely aware of the manner in which it represents ethnicity. Two African American Christmas tree salesmen, for example, take turns performing "gangsta" and "Uncle Tom" stereotypes, suggesting that dominant ideas about "blackness" are rooted in performance. And one of the film's main struggles is over how the white-collar Harold and can earn the respect of his macho Latino father-in-law. The struggle gestures toward a consideration of the issues of interethnic marriage as well as a comparison between Asian American and Latino models of masculinity. These issues are never really teased out, though, and the film is primarily a compendium of raunchy humor and 3D spectacle. But even though *Guantanamo Bay* and *3D Christmas* are less successful than *White Castle,* it is still a breath of fresh air to see wholly mainstream and youthful "stoner" comedies with Asian American leads and large multiethnic casts. Unlike so many young party films, which imagine a largely homogenous white demographic, the *Harold and Kumar* franchise serves as proof that movies with nonwhite casts can be commercially viable *and* provide insight into American race relations.

COSMOPOLITAN COMEDY: RUSSELL PETERS

More than any other figure discussed in this book, Indian Canadian comic Russell Peters (discussed briefly in the introduction) exemplifies the possibilities of multiethnic humor, in part because he places American ethnicity in a wider transnational context. Peters's parents were born in India; he was raised in Canada, and he currently lives in the United States. Despite his multiethnic and transnational concerns, Peters's humor is steeped in American sensibilities and is easily accessible to American audiences. His humor thus reflects not only the diverse populations of the United States and Canada but also the ways in which America is part of a multidirectional global web of commerce and culture. Accordingly, Peters is popular all over the world, particularly in Canada, Asia, and the Middle East, although he is also well-known in the United States and is one of the few nonblack performers to have appeared on *Def Comedy Jam*. Much of his humor is built on his experiences interacting with members of different ethnic communities and traveling to other countries. Therefore, unlike many other ethnic humorists, Peters's humor is about much more than his own ethnic community of South Asian immigrants. Throughout his stand-up routines, Peters jokes about several Asian groups, Arabs, African Americans, Latinos, Africans, Armenians, Jews, and, of course, white people. Peters is a skilled mimic, and his humor often relies on ethnic accents and stereotypes. He digs deeper than the surface stereotype, though, and provides a more complex cultural insight. Much of his humor, for instance, is built on the awkward social situations that may arise when individuals with different cultural backgrounds interact. This humor encourages intercultural dialogue but understands that such dialogue is often fraught with anxiety and has the potential for conflict.

One of the most striking features of Peters's humor is the manner in which he engages with live audience members and attempts to provide some type of humor about every ethnic group that is represented in his audience. Fans come to Peters's act expecting to hear jokes about their own community. After playing a show in Dubai, for instance, Peters explains that he "kept getting e-mails from Arab kids going, 'Hey, why did you forget about the Arabs?' It's funny because people are complaining to me, asking me why I didn't pick on them."[17] On his website, www.russellpeters.com, Peters addresses this issue at more length. Here, he responds to the frequently asked question, "How come you didn't say anything about my community?" In his answer, Peters explains that "I'll only talk about people and cultures that I know about. I won't just say something for the sake of saying it. I'm always paying attention to the fans and learning new things about them and their communities. Give me time, I'll have something for you." This answer exemplifies the role that education plays in his humor; rather than base his comedy on perceived stereotypes, Peters attempts to learn about different cultures, primarily through traveling to various places. Stories from his travels often work their way into his act.

This emphasis on transnational education and travel positions Peters as a cosmopolitan humorist. In the opening to his *Cosmopolitanism: Ethics in a World of Strangers,* Appiah explores the writings of the nineteenth-century explorer Sir Richard Burton and reads Burton as a sort of protocosmopolitan. Appiah asserts that as a result of his travels, Burton "could see the world from perspectives remote from the outlook in which he had been brought up."[18] We can read Peters in a similar way; because of his transnational affiliations and the fact that he tours the world and engages with people in many different places, Peters is familiar with a wide range of cultures. Peters himself cultivates this identity, for he typically begins each show by polling the audience to get a sense of its cultural makeup. Then, he usually provides one or two routines based on each represented group. This cosmopolitan aspect of Peters's humor is reinforced by the DVD cover of his stand-up special *Russell Peters: Outsourced* (2006). The cover displays a photo of Peters leaning on a giant globe. While the title *Outsourced* speaks specifically to his Indian identity, the image of Peters and the globe suggests that he is a comic not just for his own ethnic demographic but for the world.

Furthermore, Peters has become a sort of poster-comic for international humorists. He hosted, for example, both the Showtime stand-up special *Russell Peters Presents* (2010), which included various ethnic and international comedians, and the Showtime series *Comics without Borders* (2008), which featured a wide array of humorists from different national and ethnic backgrounds. *Comics without Borders* follows a formula very similar to HBO's *Def Comedy Jam* (discussed in chapter 1), with Peters acting as emcee and introducing various comics. However, while *Def Comedy Jam* presents itself primarily as a black space, *Comics without Borders,* as its title suggests, looks past rigid group boundaries and defines itself by its diversity and its absence of a single ethnic point of view. Peters's identity as world traveler is highlighted in the opening credit sequence, which shows an animated Peters flying, in a hot-air balloon, all over the world to locate various comedians. Unfortunately, other than Peters's brief stand-up segments at the opening of each episode, in which he usually interacts with the audience, most of the humor on *Comics without Borders* is merely mediocre, and the show lasted for only eight episodes. Furthermore, the series fails to live up to its transnational aspirations, for many of the comics are simply African Americans or white Americans, and they seem unaware that they are part of a show emphasizing international humor. While this is certainly disappointing, the failure of *Comics without Borders* only further reinforces how unique of a humorist Peters himself is.

Like most ethnic comedians, Peters makes frequent use of his own ethnic background in his act, and like Margaret Cho and other second-generation immigrant comics, he often provides humorous caricatures of his less assimilated family members. But Peters also talks about India in more complex ways. In *Outsourced,* for example, Peters explains how he can have a name like Russell Peters even though both of his parents were born in India. An Indian audience member expresses disbelief that Peters has not changed his name, so Peter asks, "Do you know Indian history at all? . . . The British were there for four hundred years. You don't think they fucked one or two of us? If they can steal all our jewelry, they can bang one or two of us." Even though it gets a laugh from the crowd, this statement is not really a joke. Rather, it is an assertion, via comic language, of India's colonial history. While he does not dwell on the issue, the comment also speaks directly to the sexual and economic exploitation of Indians at the hands of their colonizers. Peters's comedy becomes actual pedagogy as he draws on Indian history to contextualize his own ethnic identity, which is the product of multiethnic influences.

In keeping with this multiethnic perspective, Peters does not define his own ethnic position in a simple manner. Also in *Outsourced,* Peters says that Indians tend to perspire heavily and that after getting off of a long flight to Vietnam, he smelled bad. According to Peters, a Vietnamese man pointed at him and said, "You stink. You're Indian. Indians stink." Peters's reply is, "I'm Canadian. This is how Canadians smell." The joke complicates the biological determinism of racist thought by asserting the influence of culture and personal experience. In the comedy special *Red, White, and Brown* (2008), he explores this theme more explicitly in a routine called "Race vs. Culture." "My whole life," Peters explains,

"I have been thinking of myself as Indian . . . but then I realized something. I was born and raised in Canada. . . . The only Indian thing about me are my parents and my skin tone." Peters elaborates on this discovery by relating a series of humorous stories about traveling to India. "As soon as they opened the door to that plane," Peters explains, "I turned Canadian so fast." Finally, Peters asserts that he is culturally North American and racially Indian. While Peters uses different terminology, what he is really exploring here is akin to Werner Sollors's differentiation between communities of descent and communities of consent. Unlike so many contemporary ethnic humorists, Peters does not rely on rigid, descent-defined ethnic boundaries in his identity performance. This is perhaps why he has been able to speak so successfully to members of multiple ethnic positions.

As the above routines suggest, Peters's humor demonstrates his commitment to ethnic specificity. In spite of this, though, it should be noted that the ethnic stereotype is still a fundamental building block in many of his routines. The stereotypes that he uses, however, are often structured in such a way that they contribute to the ethnic pride of his audience members. This in itself is nothing new, for ethnic comedians often discuss stereotypical traits of their own group and turn those traits into positives. African American comics, for example, are well known for turning the stereotype of the "lazy coon" into a positive feature by suggesting that blacks are more in step with nature and less uptight than whites (see chapter 1). Peters, though, constructs a cosmopolitan identity and is able to invert these stereotypes in relation to a large number of ethnic groups and thus speaks on behalf of multiple subject positions. Various other comedians discussed in this work, particularly Dave Chappelle, have managed to create a thoughtful humor that includes other ethnic groups. Chappelle, though, uses multiethnic humor primarily to interrogate the place of blackness in a diverse culture. Peters, in contrast, is able to suspend his own ethnic identity and speak solely about other groups.

Peters's use of multiple ethnic stereotypes works because, rhetorically, he portrays the possession of a stereotypical trait as something desired and even something that ethnic groups can compete over. In *Red, White, and Brown*, for example, Peters provides a lengthy discussion of "cheapness," a trait that is most often assigned to Jews. Peters argues that rather than Jews, Indians are actually the cheapest people in the world, followed closely by the Chinese. Then, in an aside, Peters says that Jews can have third place in the hierarchy of cheapness so that "they won't feel like they're losing *everything*." Peters does not explain the comment, but it speaks to the growing impressions, discussed in more detail in chapter 2, that Jews, especially in the United States, are being viewed less and less as an ethnic minority and more as just a slightly different sort of white person. As they intermarry and assimilate, Peters is clearly suggesting that Jews are "losing" something and that holding on to an ethnic stereotype may actually be a way of maintaining ethnic identity.[19] Peters constructs cheapness as positive trait for Indians, explaining that, for an Indian, the word "cheap" is synonymous with "smart."

In this routine, Peters also discusses the cheapness of African Americans and asserts that white people are afraid of being seen as cheap. The largest part of this bit, however, is actually about a cheap Chinese person who will sneak a camera into a designer clothing store so that he can have his own knock-off versions made in China. During this routine, the camera often pans to Chinese members of the audience, who laugh appreciatively. A bit like this is unique because it simultaneously encourages intra-ethnic cohesion and interethnic dialogue. The good-natured stereotypes work in a manner similar to the humor found on shows like *Def Comedy Jam*, in which audience members can laugh appreciatively at perceived idiosyncrasies within their own culture. At the same time, though, Peters talks about so many different ethnic groups that the routine also encourages identification across ethnic lines. Cheapness, for Peters, is something that black, Jewish, Indian, and Chinese people can all agree on. Furthermore, if all of these groups are considered cheap, then the stereotype itself begins to lose its power. Stereotypes are typically broad generalizations about a particular group of people. If multiple groups or ethnicities seem to share the trait, however, then the stereotype becomes moot.

While Peters's humor both encourages and embraces cross-cultural dialogue, it also acknowledges the difficulty of such conversation. Many of his routines, for example, are built around confusing or awkward social situations that are caused by cross-cultural contact. In *Outsourced*, for instance, Peters discusses how many authentic Indian names can generate humor when they are used in English. For instance, the name Dip Sukh (pronounced very closely to "deep suck") has clear sexual connotations in English. Peters acknowledges that names such as this have different meanings in their original language, and he does not explicitly endorse English speakers who will laugh at such names. He does, however, take it upon himself to warn Indian immigrant parents that the names they give their children may have unforeseen consequences in another cultural context. Like a lot of derisive ethnic humor, this routine generates its laughter by pointing out idiosyncrasies in other cultures. The way Peters frames the bit, though, makes the humor about the unexpected results of intercultural contact rather than simply ridiculing other cultural positions.

Also in *Outsourced* Peters relates a story about eating at a Kentucky Fried Chicken restaurant in China that even more explicitly highlights the humor and confusion that may arise out of interethnic contact. Peters prefaces the story by explaining that native speakers in China often use the phrase "nay-ga" when they are thinking, much in the same way that English speakers will use "like" or "um."

When pronounced with a Chinese accent, "nay-ga" sounds uncomfortably close to "nigger." The story Peters tells involves himself standing in line at the KFC; also in line are a Nigerian woman and a Chinese woman with her young son. The Chinese child is considering the menu and often looking back at his mother, the whole time saying "nay-ga, nay-ga, nay-ga, nay-ga." The Nigerian woman, though, thinks that the boy is looking at her and saying "nigger" over and over again. The Nigerian woman then looks at Peters as if she wants him to "beat the kid's ass" for directing a racial slur at her. Awkwardness abounds. The routine establishes an elaborate instance of cultural misunderstanding. Rather than basing the humor solely on cultural differences, Peters's story demonstrates the anxieties of intercultural contact. The comedy is not at the expense of any single group but is rather the result of living in a multicultural/transnational society. As a cosmopolitan, though, Peters is able to understand these cultural differences and explain them to audience members.[20] The routine, like all of Peters's humor, ultimately endorses an awareness and engagement with cultural difference as a means to live more comfortably alongside each other.

While much of Peters's humor is clearly transnational, he also manages to adapt it to a specifically American ethnic landscape. Peters is able to use his cosmopolitan identity to explore American race relations in fascinating ways. As we have seen in previous chapters, American ethnicity is still often viewed through a rigid black/white binary. Peters, however, constructs his identity as "brown," as suggested by the title of his stand-up special *Red, White and Brown*.[21] This "brownness" gives Peters's ethnicity a fluidity that allows him to speak across cultural lines. This is most apparent in his January 2008 appearance on HBO's *Def Comedy Jam,* where he adapts his act to account for his primarily African American audience. Peters remarks that "in America it's always about black and white, but . . . everybody suffers racism. If you ain't white, you're getting that racist shit." Peters then mockingly describes racist whites who are confused by his ethnicity and insult him with slurs such as "sand nigger" and "dune coon." Both insults rely on terms typically reserved for African Americans; the fact that racist whites use them to describe Indians or Arabs reveals their adherence to a black/white racial dichotomy. While in this instance, Peters's brownness is reconfigured by racist whites as a variation on blackness, at other times it works as a middle-space, allowing Peters to work as a sort "double agent" for both white and black communities. In the same *Def Comedy Jam* performance, for example, Peters informs his primarily black audience that white Americans have become "clever with their racism" now that the "n-word" is off limits. Peters tells a story in which a white cab driver in Boston referred to African Americans as "Mondays," explaining that "nobody likes Mondays." The lesson of the bit is that African Americans, in Peters's words, "need to be hip" to this sort of secret language among whites. It is due to his position as a brown man that Peters is able to navigate the polarities of black and white and to serve as an informant on white racism for his African American audience. The routine here emphasizes the fact that, despite Peters's frequent reliance on stereotypes, his humor is vehemently antiracist.

Many of the comic productions discussed throughout this book—but particularly those covered in this final chapter—work to both extend and depart from the tradition of American ethnic humor. On the one hand, these works utilize the traditional building blocks of ethnic humor (exaggerated stereotypes, self-deprecation, criticism of the white majority), but they also complicate that tradition by not claiming to represent the point of view of any singular ethnic tradition and by placing multiple nonwhite ethnic communities in conversation with each other. As I will suggest in the following conclusion, these works do not necessarily embody the future of American ethnic humor, but they do represent the complexity of contemporary America—both in terms of demographic and in ground-level race relations—in a more nuanced manner than even the best ethnic humor of the past. Perhaps most important, they also demonstrate the ways in which humor can both reflect and participate in the complex intercultural dialogues that emerge when multiple ethno-racial groups come into contact with each other.

CONCLUSION

Emerging Ethnic Humor in Multiethnic America

IN EARLY 2012, as I finalized the revisions for this book, I began following a story about the dismantling of the ethnic studies program, and more specifically the Mexican American studies program, in the Tucson, Arizona, public school district. In 2012, a new state law went into effect that prohibits teaching material that the school board considers antiwhite or that, as summarized by *New York Times* writer Michael Winerip, "advocate[s] ethnic solidarity instead of treating pupils as individuals."[1] Despite studies that suggest the program actually increased Latino student retention and college admission rates, school administrators effectively banned several Mexican American books and dismissed the program's director, Sean Arce. On April 2, *The Daily Show with Jon Stewart* aired a special segment on the story in which Latino correspondent Al Madrigal interviewed school board member and defender of the new law Michael Hicks. Hicks comes across very poorly in the interview. For example, he admits that all of his knowledge of the Mexican American studies program is based on hearsay, and at one point he states that "if there's no more white people in the world, then OK, you can do what you want." Elsewhere in the interview, Hicks mistakenly refers to Rosa Parks as "Rosa Clark." While *The Daily Show* surely edited the interview to make Hicks appear as foolish as possible, there are very few contexts in which his comments would not be, at the very least, problematic.

The Daily Show segment fermented a new wave of protests of the law from within the Tucson community, and it led to greater national coverage in mainstream media outlets. The story itself illustrates that while multiculturalism has indeed been institutionalized since the 1960s, as evidenced by the existence of such ethnic studies programs all over the country, cultural and ethnic "diversity" is by no means a universal value. The meaning of ethnic identity in political and social life is still a question that is highly contested in the public sphere. Also, on a basic level, the story indicates that race—even in era that many are quick to label as "postracial"—still has the power to divide and cause controversy. And perhaps most important for this project, *The Daily Show*'s ability to not only provide a satirical commentary but also to inspire protests and increase media coverage indicates the role that humor can play in conversations about race and ethnicity. While initially ethnic humorists react to "real world" events and debates, their comedy is ultimately embedded within the discourse on race itself, an inextricable part of it. In the contemporary American landscape, ethnic relations and ethnic humor have a symbiotic relationship.

Indeed, throughout this book I have argued that comic constructions of American ethnicity are changing right along with America itself. Since the 1970s, issues of diversity and multiculturalism have become increasingly central components in the national dialogue about race. During the same time, the demographic itself has become more and more diverse: immigrants from Mexico, the Caribbean, South America, Africa, Asia, and the Middle East enter the United States every year, and they are increasingly participating in both local and national discourses. Americans are reacting to these demographic and discursive changes in multiple and often contradictory ways. One thing is clear though: it is becoming nearly impossible to view American ethnic relations through the binary lens of the color line, and many humorists are looking for ways to place their own ethnic identity within a larger multiethnic context. This is particularly true for members of the groups discussed in the first three chapters. African Americans are finding that their position as the dominant minority is threatened by the increased numbers of Asian Americans and especially Latinos. Jewish Americans are expressing anxiety about their perceived position as generic whites and are more fervently asserting their own unique place in the American multiethnic spectrum. And even some "generic" white Americans are beginning to work against the tendency to view whiteness as an unmarked norm. And as we saw in chapters 4 and 5, multiculturalism and notions of diversity have become central to comic works that do not claim to represent the point of view of any single ethnic group. Producers of mainstream sitcoms and children's films have learned that unthreatening and harmonious visions of diversity can be extremely profitable. Other comic artists have used America's multiethnic demographic to interrogate and explore intercultural dialogue in fuller and more complex ways.

The multiethnic humor discussed in the previous chapter—exemplified by *Weeds*, the *Harold and Kumar* films, and the comedy of Russell Peters—is a fascinating development, and many more works will almost certainly continue the trend. However, such multiethnic humor will represent only one part of the future of American ethnic humor. Ethnic humor in the future will likely be much the way it is in the present: contradictory, complex, challenging, and often fraught with anxiety. The most sophisticated humorists will follow in the paths carved by comics like Peters, Dave Chappelle, Sacha Baron Cohen, and Trey Parker and Matt Stone. These humorists will be willing to look beyond the rigid boundaries of ethnic identification and use humor to explore ethnic identity in more complex ways. Other humorists, though, will continue to use comedy to actively reinforce the pluralist model of ethnic America, in what Kwame Anthony Appiah calls "a celebration of the beauty of a collection of closed boxes."[2] Moreover, the simplistic and idealized "corporate multiculturalist" humor discussed in chapter 4 will not go away anytime soon.

Very recently, we have also begun to see an increase in ethnic humor created by members of other ethnic groups, particularly Latinos and Asian Americans. The remainder of this conclusion will consider the ways in which Latino and Asian American humor contribute to contemporary American ethnic humor and draw from the comic traditions of other ethnic groups. I do not include individual chapters on Latino or Asian American humor primarily because they have historically occupied a less prominent position in American popular culture and, unlike Jewish and African American humor, have been visible in American media for a shorter period of time. This is not to say that the humor from these groups is inferior to or less interesting than that created by African or Jewish Americans. Rather, I suggest that Latino and Asian American humor are still in the process of *emerging* in the pop-cultural landscape. While there are certainly long comic traditions within Latino and Asian American communities, humorists from these traditions are only beginning to appear in significant numbers in mainstream media venues and only a handful are achieving crossover appeal. Before 2000, there had been very few well-known Latino humorists and hardly any Asian American humorists. However, the past decade has seen unprecedented numbers of comic performers from both groups, suggesting that the presence and significance of Latino and Asian American humor will continue to grow.

The existence of Latino and Asian American humor in the American media marketplace is a direct result of the increasing numbers of both groups in the population as well as of the increasing tendency of mainstream American culture to embrace—at least in the abstract—the ideals of diversity and multiculturalism. However, owing to the fact that both groups are only beginning to gain a foothold in popular culture, Asian American and Latino/a humorists are often less concerned with representing multiethnic issues and are more concerned with carving out a space for themselves in the media. This development fits into the most common trajectory of ethnic American humor: Before most ethnic humorists fully engage with other groups, they find it necessary to define their own comic spaces and articulate the tropes of their emerging comic aesthetic. In this sense, Latino and Asian American humor today are in a similar (although by no means identical) position to the first wave of crossover African American humorists in the late 1960s and early 1970s.

As I explain in chapter 1, in the 1960s and 1970s, as a result of the civil rights and identity politics movements, authentic African American humor, exemplified by the work of Richard Pryor, began to achieve massive crossover appeal. Most black comics, though, maintained what I call a "just us" comic aesthetic, in which, despite integrated audiences, they used various means to articulate their humor as primarily black communal productions. Such communal black comedy reached its apex with stand-up shows like *Def Comedy Jam* and films such as *The Original Kings of Comedy.* It is only very recently and most significantly through the work of Dave Chappelle, that we began to see comedy that considered blackness in a larger multiethnic context. This history could offer a possible model for our understanding of Latino and Asian American humor. Like the African American humorists in the late 1960s, Latino and Asian American humorists are only beginning to achieve crossover success. Furthermore, their humor, particularly for Latinos, depends on a "just us" comic aesthetic, which focuses on either intragroup issues or, again like African American comics, on binary comparisons with an imagined, monolithic white culture. It is likely, then, that in coming years, Latino/a and Asian American humorists will emerge who, like Dave Chappelle, will place their ethnic affiliation in a larger, multiethnic context.

There are of course limits to how strictly we can use the history of African American humor as a lens through which to understand Latino and Asian American humor. The "black experience," determined in large part by centuries of slavery and enforced segregation, is significantly different from the varied immigration experiences of Asian Americans and Latinos. Because of these differences, the content of Latino and Asian American humor is often quite different from African American humor. Despite cultural differences, however, both Latino and Asian American humorists often explicitly acknowledge the influence of African American humor on their own comedy. This is most apparent, as I suggest briefly in chapter 1, in the numerous stand-up comedy tours that are openly modeled after the African American–focused *The Original Kings of Comedy*, such as *The Original Latin Kings of Comedy* (2002), *The Latin Divas of Comedy* (2007), and *The Kims of Comedy* (2005). Through their titles alone, these concert films (and the tours on which they are based) tie themselves explicitly to African American humor. The open acknowledgment of black influence—while it is surely done to capitalize on the commercial success of *The Original Kings*—is itself a multiethnic move that suggests a certain level of intercultural dialogue. The content of these shows, however, tends to assert ethnic pride and, despite increasingly integrated audiences, be directed primarily at Latino or Asian American demographics. Interethnic conversation is not a feature. In its current form, then, most Latino and Asian American humorists acknowledge diversity but ultimately adhere to Werner Sollors's conception of ethnic humor as "a form of boundary construction."[3]

THE RICHARD PRYOR OF HISPANIC CULTURE?

Latino humor is more prominent now than ever before, but in the intervening years since Desi Arnaz played the heavily accented Ricky Ricardo on *I Love Lucy,* a handful of other Latino/a humorists achieved celebrity and popularity. In the 1970s, Freddie Prinze was a prominent stand-up comedian and crossed over to sitcom success on *Chico and the Man* (1974–1978) before his suicide at age twenty-two. Cheech Marin gained fame in the late 1970s and 1980s, primarily through his partnership with Tommy Chong and their series of Cheech and Chong films. Paul Rodriguez and John Leguizamo also achieved a level of prominence in the 1980s and 1990s. It is only during the past ten years, however, that a recognizable Latino brand of humor has become apparent through a wide range of performers, including Carlos Mencia, Gabriel Iglesias, Alex Reymundo, Cristela Alonzo, Joey Medina, and dozens of others. Mexican American comedian George Lopez, who in addition to a prolific stand-up career has had a network sitcom and late-night talk show, is surely the biggest Latino humorist in American culture, although he has not yet reached the levels of stardom of the most famous black comedians like Richard Pryor, Bill Cosby, Eddie Murphy, Chris Rock, or Whoopi Goldberg.

Despite Lopez's success in a wide range of media formats, Latino humor is still, by and large, relegated almost solely to the stand-up stage. This is a primary indicator that the humor is still in the process of emerging in popular culture. Stand-up specials are relatively cheap to produce and are easy to market to niche audiences, but they do not receive the same audience share as sitcoms or films. In order to fully emerge in the popular consciousness, we need to see something akin to the massive proliferation of African American humor throughout all media venues. African American humor is not only available through stand-up but has permeated the culture with dozens of sitcoms. Furthermore, there is a wide range of African American film humor, such as the *Barbershop* and *Friday* franchises, the numerous Wayans brothers–produced spoofs (*Scary Movie, Dance Flick,* etc.), and a seemingly inexhaustible supply of Tyler Perry films. While many of these works are marketed primarily to black audiences, they also manage to package and sell the idea of "blackness" and thus achieve crossover success as well. Latino humor has yet to break through to such mainstream markets.

This breakthrough is likely not far away, however, for the position of Latinos in American culture is changing drastically. During the past ten to fifteen years, Latinos have surpassed African Americans as the country's largest minority group. On the one hand, this means that Latinos and African Americans sometimes see

George Lopez is the biggest name in contemporary Latino humor. (Credit: ©Showtime 2004. Photographer: Cliff Lipson. Courtesy of Photofest.)

each other as competitors over increasingly scarce jobs, resources, and political power. On the other hand, as many Latinos explore their new position in the culture, they often informally depend on African Americans as a model. We see this in the work of the most prominent Latino humorists. For instance, in the opening to his stand-up special *Why You Crying?* (2005), Lopez explains that he feels honored to perform in the same arena in which Richard Pryor had performed. The Honduran American comic Carlos Mencia goes even further, claiming—with at least a touch of delusion—to be "the first Richard Pryor of the Hispanic culture."[4] The influence of African American humor is also readily apparent in the content of Latino humor, which mostly adheres to a "just us" aesthetic. Like *The Original Kings of Comedy, The Original Latin Kings of Comedy* enforces its "just us" worldview by frequently panning to the audience in order to emphasize the film as a Latino community event. *The Original Latin Kings* excludes non-Latino spectators even more explicitly than most African American humor, for while English is the primary language, many of the jokes are actually delivered in Spanish. Furthermore, like African American comedy, Latino humor is often based on comic comparisons between white and Latino cultures. While this is not necessarily derived from African American humor, it does bear a striking resemblance to the "white people be like" jokes that are typical of black comedy shows such as *The Original Kings* and *Def Comedy Jam*.[5]

Lopez exemplifies this trend most forcefully. In his comedy special *George Lopez: Tall, Dark, and Chicano* (2009), for instance, he provides an extended routine based on stereotypical comparisons between the ways white and Latino parents raise their children. White parents, Lopez says, coddle their children, creating a race of whiny weaklings. Latino children, in contrast, are tough, self-sufficient, yet still respectful of their elders. They might, for example, "go missing for days" without their parents noticing or caring; white children, on the other hand, are not allowed to leave the yard, and whenever they are missing, an Amber Alert immediately goes into effect. In the bit, Lopez reinforces the white/Latino binary by discussing white children with *very* white names, such as Tanner, Bryce, Skylar, or Chance. In the same special, Lopez speaks of the white tendency to appropriate and Americanize Latino foods by transforming ethnically distinct tortillas and burritos into boring health foods like "flat bread" and "wraps." Like numerous African American comedians before him, Lopez depends on a homogenous and totalizing view of whiteness, which is characterized by a bland and unhip sense of privilege.

Of course Latino humor is not identical to the dominant strain of African American humor, for it deals most explicitly with issues facing the Latino community. Because the largest numbers of American Latinos are Mexican American, the topic that is dealt with most often is illegal immigration. The *Original Kings*–style stand-up show *Legally Brown* (2011), for example, is framed around the concept of illegal immigration, with Rick Najera portraying a fictional border patrol agent who will be waiting to deport all of the comedians after the show. Similarly, on *Stand-Up Revolution* (2011), Gabriel Iglesias jokes about his entire tour bus being pulled over by an immigration officer. And in *America's Mexican* (2007), George Lopez says plainly, "Let me say this about immigration so that you finally hear it from a Latino: we ain't going nowhere!" While all of these humorists critique conservative anti-immigration policies, Latino humor is often more conservative than most African American comedy.

African American humor largely articulates disillusionment with American culture and with such ideological myths as the American Dream. On the other hand, as Guillermo Avila-Saavedra argues, Latino/a comics tend to "frame the Latino immigrant experience within recurring U.S. mythologies such as the self-made man and overcoming adversity."[6] Lopez's sitcom *George Lopez* (2002–2007), for example, tells a story of upward mobility, as Lopez's character is a hard-working Mexican American who gets promoted from factory worker to plant manager. Another *Original Latin King,* Alex Reymundo, deliberately connects himself to the conservative South with concert titles such as *One Funny Hick-Spanic* (2007) and *Alex Reymundo: Red-Nexican* (2009). Reymundo also regularly tours with Ron White, from the *Blue Collar Comedy Tour,* discussed in chapter 3. The redneck/Latino connection suggests that while Latinos are often excluded from mainstream American culture, they nonetheless embrace the "simple" American values of hard work and self-reliance that are associated with the American South.

Aside from Reymundo's affiliation with white southern culture, Latino humor remains fairly insular. Despite the influence that African American humor has clearly had on Latino comedians, Latino humor does not have a figure, like Dave Chappelle, who has placed Latino culture in sustained conversation with other group positions. Some may view Carlos Mencia as a possible exception to this trend. Mencia infamously bases his humor on race, and his work contains routines about African Americans, Asians, and Arabs, as well as Latinos. Furthermore, his Comedy Central series *Mind of Mencia,* a hybrid between stand-up and sketch comedy, is clearly modeled after *Chappelle's Show.* The actual content of Mencia's humor, however, is both unsophisticated and unoriginal. This opinion is largely shared by both critics and other comedians. Scholars and journalists have generally ignored him or written him off as a sophomoric Chappelle clone, and numerous other comedians, including George Lopez, have accused him of stealing jokes.[7]

Mencia's on-stage persona is abrasive and confrontational, and most of his jokes are delivered through screams. While his act is openly about race, he succeeds neither at providing thoughtful ethnic commentary nor at being particularly funny. For example, in *Not for the Easily Offended* (2005), Mencia provides an extended bit about how people enrolled in online colleges could simply get their "Asian friend" to take the test for them. Mencia then provides a stereotypical impersonation of a generic, accented Asian doing homework: "I rove tests. . . . Today you gonna get a A prus." A bit like this is a simple caricature, and does not really even qualify as a joke, for there is no play, punch line, or other formal device that would make it so. His impersonation of a nerdy, test-loving Asian American student calls up the stereotype of the "smart Asian," but Mencia does nothing to interrogate or contextualize the stereotype, and he certainly does nothing to challenge it. Dave Chappelle, to whom Mencia is most often compared, performs a similar Asian stereotype in his "Racial Pixies" sketch—discussed in chapter 1—but here, Chappelle explores the ways that racial stereotypes affect their targets internally, and he ultimately works to deflate the power of ethnic stereotypes. Mencia, in contrast, simply seems to believe that the stereotype is true.

An even more problematic routine occurs in *Performance Enhanced*, which aired during the 2008 presidential election. Here, Mencia argues that if Obama gets elected, "black people can no longer bitch about racism, and the race card will no longer exist." He goes on to assert that affirmative action policies can be dismantled and that "we" will now be able to judge black people based on merit without being accused of racism. The routine suggests, despite his "blue" language, that Mencia's ethnic politics are extremely conservative, and he has little understanding of or concern for the ways in which racism manifests itself in American culture. The bit, especially when seen in conjunction with the "smart Asian" stereotype discussed above, also illustrates the limitations of Mencia's multiethnic humor. As we saw in the previous chapter, an artist like Russell Peters is able to discuss multiple ethnic groups and even ethnic stereotypes as a way of encouraging an intercultural dialogue and highlighting similarities between seemingly dissimilar ethnic positions. Mencia, on the other hand, relies primarily on ridicule in his discussion of other ethnic positions. His screaming delivery of these bits also makes the humor seem genuinely mean-spirited rather than playful. Clearly, Mencia has fans; he has starred in four comedy specials, and his television series aired for four seasons. But his alienation from the rest of the Latino humor community (and really from the rest of the *humor* community) and his superficial representations of ethnicity make him a poor candidate for a humorist who can place Latino humor in a larger multicultural dialogue.

Gabriel Iglesias may be a more likely candidate. With two hour-long stand-up specials and his own Comedy Central stand-up series, Iglesias has emerged as a leader in Latino humor. His comedy is rooted in the Mexican American community, and like other Mexican American comics, he delivers occasional punch lines in Spanish, jokes about immigration, and provides self-deprecating yet ultimately flattering depictions of Mexican American culture. At the same time, Iglesias's humor is not defined solely by his ethnicity. Describing himself as "fluffy," Iglesias is physically very large and bases much of his humor on his weight and his eating habits. He is also a skilled mimic and, within a single routine, may impersonate a Valley girl, a redneck, and a stereotypical Latino as well as various noises, such as cars, roller coasters, and bodily functions. Iglesias's humor, like Dave Chappelle's, is also aided by his laid-back and likable character, which stands in sharp contrast to the aggressive demeanor of Lopez and Mencia.

His persona and appearance (he usually wears bright Hawaiian shirts, giving him a "party animal" look) make Iglesias a figure ripe for major crossover appeal.

And while Iglesias's humor thus far does not engage in sustained multiethnic conversation, his comedy does suggest a more fluid vision of Latino culture than that of most of his contemporaries. For example, in his stand-up special *I'm Not Fat . . . I'm Fluffy* (2009), Iglesias tells multiple stories about his attempts to use his Mexican American identity—and more specifically his ability to speak Spanish—to get himself out of unpleasant situations. In the first example, Iglesias is stopped by a school principal when he tries to drop off his girlfriend's son in the wrong area. Iglesias impersonates the principal, and it is clear from his impersonation that she is supposed to be a white female. Iglesias attempts to ignore the woman's demands by switching to Spanish and feigning ignorance. The principal, voiced by Iglesias, immediately repeats her instructions in a comically bland, unaccented Spanish. At the end, she says, "no soy un pendeja." A subtitle translates the line as, "I'm not stupid." In the same special, he tells another story about an unpleasant conversation with a telephone customer service operator, whom Iglesias impersonates in the manner of a stereotypical "sassy black woman." When the woman does not cooperate with Iglesias, he hangs up and calls back, this time choosing "Spanish" from the automated menu. However, to his chagrin, the same African American woman picks up the line, exclaiming, "I speak Spanish too, motherfucker!"

While the humor of these routines depends on white and African American stereotypes, the jokes also raise questions about Latinos' ability to construct rigid ethnic boundaries in contemporary American culture. As I have suggested, the use of Spanish is one of the fundamental ways in which Latino/a humorists maintain a "just us" comic aesthetic. Spanish often serves as a cultural barrier with which Latinos can draw a firm line between themselves and white people. In *Tall, Dark, and Chicano*, for example, Lopez asserts that most Latinos *do* speak English, "we just don't want to talk to you [white people]." In the routines above, Iglesias attempts to use Spanish to construct a similar barrier, but finds out that, despite his ethnicity, he does not "own" Spanish. Indeed, as the Latino population continues to grow, more and more non-Latinos, especially in the Southwest, are finding that Spanish is a necessity in order to do business in communities with heavy Latino populations. If Spanish serves as the primary cultural barrier, then these routines suggest, in a manner reminiscent of Dave Chappelle's "I Know Black People" sketch, that Latino culture exists at the crossroads of multiple ethnic affiliations, not as a closed-off unit.

It is of course impossible to tell whether or not Iglesias will continue to develop these sorts of jokes into a genuine multiethnic humor, or if he will gain access to a forum beyond the stand-up stage to present his talents to a wider audience. His brief Comedy Central stand-up series *Gabriel Iglesias Presents:*

Stand-Up Revolution (2011), however, does suggest that Iglesias is at least willing to look beyond the strict boundaries of Mexican American identification. The series is loosely modeled after *Def Comedy Jam* and features Iglesias performing a short stand-up routine and then introducing other comedians. In various ways, the show roots itself in Latino culture and features primarily Latino/a comedians. However, Iglesias gives space on the show to comedians from other demographics, such as Native American comic Larry Omaha, Indian American Paul Varghese, and Iranian American Maz Jobrani. While there is not an explicit cross-cultural exchange between these diverse comedians, the potential for such an exchange is present on a series like this. The diversity of the cast also suggests that, like Russell Peters, Iglesias could possibly serve as a spokesperson for a multiethnic coalition of "brown" comedians. This is of course dependent on Comedy Central and other corporate entities allowing a space for Iglesias to develop his humor. As of this writing, unfortunately, *Stand-Up Revolution* is not slated for a second season.

LOCATING AN ASIAN AMERICAN HUMOR

While individual ethnic humorists may have their own style and concerns, there are usually a shared set of comic devices and/or social issues that hold together the humor of a specific ethnicity. African American humorists often depend on comic comparisons between white and black cultures; Jewish humorists utilize self-deprecation and comic pessimism; Latino humorists frequently switch to Spanish and joke about immigration. These common traits allow us to locate and define a specific *brand* of black, Jewish, or Latino humor, which serves to not only hold together various humorists of a particular ethnicity but also to aid in the marketing and selling of a specific set of ideas about ethnicity. In contrast, it is more difficult to locate common tropes in the comedy created by Asian Americans. In particular, the internal diversity of Asian Americans complicates our ability to firmly delineate Asian American humor. For instance, as a whole, Asian Americans have education and income levels comparable to or greater than white Americans, but subgroups such as Hmong and Vietnamese Americans have substantially higher poverty rates. Most Japanese American families have been in the country for generations, whereas Indian and Korean Americans are more recent immigrants. This diversity makes it nearly impossible to make generalizing statements about Asian American culture or Asian American humor.[8]

Perhaps owing to this internal diversity, as well as the fact that they are the fastest growing group in the country, Asian Americans can sometimes serve as a signifier for the broader diversity of the entire nation. As we saw in the previous chapter, two of the most significant contributions to multiethnic humor—Russell Peters and the *Harold and Kumar* films—highlight Asian American issues. However, both Peters and the *Harold and Kumar* films focus on a broad spectrum of ethnic affiliations. They do not market themselves as a specifically Asian American humor. Asian American humor thus lacks a multimedia superstar—like George Lopez, or any number of black comedians—who can serve as a comic representative of the Asian American community. While Peters is the most obvious candidate, his international concerns and cosmopolitan brand of humor allows him to speak to and on behalf of not only Asians and Asian Americans but also Arabs, Latinos, and even African Americans. While this cosmopolitan thrust makes Peters a fascinating humorist overall, his humor is not, nor does it aim to be, representative of a distinct "Asian American" brand of comedy.

A similar point could be made about Margaret Cho, a Korean American comic who is even more prominent than Peters. In the 1990s, Cho starred in the short-lived sitcom *All-American Girl* (1994–1995), which was one of only a handful of television series with an Asian American main character. Because of poor ratings and criticism from the Asian American community, the series was cancelled after one season. Since then, Cho has had a prolific stand-up career. Her first stand-up special, *I'm the One That I Want* (2000), focuses most explicitly on Asian American issues, as Cho details the production of and media response to *All-American Girl.* In this special, Cho provides a pointed critique of dominant representations of shy and submissive Asian and Asian American women, explicitly referencing the Disney vehicle *Mulan* (1998). In her critique of Asian stereotypes, Cho performs a series of bows and giggles and affects a strong Asian accent, saying lines such as, "When I grow up in Korea, we live on the rice patty. And we have-a no food." The meek stereotype stands in sharp contrast to Cho's aggressive and often raunchy humor and serves as a compelling example of the ways in which humor can explore the intersections of gender and ethnicity. Since this special, however, Asian American issues have become less central to Cho's comedy, and she has taken on the role of spokesperson for the gay and lesbian community. She still addresses her ethnicity, but Asian American concerns have taken a backseat in her most recent humor. Like Peters, then, Cho does not perform as a comic representative of the Asian American community.

Among lesser-known Asian American humorists, there have been various attempts at creating a brand of Asian American humor. We see this most explicitly in the Asian American stand-up concert film *The Kims of Comedy*, as well as in the stand-up television series *Comedy Zen* (2006), which aired on "ImaginAsian TV" and was thus specifically targeted for an Asian American audience. These works adhere to a "just us" aesthetic and, like many Latino humorists, use African American humor as a model. *The Kims of Comedy* openly refers to *The Original Kings of Comedy* and, like that film, maintains a "just us" aesthetic by frequently panning to the predominantly Asian American audience. However, its similarities with African American humor are limited: even as the title of the film acknowledges an African American influence, it also distances itself from black culture. Based on the common Korean surname Kim, the title suggests a playful and ironic relationship between African American and Asian American humor. This ironic or tongue-in-cheek connection is driven home in the final moments of the film when comedian Ken Jeong brings out an acoustic guitar and sings a Christian / Korean American revision of many famous hip-hop songs, such as Run DMC's "It's Tricky" and Dr. Dre's "Nuthin but a 'G' Thang." The humor here is driven by the awkward juxtaposition of an Asian American singing, in a decidedly light style, music that is typically associated with a black urban sensibility. In other works, Indian American comedian Aziz Ansari has a similar approach, for he often tells stories about socializing with popular black musicians like Kanye West, Jay-Z, or R. Kelly. These stories, however, emphasize how "nerdy" Ansari is compared to the "cool" black musicians. Rather than suggesting that African American culture can serve as a real model for Asian American culture, this sort of humor suggests that while the two groups are held together by their minority status, they are also wildly dissimilar.

Although it does not provide an overt influence, Jewish American humor may ultimately serve as a better model in locating an Asian American comic aesthetic. As I suggest in my discussion of the *Harold and Kumar* films in the previous chapter, many of the stereotypes about Jewish and Asian Americans overlap. In the early to mid-twentieth century, Jewish Americans, owing to their high education and income levels, were constructed in the national imagination as a "model minority" in much the same way that Asian Americans are today. The content of Asian American humor occasionally uses the comic devices of Jewish humor, such as irony and self-deprecation, but the connection is more apparent in Asian American comedians' attitude toward their own ethnicity. Most contemporary Asian American humorists are second generation and seem to have assimilated fairly fluidly into American culture. Like many Jewish Americans, Asian American humorists can have a relaxed relationship with their ethnic identity and avoid being completely defined by it. Aziz Ansari, discussed briefly above, is a good example of this. He occasionally discusses his ethnic background, but his best-known routines are about teasing his cousin on Facebook, his obsession with bed sheet thread counts, and, as previously mentioned, his awkward social interactions with famous rappers and R&B singers. Ansari makes no attempt to hide his Asian American ethnicity, but he clearly has the freedom, like Jewish American and other white comedians, to treat it as only one facet of his comic persona.

This flexible approach to ethnic affiliation manifests itself in the most common trope of Asian American humor, which is the humorist's tendency to impersonate his or her less-assimilated immigrant parents. Margaret Cho is perhaps most famous for this, for she includes impersonations of her heavily accented mother in nearly every one of her stand-up acts. Russell Peters also regularly impersonates his Indian-accented father and has even assigned to his father, who is recently deceased, a catchphrase: "Somebody's going to get a hurt real bad." Likewise, Bobby Lee mimics his Korean father; and half-Korean comic Steven Byrne and half-Filipino comic Jo Koy both impersonate their Asian mothers to comic effect. These parental impersonations are all good-natured, but the parents in the routines come across as quaint and slightly clueless ethnic others. The accented impersonations all contrast with the unaccented voices of the comedians themselves. Similarly, much of the humor has to do with arguments between child and parent about the differences between American and Asian customs. Overall then, these routines serve to de-ethnicize the second generation Asian American comics themselves. By highlighting their ethnic parents, Asian American comedians claim ethnic difference but also distance themselves from it. Clearly, this sort of humor is available only for second-generation Asian American comedians; it will be interesting to see what approach third- and fourth-generation Asian American humorists—who will not be raised by less-assimilated immigrants—will take to their ethnic affiliation. Very often, as we have seen in Jewish American and many other "white ethnic" groups, third- and fourth-generation individuals often embrace ethnic difference as a sort of revolt against the assimilationist motives of the previous generation(s). Time will tell whether Asian American humorists will follow a similar path.

As the above examples illustrate, Asian American humorists (like Latinos) are primarily restricted to the stand-up stage, and there is a scarcity of Asian American humor in other media productions. Since the cancellation of Margaret Cho's short-lived sitcom, Asian Americans have been relegated to supporting roles in comic television series, such as Aziz Ansari in *Parks and Recreation* and Kunal Nayyar in *The Big Bang Theory*.[9] Asian American performers are even more scarce in film. Outside of the martial arts genre, they are virtually invisible in mainstream American film and almost always relegated to small parts, such as Ken Jeong's problematic portrayal of an effeminate Asian gangster in *The Hangover* films (2009 and 2011). However, the case of the successful and innovative *Harold and Kumar* franchise demonstrates that Asian Americans *can* play leading roles in mainstream American film and that white audiences will go to see such films. As the Asian American population continues to grow, it will be interesting to see how Asian American humorists develop in terms of their changing status in the national imagination. In addition to speaking to and for an extremely diverse Asian American population, they will most likely find it increasingly necessary to articulate their ethnic identity in relation to other groups. Defining a specific brand of Asian American humor may not get any easier, but Asian American humorists will certainly become more central to the contemporary comic landscape.

While undeniably significant in their own right, the emergence of Latino and Asian American humorists also raises important questions about the role that ethnic humor plays in American popular culture. Once we categorize and define African American, Jewish American, white, Latino, and Asian American humor, it becomes clear that we need not stop there. The actual landscape of American humor is as diverse as the American population, whose constituency goes well beyond the above-mentioned categories. For example, we have already seen a rise in Muslim and Arab American humor in response to the anti-Muslim attitudes fostered by the attacks of September 11, 2001, and the subsequent "War on Terror."[10] Humorists such as Ahmed Ahmed, Maz Jobrani, and Maysoon Zayid, among others, represent a new wave of Arab American humorists who use their comedy to challenge prominent Arab stereotypes. Furthermore, many biracial humorists, including Dean Obeidallah, Jo Koy, Steve Byrne, and the comedy team of Keegan-Michael Key and Jordan Peele are actively speaking about their mixed-race heritage. In contrast, even twenty years ago, most biracial or multiracial entertainers would either "pass" as undifferentiated whites or wholly embrace their nonwhite ancestry in order to make ethnicity a central aspect of their humor.[11] The category of "African American," has also been complicated by recent waves of immigrants from Africa and the Caribbean. For example, Haitian American stand-up comic Wil Sylvince appears in many venues typically associated with African Americans, such as on *Def Comedy Jam* or *Showtime at the Apollo*, but his presence complicates his audience's ability to view blackness as a monolithic category.

The above examples suggest an increasing diversification of American ethnic humor. In light of this diversification, it may seem as if the American humor marketplace is becoming more fractured than ever. In an age of niche marketing and instant streaming access to virtually every comedian who has ever been filmed, it is plausible to assert that, rather than there being a recognizable American ethnic humor, there are only a series of small, group-specific ethnic humors. Not only are there African American, Jewish American, and white American humors, but also Asian American, Latino, Caribbean American, Native American, mixed-race, Arab American, and any other number of "hyphenated" American humors that we choose to name, including numerous subgroups within the previously mentioned categories. Viewed through the lens of this fracturing, contemporary ethnic humor appears to be very similar to Appiah's "celebration of the beauty of a collection of closed boxes." This of course suggests a move in the opposite direction from the trend in intercultural dialogue and multiethnic humor that I have teased out throughout this project. I predict that, just as some African American and Jewish American comedians have already done, comedians from these diverse subject positions will also participate in a more sustained multiethnic dialogue. One wonders, though, if it is possible to locate a distinctly

American humor amid all of this ethnic fracturing. The question resonates with a larger, ongoing discussion about the nature and potential problems of American multiculturalism. As we celebrate our differences and delineate between them, then what can hold us all together as Americans?

The issue is a thorny one, for in recognizing diversity, we are also deeply suspicious of narratives or worldviews that attempt to speak on behalf of an entire nation. Such narratives run the risk of universalizing and thus glossing over cultural differences and racial inequalities. David Hollinger addresses the question at length and ultimately promotes a vision of "civic nationalism" that embraces diversity yet does not lose sight of our shared lot as Americans. "Being an American amid a multiplicity of affiliations," Hollinger argues, "need not be dangerously threatening to diversity. Nor need it be too shallow to constitute an important solidarity of its own."[12] Statements like this sound good, but it is quite difficult—lacking an immediate national tragedy such as 9/11—to envision what entails such a civic nationalism. In the context of this project, what might an American ethnic humor, based on solidarity rather than ethnic boundaries, look like? The multiethnic and cosmopolitan humor discussed in chapter 5, in which humor is derived from conversation among members of multiple ethnic affiliations, may be an important step in that direction, but neither agreement nor cohesion are required for such conversations. Even when an understanding is achieved across cultural lines, this does not easily translate into an American ethnic humor.

There is no easy resolution here, but I argue that it is possible for humorists to be deeply entrenched in their ethnic affiliation and simultaneously embrace a distinctly American identity. This balancing may translate into a sort of national ethnic humor. I will end with a discussion of one last comedy routine, from Chris Rock's 2004 stand-up special *Never Scared*, that may suggest the features that such a national ethnic humor might have. Elsewhere in this book, I have critiqued Rock for his reluctance to look beyond the white/black binary that drives most African American humor. In this bit, however, Rock manages to transition from a white/other vision of American race relations into a broader discussion of a distinctly American phenomenon that transcends ethno-racial difference. At the beginning of the routine, Rock argues that "only the white man can profit from pain." According to this logic, black people can become rich only by doing "positive" things, whereas white people make billions of dollars by dealing in undeniably harmful commodities. For example, Rock asks, "could you imagine if the Philip Morris family was a bunch of Jheri-curled niggers from Mississippi? Do you know how illegal a pack of cigarettes would be?" Rock provides a similar discussion of alcohol and guns, and after each example, he repeats, in preacher-like fashion, the refrain "but it's all right 'cause it's all white!" The bit, so far, is an insightful piece of racial commentary that speaks directly to issues of systemic inequality, and it is the sort of routine at which Rock excels.

Moments later, however, he transitions into a larger American critique. "The number one reason people hate America," Rock argues, "is our religion. Americans worship money. We worship money . . . and we all go to the same church: the church of ATM." Notice how Rock's word choice changes here. In the bit about white people profiting from pain, Rock is careful to differentiate between whites and blacks in order to illustrate his point about racial inequality. In the joke about worshiping money, however, he talks about "Americans" and uses inclusive language, such as "our" and "we." Similar routines about American materialism and wealth obsession can of course be found in the works of white comedians like Louis C.K., George Carlin, or Bill Hicks, but white humorists very often make broad statements about American culture, and as we saw in chapter 3, whiteness typically works as a signifier for universality. The significance here is not Rock's blackness but rather the way in which he situates his broad critique of American culture alongside a related critique of American race relations. Rock has a deep understanding of racial differences in America, yet at the same time, he acknowledges that there are other things that hold us all together as Americans.

This sort of comic jeremiad is probably not quite what Hollinger has in mind in his discussion of civic nationalism, but Rock manages to speak of America as a distinct ethnos. Furthermore, he uses self-deprecation, one of the fundamental building blocks of a communal ethnic humor, as a means of articulating it. That the bit is based on a perceived problem in American culture, I would argue, in no way negates the joke's nationalist impulse. First of all, a joke simply asserting ethnic pride would probably not be very funny. And more important, Rock begins the joke by creating a sort of us-versus-them binary by explaining that our worship of wealth is "the number one reason people hate America." These "people," we can assume, are either not Americans at all or choose not to identify as Americans. In keeping with Werner Sollors's conception of ethnic humor as "a form of boundary construction," Rock builds rhetorical boundaries around America and creates a community of laughter. Within this community there are an endless of array of smaller ethnic affiliations. However, despite these differences, we can all laugh at ourselves, both as Americans and as members of numerous other subgroups. As we do so, this laughter can also teach us something about our culture. Ethnic humor, regardless of who creates it, is a response to our multiethnic environment. Ethnic humor can thus serve as an avenue through which we can learn more about what separates us, what holds us together, and how we would like to see ourselves.

NOTES

INTRODUCTION

1. The Yiddish term *goyish* officially refers to anyone or anything that is not Jewish, but in contemporary parlance the term is used to refer almost exclusively to white Christians.
2. Lenny Bruce, *The Essential Lenny Bruce,* compiled and edited by John Cohen (New York: Bell Publishing, 1970), 31.
3. All statistics come from the U.S. Census Bureau website: http://www.census.gov/population/race.
4. For a full survey of humor theory, see Michael Billig, *Laughter and Ridicule: Towards a Social Critique of Humour* (London: Sage Publications, 2005); Leon Rappoport, *Punchlines: The Case for Racial, Ethnic, and Gender Humor* (Westport, CT: Praeger, 2005); and Simon Critchley, *On Humour: Thinking in Action* (New York: Routledge, 2002).
5. Thomas Hobbes, "Human Nature: Or, the Fundamental Elements of Policy," in *The English Works of Thomas Hobbes,* vol. 4, ed. Sir William Molesworth (London: John Bohn, 1840), 46.
6. Sigmund Freud, *Jokes and Their Relation to the Unconscious,* trans. James Strachey (New York: W. W. Norton, 1960), 101.
7. Christie Davies, "Exploring the Thesis of the Self-Deprecating Jewish Sense of Humor," in *Semites and Stereotypes: Characteristics of Jewish Humor,* ed. Avner Ziv and Ana Zajdman (London: Greenwood Press, 1993), 33.
8. For a fuller discussion of the implications of self-deprecating humor, see Davies, "Exploring the Thesis of the Self-Deprecating Jewish Sense of Humor," and Rappoport, *Punchlines.*
9. Werner Sollors, *Beyond Ethnicity: Consent and Descent in American Culture* (New York: Oxford University Press, 1986), 132.
10. Bambi Haggins, *Laughing Mad: The Black Comic Persona in Post-Soul America* (New Brunswick, NJ: Rutgers University Press, 2007), 243.
11. John Lowe, "Theories of Ethnic Humor: How to Enter Laughing," *American Quarterly* 38, no. 3 (1986): 439.
12. Full contexts for African American and Jewish American humor will be provided in chapters 1 and 2, respectively. For comparisons between the two, see Joseph Boskin, "Beyond Kvetching and Jiving: The Thrust of Jewish and Black Folk Humor," in *Jewish Wry,* ed. Sarah Blacher Cohen (Bloomington: Indiana University Press, 1987), 53–79; and Rappoport, *Punchlines,* chap. 5.
13. The following history is suggested by Joseph Boskin and Joseph Dorinson, "Ethnic Humor: Subversion and Survival," in *What's So Funny? Humor in American Culture,* ed. Nancy A. Walker (Wilmington, DE: Scholarly Resources, 1998), 205–224.
14. For a full discussion of early minstrel shows, see Eric Lott, *Love and Theft: Blackface Minstrelsy and the American Working Class* (Oxford: Oxford University Press, 1995). For a discussion

of Jewish stage representations, see Harley Erdman, *Staging the Jew: The Performance of an American Ethnicity, 1860–1920* (New Brunswick, NJ: Rutgers University Press, 1997).

15. Donald Bogle, *Toms, Coons, Mulattoes, Mammies, and Bucks: An Interpretive History of Blacks in American Films* (New York: Continuum International, 1994); and idem, *Primetime Blues: African Americans on Network Television* (New York: Farrar, Straus and Giroux, 2001).

16. As William Knoedelseder explains in his history of stand-up comedy during the 1970s and 1980s, appearances on Johnny Carson's *Tonight Show* were the primary avenue for a stand-up comedian to achieve mainstream success. Carson, however, did not think that women made successful comedians and would rarely—with the exception of Joan Rivers—allow them on his show. William Knoedelseder, *I'm Dying Up Here: Heartbreak and High Times in Stand-up Comedy's Golden Era* (New York: Public Affairs Books, 2009), 78–79. This trend continues into the present day. In January 2012, David Letterman's comedy booker Eddie Brill was fired after admitting in a *New York Times* interview that he preferred male comedians because, according to him, most female comedians try to act like men and are "less authentic." Jason Zinoman, "The Comedy Gatekeeper Who Makes Letterman Laugh," *New York Times*, January 11, 2012, http://www.nytimes.com/2012/01/12/arts/television/eddie-brill-and-the-comics-on-david-lettermans-show.html?_r=1.

17. There is also a lack of scholarly literature exploring the intersections of ethnicity and gender in American humor. For discussions of important female humorists, see Kathleen Rowe, *The Unruly Woman: Gender and the Genres of Laughter* (Austin: University of Texas Press, 1995); and Joanne R. Gilbert, *Performing Marginality: Humor, Gender, and Cultural Critique* (Detroit: Wayne State University Press, 2004). Gilbert provides a brief discussion of female ethnic humor on 81–83. Also see Bambi Haggins's discussion of black female comics, particularly Whoopi Goldberg, in chapter 4 of *Laughing Mad*.

18. Mel Watkins, *On the Real Side: A History of African American Comedy* (Chicago: Lawrence Hill Books, 1999).

19. For a complete history of early Jewish American humor, see Lawrence J. Epstein, *The Haunted Smile: The Story of Jewish Comedians* (Oxford: Public Affairs, 2001).

20. Lott, *Love and Theft*, 18.

21. Michael Billig, "Humour and Hatred: The Racist Jokes of the Ku Klux Klan," *Discourse & Society* 12, no. 3 (2001): 267–289.

22. See Bogle, *Toms, Coons*.

23. As Roger Daniels explains, the intended effects of this law were to benefit future immigrants from eastern and southern Europe. Neither Lyndon B. Johnson nor the writers of the bill foresaw the extent of increased immigration from Asia and Latin America. Roger Daniels, *Coming to America: A History of Immigration and Ethnicity in American Life* (New York: HarperCollins, 2002), 341.

24. Daniels explains that the Asian American population grew from "less than four-tenths of 1 percent" of the overall population in 1940 to approximately 1.5 percent in 1980 and 4 percent in 2000. Additionally, before the 1960s, Americans with Korean, Vietnamese, or Indian ancestry were practically nonexistent; today, these groups make up sizable portions of the Asian American community (ibid., 350–351). During the same time period, immigrants from the Caribbean and South America greatly increased as well. For example, owing to the influx of Cuban refugees following the Cuban revolution, the Cuban American community grew from 120, 000 in 1960 to 1.2 million in 2000 (ibid., 372–376).

25. J. Eric Oliver, *The Paradoxes of Integration: Race, Neighborhood, and Civic Life in Multiethnic America* (Chicago: University of Chicago Press, 2010), 2.

26. See Ramon A. Gutierrez, "Ethnic Studies: Its Evolution in American Colleges and Universities," in *Multiculturalism: A Critical Reader*, ed. David Theo Goldberg (Cambridge: Wiley-Blackwell, 1994), 157–167.
27. See Mary C. Waters, *Ethnic Options: Choosing Identities in America* (Berkeley: University of California Press, 1990).
28. Oliver, *Paradoxes of Integration*, 4–5.
29. Jennifer L. Hochschild and Reuel R. Rogers, "Race Relations in a Diversifying Nation," in *New Directions: African Americans in a Diversifying Nation*, ed. James S. Jackson (Ann Arbor: Program for Research on Black Americans, University of Michigan Press, 2000), 56–57.
30. David Hollinger, *Postethnic America: Beyond Multiculturalism* (New York: Basic Books, 2005), 36–37.
31. Ibid., 3.
32. Paul Gilroy, *Against Race: Imagining Political Culture beyond the Color Line* (Cambridge, MA: Harvard University Press, 2000), 13.
33. Kwame Anthony Appiah, *The Ethics of Identity* (Princeton, NJ: Princeton University Press, 2005), 256.
34. Paul Gilroy, *Postcolonial Melancholia* (New York: Columbia University Press, 2005), 67.
35. Kwame Anthony Appiah, *Cosmopolitanism: Ethics in a World of Strangers* (New York: W. W. Norton, 2006), 85.
36. Christie Davies, *Ethnic Humor around the World: A Comparative Analysis* (Bloomington: Indiana University Press, 1996), 9.
37. Baron Cohen is actually British, but I argue that because he bases much of his humor in U.S. culture and has achieved massive popularity in America that it is valid to place his humor in an American context.

1. "JUST US": AFRICAN AMERICAN HUMOR IN MULTIETHNIC AMERICA

1. Perhaps as homage to Pryor's "just us" joke, the plot of the 2000 film *Dancing in September* (about African American images in the media) focuses on a fictional African American sitcom titled *Just Us*.
2. Mel Watkins, *On the Real Side: A History of African American Comedy* (Chicago: Lawrence Hill Books, 1999), 562. This is not to say that Pryor was the first African American comic to achieve popularity with both black and white audiences. As Watkins maintains, Dick Gregory, Bill Cosby, and Flip Wilson, among others, preceded Pryor in this sense. Pryor, however, brought to white audiences an authentic black folk humor that had previously been contained within the black community itself.
3. Siva Vaidhyanathan, "Now's the Time: The Richard Pryor Phenomenon and the Triumph of Black Culture," in *New Directions in American Humor*, ed. David E. E. Sloane (Tuscaloosa: University of Alabama Press, 1998), 48.
4. Werner Sollors, *Beyond Ethnicity: Consent and Descent in American Culture* (New York: Oxford University Press, 1986), 132.
5. Bambi Haggins, *Laughing Mad: The Black Comic Persona in Post-Soul America* (New Brunswick, NJ: Rutgers University Press, 2007), 72.
6. Ibid., 73
7. This type of dismissal can be found in Pryor as well. In *Richard Pryor: Live in Concert*, for example, Pryor briefly impersonates a stuttering Chinese man. Unlike his nuanced impersonations of various white and black voices, which provide real commentary on American race relations, Pryor's stuttering Chinese man is simply an object of ridicule.
8. W.E.B. Du Bois, *The Souls of Black Folk* (New York: Dover Publications, 1994), 2.

9. Watkins, *On the Real Side*, 27.

10. Ibid., 32

11. Quoted in Watkins, *On the Real Side*, 52.

12. Christine Acham, *Revolution Televised: Prime Time and the Struggle for Black Power* (Minneapolis: University of Minnesota Press, 2004), 7.

13. For a fuller discussion of these and other *Original Kings* inspired works, see the conclusion to this book.

14. Paul Gilroy, *Against Race: Imagining Political Culture beyond the Color Line* (Cambridge, MA: Harvard University Press, 2000), 24.

15. Gary M. Segura and Helena Alves Rodrigues, "Comparative Ethnic Politics in the United States: Beyond Black and White," *Annual Review of Political Science* 9 (2006): 376.

16. David Hollinger, *Cosmopolitanism and Solidarity: Studies in Ethnoracial, Religious, and Professional Affiliation in the United States* (Madison: University of Wisconsin Press, 2006), 43. See, in particular, the first two chapters, "Amalgamation and Hypodescent" and "The One Drop Rule and the One Hate Rule."

17. Paul Mooney, *Black Is the New White* (New York: Simon Spotlight Entertainment, 2009), 3, original emphasis.

18. For a discussion of Mooney and Pryor's work on *Sanford and Son* and *The Richard Pryor Show*, see chapters 4 and 6 of Acham, *Revolution Televised.*

19. Mooney explains Homey D. Clown as a sort of metaphor for the plight of the black entertainer: "Homey has a motto [Homey don't play dat], which may as well be words to live by for every comedian who doesn't want to play the coon. 'Homey may be a clown,' Damon says in character more than once, 'but he don't make a fool out of himself.'" Mooney, *Black Is the New White*, 217.

20. Ibid., 141, original emphasis. Hostile viewers (and a quick look at Mooney's message board on IMDb [http://www.imdb.com] reveals that Mooney has many hostile viewers) may be tempted to argue with Mooney's claims about the blackness of Jesus, Cleopatra, or rice, but such arguments will only lead us into thorny areas about the definition of "blackness" and our ability to apply that definition to historical periods.

21. Ibid., 247.

22. Ibid., 248.

23. Herman Gray, *Watching Race: Television and the Struggle for "Blackness"* (Minneapolis: University of Minnesota Press, 1995), 12.

24. In his memoir, Mooney also refers to this as "the nigger moment." *Black Is the New White*, 130.

25. At the 2005 BET Comedy awards Mooney called this bit "The Nigga Wake-Up Call," but in the film *Know Your History*, Mooney clearly pronounces the word "nigger."

26. Segura and Rodrigues explain that "African-Americans . . . view Latinos and their growing numbers as a threat to their social, economic, and political benefits. Furthermore, Latinos do not view African-Americans as an oppressed group in the same way other Americans may view them" ("Comparative Ethnic Politics," 387).

27. Mooney, *Black Is the New White*, 16.

28. Rock's sentiments here are resonant with James Baldwin's 1967 *New York Times* essay "Negroes Are Anti-Semitic Because They're Anti-White," http://www.nytimes.com/books/98/03/29/specials/baldwin-antisem.html.

29. Mooney, *Black Is the New White*, 258.

30. See Haggins, *Laughing Mad*, and Glenda R. Carpio, *Laughing Fit to Kill: Black Humor in the Fictions of Slavery* (New York: Oxford University Press, 2008). Chappelle's work has also

inspired a collection of scholarly articles devoted to his comedy: *The Comedy of Dave Chappelle: Critical* Essays, ed. K. A. Wisniewski (Jefferson, NC: McFarland, 2009).

31. Wisniewski, introduction to *The Comedy of Dave Chappelle*, 5.

32. Graham Chia-Hui Preston, "Dave Chappelle, the Wu-Tang Clan and Afro-Asian America," in *The Comedy of Dave Chappelle*, 60.

33. Haggins, *Laughing Mad*, 196.

34. Novotny Lawrence, "Comic Genius or Con Man? Deconstructing the Comedy of Dave Chappelle," in *The Comedy of Dave Chappelle*, 32.

35. Kwame Anthony Appiah, *The Ethics of Identity* (Princeton, NJ: Princeton University Press, 2005), 246.

36. Susan Stanford Friedman, "Beyond White and Other: Relationality and Narratives of Race in Feminist Discourse," *Signs: Journal of Women and Culture in Society* 21, no. 1 (1995): 17.

37. Katrina Bell-Jordan, "Speaking Fluent 'Joke': Pushing the Racial Envelope through Comedic Performance on *Chappelle's Show*," *Performance Research* 12, no. 3 (2007): 83.

38. In *Know Your History*, Paul Mooney performs a bit about white people "taking" black celebrities. Mooney states, for example, that white people took Tina Turner, Oprah Winfrey, and James Brown.

39. Bambi Haggins, "In the Wake of 'The Nigger Pixie': Dave Chappelle and the Politics of Crossover Comedy," in *Satire TV: Politics and Comedy in the Post-Network Era*, ed. Jonathan Gray, Jeffrey P. Jones, and Ethan Thompson (New York: New York University Press, 2009), 239.

40. The television writer is Bryan H. Tucker, not, as some critics have assumed, Chappelle's writing partner Neal Brennan.

41. The answers are, respectively, a woman's rear end, a single cigarette, and a woman who performs fellatio.

42. Haggins, *Laughing Mad*, 187.

43. Lawrence, "Comic Genius," 38.

44. See, for example, Christopher John Farley, "Dave Speaks," *Time*, May 23, 2005. Also see Chappelle's February 2006 interview with James Lipton on season 12, episode 9 of the television series *Inside the Actors Studio*. The full interview can be seen on YouTube at http://www.youtube.com/watch?v=84NjYRTHpfU.

45. Lawrence, "Comic Genius," 46, and Kimberly A. Yates, "When 'Keeping It Real' Goes Right," in *The Comedy of Dave Chappelle*, 154.

46. Brian Gogan, "Laughing Whiteness: Pixies, Parody, and Perspectives," in *The Comedy of Dave Chappelle*, 75.

47. The following routine can be found, under the title "Dave Chappelle in London," on YouTube at http://www.youtube.com/watch?v=TV2v37u39NY.

48. Avi Santo, "Of Niggas and Citizens: *The Boondocks* Fans and Differentiated Black American Politics," in *Satire TV*, 252.

2. THE NEW JEWISH BLACKFACE: ETHNIC ANXIETY IN CONTEMPORARY JEWISH HUMOR

1. See, in particular, Eric. J. Sundquist, *Strangers in the Land: Blacks, Jews, Post-Holocaust America* (Cambridge, MA: Harvard University Press, 2005); and Cheryl Lynn Greenberg, *Troubling the Waters: Black-Jewish Relations in the American Century* (Princeton, NJ: Princeton University Press, 2006).

2. Vincent Brook, *Something Ain't Kosher Here: The Rise of the "Jewish" Sitcom* (New Brunswick, NJ: Rutgers University Press, 2003), 83.

3. Mel Watkins, *On the Real Side: A History of African American Comedy* (Chicago: Lawrence Hill Books, 1999), 485.
4. Eric L. Goldstein, *The Price of Whiteness: Jews, Race, and American Identity* (Princeton, NJ: Princeton University Press, 2006), 211.
5. Even though he is British, Baron Cohen has achieved mainstream popularity in America, and much of his humor is either derived from or satirizes American culture. Even though there are notable differences between American and British Jewry, I thus feel it is appropriate to discuss his humor in the context of American ethnicity.
6. Brook, *Something Ain't Kosher Here*, 148–168.
7. Ibid., 155. For Brook, this *receptive* Jewish multiculturalism stands in contrast to an *assertive* Jewish multiculturalism, in which Jews "argue for a transformation not so much of Jewishness as of multiculturalism" (ibid., 156).
8. Sarah Blacher Cohen, "The Varieties of Jewish Humor," in *Jewish Wry: Essays on Jewish Humor*, ed. Sarah Blacher Cohen (Bloomington: Indiana University Press, 1987), 2.
9. Goldstein, *The Price of Whiteness*, 3.
10. Greenberg, *Troubling the Waters*, 7.
11. For a detailed history of Irish Americans' use of blackface, see Eric Lott, *Love and Theft: Blackface Minstrelsy and the American Working Class* (Oxford: Oxford University Press, 1995). In some ways, the Irish American use of blackface anticipates that of Jewish Americans. In the midnineteenth century, Irish Americans were considered, like American Jews sixty years later, only marginally white. After whiteness was achieved, Irish Americans largely stopped donning blackface.
12. Michael Rogin, *Blackface, White Noise: Jewish Immigrants in the Hollywood Melting Pot* (Berkeley: University of California Press, 1996), 5.
13. Ibid., 27. While Rogin's thesis is widely influential, it has also undergone some serious criticism. Joel Rosenberg, for example, argues that Jewish blackface "was not always easily readable as an expression of hostility or derision—at times, it has been seen as a gesture of homage or sincere identification" ("Rogin's Noise: The Alleged Historical Crimes of *The Jazz Singer*," *Prooftexts: A Journal of Jewish Literary History* 22 [2002]: 225). In this sense, contemporary Jewish blackface may also be seen as a continuation of, or return to, the motives of early-twentieth-century Jewish entertainers.
14. Brook, *Something Ain't Kosher Here*, 83.
15. Goldstein, *The Price of Whiteness*, 236.
16. Simcha Weinstein, *Shtick Shift: Jewish Humor in the 21st Century* (Fort Lee, NJ: Barricade Books, 2008), 33.
17. Lawrence J. Epstein, *The Haunted Smile: The Story of Jewish Comedians* (Oxford: Public Affairs, 2001), 252.
18. Sarah Silverman, *The Bedwetter: Stories of Courage, Redemption, and Pee* (New York: HarperCollins, 2010), 4.
19. Ibid., 4–5.
20. Ibid., 52–53.
21. Ibid., unpaged photo insert.
22. Ibid., 226.
23. Throughout, I will refer to Sarah Silverman the humorist as Silverman and to her uncouth stage persona as Sarah.
24. The JAP—and her relationship with her overindulgent father—is a counterpart to the overbearing Jewish Mother stereotype.
25. Alan Dundes, *Cracking Jokes: Studies of Sick Humor Cycles and Stereotypes* (New York: Ten Speed Press, 1987), 68.

26. Sarah Blacher Cohen, "The Unkosher Comediennes: From Sophie Tucker to Joan Rivers," in *Jewish Wry: Essays on Jewish Humor*, ed. Sarah Blacher Cohen (Bloomington: Indiana University Press, 1987), 105.
27. Ibid.
28. Neal Gabler notes how in the early years of the Hollywood film industry, the "least veiled anti-Semitism was reserved for such social clubs," inspiring Jewish film producers to create Hillcrest, a club for wealthy Hollywood Jews. Gabler, *An Empire of Their Own: How the Jews Invented Hollywood* (New York: Doubleday, 1988), 273.
29. "Face Wars" did not receive as much criticism as one might expect. To my knowledge, neither academics nor mainstream journalists have offered any extended discussion of the episode. Some bloggers, however, did express outrage over Silverman's use of the blackface mask. See, in particular, username Kevin's discussion titled "The Blackface Files Return" on the blog www.slanttruth.com, http://slanttruth.com/2007/10/23/the-blackface-files-return.
30. Sanford Pinsker, *The Schlemiel as Metaphor: Studies in Yiddish and American Jewish Fiction* (Carbondale: Southern Illinois University Press, 1991), 6. The *schlimazl*, in contrast, suffers misfortunes through no fault of his own.
31. Ibid., 13.
32. Ruth Wisse, *The Schlemiel as Modern Hero* (Chicago: University of Chicago Press, 1971), 3.
33. For an extended discussion of the ways in which Jewish conceptions of masculinity may serve to challenge classic Western ideals, see Daniel Boyarin, *Unheroic Conduct: The Rise of Heterosexuality and the Invention of the Jewish Man* (Berkeley: University of California Press, 1997).
34. In real life, Larry David was famously married to a Jewish woman, Laurie David. They divorced in 2007.
35. This sentiment has a long history among Jewish artists and humorists, including Woody Allen and Franz Kafka. See Vincent Brook, "'Ya'll Killed Him, We Didn't!': Jewish Self-Hatred and *The Larry Sanders Show*," in *You Should See Yourself: Jewish Identity in Postmodern American Culture*, ed. Vincent Brook (New Brunswick, NJ: Rutgers University Press, 2006), 307.
36. Philip Roth, *Portnoy's Complaint* (New York: Random House, 1969), 76.
37. Werner Sollors, *Beyond Ethnicity: Consent and Descent in American Culture* (New York: Oxford University Press, 1986), 132.
38. While African Americans are the marginalized group that Larry most often forms relationships with, it should be noted that he also, on occasion, forms similar bonds with Native Americans, homosexuals, and the physically and mentally disabled.
39. In the first few episodes of season 7, Larry's romantic relationship with Loretta Black dissolves. However, Larry maintains his friendship with Leon throughout seasons 7 and 8 (the most recent to date).
40. Wisse, *The Schlemiel as Modern Hero*, 3.
41. See Brendan O'Neill, "Backstory: Borat Write Thesis. It Niiiice. You Like Read?," *Christian Science Monitor*, November 21, 2006, http://www.csmonitor.com/2006/1121/p20s01-almo.html.
42. Sacha Baron Cohen, interview by Neil Strauss, "The Man behind the Mustache," NeilStrauss.com, http://www.neilstrauss.com/articles/manbehind_mustache_neilstrauss.html.
43. Steven S. Lee, "'Borat,' Multiculturalism, 'Mnogonatsional'nost,'" *Slavic Review* 67, no. 1 (2008): 22.
44. See Sander Gilman, *The Jew's Body* (New York: Routledge, 1991).
45. A similar joke can be found in one of Baron Cohen's Brüno segments when the Austrian fashion expert decides which celebrities, based on their outfits, can "stay in the ghetto" and which must take the "train to Auschwitz."

46. Baron Cohen, interview by Strauss, "The Man behind the Mustache."
47. Luenell is played by the actress and comedian Luenell Campbell; in other words, Baron Cohen did not find an actual prostitute to bring to the party.
48. Woody Allen uses a black prostitute character in a very similar manner in his film *Deconstructing Harry* (1997). Perhaps the African American woman is emerging in the Jewish imagination as a new sort of "shiksa goddess."
49. Lee, "'Borat,' Multiculturalism," 23.
50. Quoted in Richard Howells, "'Is It Because I Is Black?' Race, Humour, and the Polysemiology of Ali G," *Historical Journal of Film, Radio, and Television* 26, no. 2 (2006): 170.
51. For an insightful exploration of Ali G's ethnicity, see "Is It 'Cause I Is Black?," *Guardian*, January 12, 2000, http://www.guardian.co.uk/world/2000/jan/12/race.
52. Paul Mooney, *Black Is the New White* (New York: Simon Spotlight Entertainment, 2009), 247–248.
53. Lott, *Love and Theft*, 18.

3. "CRACKER, PLEASE!": TOWARD A WHITE ETHNIC HUMOR

1. Most scholars estimate that by 2050, whites will make up less than 50 percent of the U.S. population.
2. Ruth Frankenberg, "Local Whitenesses, Localizing Whiteness," in *Displacing Whiteness: Essays in Social and Cultural Criticism*, ed. Ruth Frankenberg (Durham, NC: Duke University Press, 1997), 9.
3. Toni Morrison, *Playing in the Dark: Whiteness and the Literary Imagination* (New York: Vintage Books, 1993), 47.
4. Richard Dyer, *White: Essays on Race and Culture* (New York: Routledge, 1997), 10.
5. There are some signs, however, that this might be changing. Jon Stewart's *The Daily Show*, in particular, has been utilizing a much more multiethnic cast of correspondents, including African Americans Wyatt Cenac and Jessica Williams, Asian American Olivia Munn, Latino Al Madrigal, and Arab American Aasif Mandvi. More often than not, these correspondents speak primarily about news stories related to their own ethnic positions, but their presence does disrupt the virtual white-out of most political comedy.
6. The most prominent exception to this rule is Bill Cosby, but even though Cosby may have, in his heyday, managed to sidestep racial issues in his act, critical discussions about him almost always focus on race.
7. David Savran, *Taking It like a Man: White Masculinity, Masochism, and Contemporary American Culture* (Princeton, NJ: Princeton University Press, 1998), 4.
8. Michael Kimmel, *Manhood in America: A Cultural History* (New York: Oxford University Press, 2006), 197.
9. George Rodriguez, "The White Anxiety Crisis," *Time*, March 11, 2010, http://www.time.com/time/specials/packages/article/0,28804,1971133_1971110_1971119,00.html.
10. It is important to note that the term "cracker" is traditionally used to refer to poor, rural whites, which are not the sort that Birbiglia is mocking in his act.
11. Werner Sollors, *Beyond Ethnicity: Consent and Descent in American Culture* (New York: Oxford University Press, 1986), 132.
12. As I suggest in chapter 1, the most dominant strain of African American humor is often characterized by a regressive gender politics.
13. Lander compiled the contents of this blog into the book *Stuff White People Like: A Definitive Guide to the Unique Taste of Millions* (New York: Random House, 2008). He has since

published a sequel titled *Whiter Shades of Pale: The Stuff White People Like, Coast to Coast, from Seattle's Sweaters to Maine's Microbrews* (New York: Random House, 2010).

14. Lisa Respers, "Finding Humor in 'Stuff White People Like,'" CNN.com, January 29, 2009, http://www.cnn.com/2009/SHOWBIZ/books/01/29/stuff.white.people.like/index.html.

15. Ibid.

16. Ibid.

17. For an extensive discussion of this lineage, see Michael Dunne and Sara Lewis Dunne, "Intertextual Rednecks: Griffith, Gardner, Wilson, Clower, and Foxworthy," in *The Enduring Legacy of Old Southwest Humor*, ed. Edward J. Piacentino (Baton Rouge: Louisiana State University Press, 2006), 248–260.

18. A full transcript of Foxworthy's speech can be found at http://www.freerepublic.com/focus/f-news/1821089/posts.

19. Anne Shelby, "The 'R' Word: What's So Funny (and Not So Funny) about Redneck Jokes," in *Confronting Appalachian Stereotypes: Back Talk from an American Region*, ed. Dwight B. Billings, Gurncy Norman, and Katherine Ledford (Lexington: University Press of Kentucky, 1999), 158. While Shelby's point is well-taken, homosexuals may be considered another group that it is still "okay" to make fun of.

20. Ibid.

21. Stephen Groening, "Cynicism and Other Postideological Half Measures in *South Park*," in *Taking South Park Seriously*, ed. Jeffrey Andrew Weinstock (Albany: State University of New York Press, 2008), 123.

22. Lindsay Coleman, "Shopping at J-Mart with the Williams: Race, Ethnicity, and Belonging in *South Park*," in *Taking South Park Seriously*, 134.

23. Toni Johnson-Woods, *Blame Canada: South Park and Contemporary Culture* (New York: Continuum, 2007), 218.

24. See, in particular, Brian C. Anderson, *South Park Conservatives: The Revolt against Liberal Media Bias* (Washington DC: Regnery Publishing, 2007).

4. IMAGINING DIVERSITY: CORPORATE MULTICULTURALISM IN THE CHILDREN'S FILM AND THE SITUATION COMEDY

1. Paul Gilroy, *Against Race: Imagining Political Culture beyond the Color Line* (Cambridge, MA: Harvard University Press, 2000), 21.

2. Ibid., 52.

3. Jennifer Fuller, "Branding Blackness on US Cable Television," *Media, Culture & Society* 32, no. 2 (2010): 302–303.

4. This is not to say that there are not moments of subversion within network sitcoms or children's films or that, according to Stuart Hall's notion of "dominant," "negotiated," or "oppositional" readings, audiences do not often find subversive messages within mainstream texts (Stuart Hall, "Encoding/Decoding," in *Culture, Media, Language: Working Papers in Cultural Studies, 1972–79* [London: Hutchinson, 1980], 128–138). In *Revolution Televised*, for example, Christine Acham illustrates the ways in which black performers and writers often managed to embed resistant messages into otherwise hegemonic texts. Christine Acham, *Revolution Televised: Prime Time and the Struggle for Black Power* (Minneapolis: University of Minnesota Press, 2004).

5. Vincent Brook, "Convergent Ethnicity and the Neo-platoon Show," *Television and New Media* 10, no. 4 (2009): 331–353.

6. Ibid., 333.

7. Ibid., 341.
8. Ibid., 348.
9. See, for example, Lynda Haas and Laura Sells, eds., *From Mouse to Mermaid: The Politics of Film, Gender, and Culture* (Bloomington: Indiana University Press, 2008); and Amy Davis, *Good Girls and Wicked Witches: Women in Disney's Feature Animation* (Eastleigh, UK: John Libbey Publishing, 2007).
10. Henry A. Giroux, *The Mouse That Roared: Disney and the End of Innocence* (New York: Rowman & Littlefield, 1999).
11. Douglas Brode, *Multiculturalism and the Mouse: Race and Sex in Disney Entertainment* (Austin: University of Texas Press, 2005), 270. Also see Douglas Brode, *From Walt to Woodstock: How Disney Created the Counterculture* (Austin: University of Texas Press, 2004).
12. Carmen R. Lugo-Lugo and Mary K. Bloodsworth-Lugo, "'Look Out New World, Here We Come'? Race, Racialization, and Sexuality in Four Children's Animated Films by Disney, Pixar, and DreamWorks," *Cultural Studies⇔ Critical Methodologies* 9, no. 2 (2009): 168.
13. Bambi Haggins, *Laughing Mad: The Black Comic Persona in Post-Soul America* (New Brunswick, NJ: Rutgers University Press, 2007), 60.
14. Giroux, *The Mouse That Roared*, 105–106.
15. Rock's grandfather was, in fact, a preacher, and in interviews Rock has acknowledged the influence of his grandfather on his humor. See "Chris Rock: I Learned Humor from Preacher Grandfather," *National Ledger*, June 21, 2010, http://www.nationalledger.com/pop-culture-news/chris-rock-i-learned-humor-fr-220140.shtml.
16. Tanya Batson-Savage provides a brief discussion of Ernie and Bernie in relation to prevalent Jamaican stereotypes in "Through the Eyes of Hollywood: Reading Representations of Jamaicans in American Cinema," *Small Axe* 14, no. 2 (2010): 42–55.
17. An exception to this is *Cars 2* (2011). While the film was still profitable, it received mostly negative reviews.
18. A key exception to this trend is one of Pixar's best films, *WALL-E* (2008), which tells the story of a dystopian future in which humankind has been forced to abandon the planet as a result of massive pollution. The main character is a robot, and the film's people, mostly white, are portrayed as lazy and extremely obese. Despite its sentimental conceits, the film borders on misanthropy.
19. Lewis appeared on the sketch comedy show *In Living Color* and in multiple Tyler Perry productions, and she provided the voice of Motown Turtle in *Shark Tale*, discussed above.
20. A second sequel, *Madagascar 3: Europe's Most Wanted* was released in summer 2012, as I finalized the revisions to this book.
21. Lawrence E. Mintz, "Ideology in the Television Situation Comedy," in *What's So Funny? Humor in American Culture*, ed. Nancy A. Walker (Wilmington, DE: Scholarly Resources, 1998), 273.
22. See, for example, Bill Carter, "The Laughter Is Fading in Sitcomland: Reality Shows, Costs, and Innovative Comedy Threaten a TV Staple," *New York Times*, May 24, 2004, http://www.nytimes.com/2004/05/24/arts/television/24UPFR.html.
23. In recent scheduling, each of the four major networks typically group their sitcoms together in a single block. NBC, for example, has long aired a three-hour sitcom block on Thursday nights.
24. Fox, of course, is an upstart network that rose in popularity in the late 1980s and early 1990s; its early identity thus depended on "alternative" programming like *The Simpsons* and *In Living Color*. Vestiges of this identity can be found on Fox's Sunday night lineup of crude and edgy animated shows, anchored by *The Simpsons* and *Family Guy*.
25. David Marc, *Comic Visions: Television Comedy and American Culture* (Malden, MA: Blackwell-Wiley, 1999), 22.

26. Ibid., 89.
27. For a fuller history of ethnic sitcoms, see Herman Gray, *Watching Race: Television and the Struggle for "Blackness"* (Minneapolis: University of Minnesota Press, 1995); Donald Bogle, *Primetime Blues: African Americans on Network Television* (New York: Farrar, Straus and Giroux, 2001); Vincent Brook, *Something Ain't Kosher Here: The Rise of the "Jewish" Sitcom* (New Brunswick, NJ: Rutgers University Press, 2003); and David Zurawik, *The Jews of Prime Time* (Hanover, NH: Brandeis University Press, 2003).
28. Mintz, "Ideology," 276.
29. Gray, *Watching Race*, 85.
30. Ibid., 88.
31. Ibid., 90.
32. See the final chapter of Jeremy Butler's *Television Style* (New York: Routledge, 2010) for a detailed comparison of multi-camera and single-camera sitcoms.
33. The traditional sitcom, though, is still here. Two of the most popular sitcoms of the twenty-first century are the Chuck Lorre productions *Two and a Half Men* (2003–) and *The Big Bang Theory*, both of which air on CBS and are filmed in a traditional multi-camera style.
34. Jeffrey Griffin, "The Americanization of *The Office*: A Comparison of the Offbeat NBC Sitcom and Its British Predecessor," *Journal of Popular Film and Television* 30, no. 4 (2008): 158.
35. Marc, *Comic Visions*, 182.
36. My description of the language and accents is drawn from username Maytha's informative review "A 'Community' of Misrepresentation" at the Arab American website www.KABOBfest.com, http://www.kabobfest.com/2009/11/a-community-of-misrepresentation.html.

5. COMEDY WITHOUT BORDERS? TOWARD A MULTIETHNIC HUMOR

1. Kwame Anthony Appiah, *Cosmopolitanism: Ethics in a World of Strangers* (New York: W. W. Norton, 2006), 85.
2. Werner Sollors, *Beyond Ethnicity: Consent and Descent in American Culture* (New York: Oxford University Press, 1986), 132.
3. David Hollinger, *Cosmopolitanism and Solidarity: Studies in Ethnoracial, Religious, and Professional Affiliation in the United States* (Madison: University of Wisconsin Press, 2006), xviii.
4. In an early episode, Nancy explains that her specific ethnic background is Welsh, but other than that, she is never referred to as anything but white.
5. Kera Bolonik, *In the Weeds: The Official Companion Book to the Hit Showtime Series* (New York: Simon Spotlight Entertainment, 2007), xi.
6. Alessandra Stanley, "Mom Brakes for Drug Deals," *New York Times*, August 5, 2005, http://www.nytimes.com/2005/08/05/arts/television/05tvwk.html.
7. The label "Grasshopper," of course, alludes to the television series *Kung Fu* (1972–1975), about a half-Chinese, half-white drifter who has learned the secrets of martial arts from his Chinese teachers Master Po and Master Kan. The allusion suggests that *Weeds*'s writers are well aware of the history of intercultural education in popular culture.
8. In an interview with Kera Bolonik, *Weeds* creator Jenji Kohan cites *Reefer Madness* (2003), Eric Schlosser's exposé on America's underground economy, as a useful source when she was writing the series pilot. Bolonik, *In the Weeds*, 90.
9. MILF is an acronym for Mother I'd Like to Fuck.
10. Dennis Lim, "The Wild Munch," *Village Voice*, July 20, 2004, http://www.villagevoice.com/2004-07-20/film/the-wild-munch/1/.
11. Harold and Kumar's hedonism, however, may reinforce the even older Asian stereotype of the indulgent, opium-smoking sultan.

12. C. N. Le, *Asian American Assimilation: Ethnicity, Immigration, and Socioeconomic Attainment* (New York: LFB Scholarly Publishing, 2007), 142. For a detailed critique of the model-minority thesis, see Deborah Woo, "Inventing and Reinventing of 'Model Minorities': The Cultural Veil Obscuring Structural Sources of Inequality," in *Asian Americans: Experiences and Perspectives*, ed. Timothy P. Fong and Larry H. Shinagawa (Upper Saddle River, NJ: Prentice Hall, 2000), 193–212.

13. bell hooks, *Black Looks: Race and Representation* (Boston: South End Press, 1992), 169.

14. Ruth Frankenberg, "Local Whitenesses, Localizing Whiteness," in *Displacing Whiteness: Essays in Social and Cultural Criticism*, ed. Ruth Frankenberg (Durham, NC: Duke University Press, 1997), 13.

15. Rosenberg and Goldstein may serve as fictional stand-ins for Jon Hurwitz and Hayden Schlossberg, the film's Jewish American screenwriters.

16. Peter Kivisto notes that "while Jews in an earlier era were the paradigmatic example among groups using university credentials as a route to economic improvement, one can see a similar tendency today among some Asian groups." Kivisto, *Multiculturalism in a Global Society* (Oxford: Blackwell Publishing, 2002), 33–34. In her discussion of "model minorities," Woo also directly compares stereotypical constructions of Jewish and Asian American identity. Woo, "Inventing and Reinventing," 205–207.

17. Guy MacPherson, "Russell Peters: Fun with Stereotypes," Straight.com, June 14, 2004, http://www.straight.com/article-95136/fun-with-stereotypes.

18. Appiah, *Cosmopolitanism*, 5.

19. David J. Schneider provides a discussion of this phenomenon in his massive work *The Psychology of Stereotyping* (New York: Guilford Press, 2004), 242–243. He explains that "self-stereotyping" often serves to increase solidarity, especially in groups that are otherwise marginalized.

20. Of course, it is Peters-as-performer who is able to navigate such cross-cultural contact. Within the story itself, Peters does nothing to alleviate the Nigerian woman's discomfort or confusion. If the awkwardness of this situation were to be easily cleared up, however, then the story would not work very well as a comedy routine.

21. For a discussion of Peters as a brown man, see Faiza Hirja, "'Somebody Going to Get Hurt Real Bad': The Race-based Comedy of Russell Peters," *Canadian Journal of Communication* 34, no. 4 (2009): 572.

CONCLUSION: EMERGING ETHNIC HUMOR IN MULTIETHNIC AMERICA

1. Michael Winerip, "Racial Lens Used to Cull Curriculum in Arizona," *New York Times*, March 19, 2012, http://www.nytimes.com/2012/03/19/education/racial-lens-used-to-cull-curriculum-in-arizona.html?_r=1&pagewanted=all.

2. Kwame Anthony Appiah, *The Ethics of Identity* (Princeton, NJ: Princeton University Press, 2005), 256.

3. Werner Sollors, *Beyond Ethnicity: Consent and Descent in American Culture* (New York: Oxford University Press, 1986), 132.

4. Quoted in Guillermo Avila-Saavedra, "Ethnic Otherness versus Cultural Assimilation: U.S. Latino Comedians and the Politics of Identity," *Mass Communication and Society* 14, no. 3 (2011): 287.

5. The phrase describing such jokes is from Bambi Haggins, *Laughing Mad: The Black Comic Persona in Post-Soul America* (New Brunswick, NJ: Rutgers University Press, 2007), 187.

6. Avila-Saavedra, "Ethnic Otherness," 286.

7. Mencia has been accused of stealing jokes from Joe Rogan, Ari Shaffir, George Lopez, and even Bill Cosby. In 2010, Joe Rogan confronted Mencia about alleged joke theft onstage at The Comedy Store. Videos of the confrontation have since leaked on to YouTube and can be found at http://www.youtube.com/watch?v=M42BflUZry8. In the documentary film *I Am Comic* (2010), Mencia admits to appropriating other comics' material and then adding a Latino spin.

8. The same point about internal diversity could of course be made about the various Latino groups in the United States, but Latino groups usually share a common language, and the greater number of Mexican Americans, as well as their spotlight in national debates about immigration policy, makes this group more dominant in popular culture.

9. There are some signs, however, that this may be changing. For example, Mindy Kaling—formerly a supporting player in *The Office*—is, as of this writing, the star of her own sitcom, *The Mindy Project* (2012–). This marks the first television series with an Asian American lead since Cho's *All-American Girl*. We will have to wait to see whether Kaling's series will have more success than Cho's.

10. See Amarnath Amarasingam, "Laughter the Best Medicine: Muslim Comedians and Social Criticism in Post-9/11 America," *Journal of Muslim Minority Affairs* 30, no. 4 (2010): 463–477.

11. See Darby Li Po Price, "Mixed Laughter," in *We Are a People: Narrative and Multiplicity in Constructing Ethnic Identity*, ed. Paul Spickard and W. Jeffrey Burroughs (Philadelphia: Temple University Press, 2000), 179–191.

12. David Hollinger, *Postethnic America: Beyond Multiculturalism* (New York: Basic Books, 2005), 163.

INDEX

ABOUT THE AUTHOR

DAVID GILLOTA is an instructor in the English and ethnic studies programs at the University of Wisconsin–Platteville.